INTELLIGENCE
REFRAMED

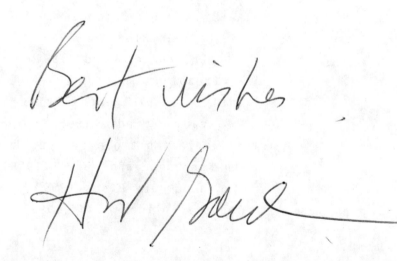

Best wishes

Howard Gardner

Other Books by Howard Gardner

The Quest for Mind (1973)
The Arts and Human Development (1973)
The Shattered Mind (1975)
Developmental Psychology (1978)
Artful Scribbles (1980)
Art, Mind, and Brain (1982)
Frames of Mind (1983)
The Mind's New Science (1985)
To Open Minds (1989)
The Unschooled Mind (1991)
Creating Minds (1993)
Multiple Intelligences (1993)
Leading Minds (1995)
Intelligence: Multiple Perspectives
(with Kornhaber and Wake) (1996)
Extraordinary Minds (1997)
The Disciplined Mind (1999)

INTELLIGENCE
REFRAMED

MULTIPLE INTELLIGENCES
FOR THE 21ST CENTURY

HOWARD GARDNER

BASIC
B
BOOKS

A MEMBER OF THE PERSEUS BOOKS GROUP

Copyright © 1999 by Howard Gardner

Published by Basic Books,
A Member of the Perseus Books Group

A CIP catalog record for this book is available from
the Library of Congress
ISBN 0–465–02610–9

Book design by Victoria Kuskowski

99 00 01 02 03 / RRD

10 9 8 7 6 5 4 3 2 1

FOR PATRICIA ALBJERG GRAHAM,
INCOMPARABLE MENTOR,
CHERISHED COLLEAGUE,
VALUED FRIEND

CONTENTS

ACKNOWLEDGMENTS

This book draws heavily on essays written in the 1990s. For their critical comments on one or more of these essays, I thank Thomas Armstrong, Eric Blumenson, Veronica Boix-Mansilla, Mihaly Csikszentmihalyi, Patricia Bolanos, Antonio Damasio, William Damon, Reuven Feuerstein, Daniel Goleman, Tom Hatch, Tom Hoerr, Jeff Kane, Paul Kaufman, Mindy Kornhaber, Mara Krechevsky, Jonathan Levy, Tanya Luhrmann, Robert Ornstein, David Perkins, Charles Reigeluth, Courtney Ross, Mark Runco, Mark Turner, Julie Viens, Joe Walters, John T. Williams, E. O. Wilson, and Ellen Winner. Jo Ann Miller, Donya Levine, Richard Fumosa, and Sharon Sharp of Perseus Books aided ably in the editorial process.

In particular, I have drawn on the following:

Gardner, H.: "Reflections on Multiple Intelligences: Myths and Messages." *Phi Delta Kappan 77*, no. 3(1995): 200–209.

_____. "Are There Additional Intelligences?" In *Education, Information, and Transformation*, ed. J. Kane. Upper Saddle River, N.J.: Prentice Hall, 1999.

_____. "Multiple Approaches to Understanding." In *Instructional-Design Theories and Models: A New Paradigm of Instructional Theory*, ed. C. Reigeluth. Mahwah, N.J.: Erlbaum, 1999.

_____. "Who Owns Intelligence?" *Atlantic Monthly*, February 1999, 67–76.

The work described in these essays has been made possible by generous funders. I would like to thank the Bauman Foundation, the Carnegie Corporation, the Nathan Cummings Foundation, Jeffrey Epstein, the Fetzer Institute, the Ford Foundation, the William T. Grant Foundation, the William and Flora Hewlett Foundation, the Christian A. Johnson Endeavor Foundation, Thomas H. Lee, the New American Schools Development Corporation, the Jesse Phillips Foundation, the Rockefeller Brothers Foundation, the Rockefeller Foundation, the Louise and Claude Rosenberg Jr. Family Foundation, the Ross Family Charitable Foundation, the Spencer Foundation, and the Bernard Van Leer Foundation, as well as a generous funder who wishes to remain anonymous.

Finally, I want to thank, though not by name, the many people in the United States and abroad who have worked with me to develop the implications of the theory of multiple intelligences. Many of you are listed in the appendices. To all of you, I express my heartfelt gratitude.

CAMBRIDGE, MA
June 1999

INTELLIGENCE
REFRAMED

1

INTELLIGENCE AND INDIVIDUALITY

EVERY SOCIETY FEATURES its ideal human being. The ancient Greeks valued the person who displayed physical agility, rational judgment, and virtuous behavior. The Romans highlighted manly courage, and followers of Islam prized the holy soldier. Under the influence of Confucius, Chinese populations traditionally valued the person who was skilled in poetry, music, calligraphy, archery, and drawing. Among the Keres tribe of the Pueblo Indians today, the person who cares for others is held in high regard.

Over the past few centuries, particularly in Western societies, a certain ideal has become pervasive: that of the *intelligent person*. The exact dimensions of that ideal evolve over time and setting. In traditional schools, the intelligent person could master classical languages and mathematics, particularly geometry. In a business setting, the intelligent person could anticipate commercial opportunities, take measured risks, build up an organization, and keep the books balanced and the stockholders satisfied. At the beginning of the twentieth century, the intelligent person was one who could be dispatched to the far corners of an empire and who could then execute orders competently. Such notions remain important to many people.

As the turn of this millennium approaches, however, a premium has been placed on two new intellectual virtuosos: the "symbol analyst" and the "master of change."[1] A symbol analyst can sit for hours in front of a string of numbers and words, usually displayed on a computer screen, and readily discern meaning in this thicket of symbols. This person can then make reliable, useful projections. A master of change readily acquires new information, solves problems, forms "weak ties" with mobile and highly dispersed people, and adjusts easily to changing circumstances.

Those charged with guiding a society have always been on the outlook for intelligent young people. Two thousand years ago, Chinese imperial officials administered challenging examinations to identify those who could join and direct the bureaucracy. In the Middle Ages, church leaders searched for students who displayed a combination of studiousness, shrewdness, and devotion. In the late nineteenth century, Francis Galton, one of the founders of modern psychological measurement, thought that intelligence ran in families, and so he looked for intelligence in the offspring of those who occupied leading positions in British society.

Galton did not stop with hereditary lineages, however. He also believed that intelligence could be measured more directly. Beginning around 1870, he began to devise more formal tests of intelligence, ones consistent with the emerging view of the human mind as subject to measurement and experimentation. Galton thought that more intelligent persons would exhibit greater sensory acuity, and so the first formal measures of intelligence probed the ways in which individuals distinguished among sounds of different loudness, lights of different brightness, and objects of different weight. As it turned out, Galton (who thought himself very intelligent) bet on indices of intelligence

---

[1]Reference notes are found at the end of the book.

that proved unrevealing for his purposes. But in his wager on the *possibility* of measuring intelligence, he was proved correct.

Since Galton's time, countless people have avidly pursued the best ways of defining, measuring, and nurturing intelligence. Intelligence tests represent but the tip of the cognitive iceberg. In the United States, tests such as the Scholastic Assessment Test, the Miller Analogies Test, and the various primary, secondary, graduate, and professional examinations are all based on technology originally developed to test intelligence. Even assessments that are deliberately focused on measuring achievement (as opposed to "aptitude" or "potential for achievement") often strongly resemble traditional tests of intelligence. Similar testing trends have occurred in many other nations as well. It is likely that efforts to measure intelligence will continue and, indeed, become more widespread in the future. Certainly, the prospect of devising robust measures of a highly valued human trait is attractive, for example, for those faced with decisions about educational placement or employment. And the press to determine *who* is intelligent and to do so at the earliest possible age is hardly going to disappear.

Despite the strong possibility that intelligence testing will remain with us indefinitely, this book is based on a different premise, namely, that intelligence is too important to be left to the intelligence testers. Just in the past half century, our understanding of the human mind and the human brain has been fundamentally altered. For example, we now understand that the human mind, reflecting the structure of the brain, is composed of many separate modules or faculties. At the same time, in the light of scientific and technological changes, the needs and desires of cultures all over the world have undergone equally dramatic shifts. We are faced with a stark choice: either to continue with the traditional views of intelligence and how it should be measured or to come up with a different, and better, way of conceptualizing the human intellect. In this book, I adopt the latter tack. I present evidence that human beings possess a range of capacities and potentials—multiple intelligences—that, both individually and in consort, can be put to many productive uses. Individuals can not only come to understand their multiple intelligences but also deploy them in maximally flexible and productive ways within the human roles that various societies have created. Multiple intelligences can be mobilized at school, at home, at work, or on the street—that is, throughout the various institutions of a society.

But the task for the new millennium is not merely to hone our various intelligences and use them properly. We must figure out how intelligence and morality can work together to create a world in which a great variety of people will want to live. After all, a society led by "smart" people still might blow up itself or the rest of the world. Intelligence is valuable but, as Ralph Waldo Emerson famously remarked, "Character is more important than intellect." That insight applies at both the individual and the societal levels.

ORGANIZATION OF THE BOOK

In Chapter 2, I describe the traditional scientific view of intelligence. I introduce my own view—the theory of multiple intelligences—in Chapter 3. While this theory was developed nearly two decades ago, it has not remained static. Thus, in Chapters 4 and 5, I consider several new candidate intelligences, including naturalist, spiritual, existential, and moral ones. In Chapter 6, I address some of the questions and criticisms that have arisen about the theory and I dispel some of the more prominent myths. I treat other controversial issues in Chapter 7. And I explore in Chapter 8 the relationships among intelligence, creativity, and leadership.

The next three chapters focus on ways in which the theory of multiple intelligences can be applied. Chapters 9 and 10 are devoted to a discussion of the theory in scholastic settings, and in chapter 11 I discuss its applications in the wider world. Finally, returning to the issues raised in Chapter 1, in Chapter 12 I explore my answer to the provocative question "Who owns intelligence?"

Since my presentation of the theory almost twenty years ago, an enormous secondary literature has developed around it. And many individuals have propagated the theory in various ways. In the appendices, I present an up-to-date listing of my own writings on the theory, writings by other scholars who have devoted books or major articles to the theory, selected miscellaneous materials, and key individuals in the United States and abroad who have contributed to the development of the theory or related practices. I provided a similar, but much smaller, listing of resources in *Multiple Intelligences: The Theory in Practice*, completed in 1992. I am humbled by the continued and growing interest in the theory, and proud that it has touched so many people all over the world.

BEFORE
MULTIPLE INTELLIGENCES

A TALE OF TWO BOOKS

In the fall of 1994, an unusual event occurred in the book-publishing industry. An eight-hundred-page book, written by two scholars and including two hundred pages of statistical appendices, was issued by a general trade publisher. The manuscript had been kept under embargo and therefore had not been seen by potential reviewers. Despite (or perhaps because of) this secrecy, *The Bell Curve*, by Richard J. Herrnstein and Charles Murray, received front-page coverage in the weekly news magazines and became a major topic of discussion in the media and around dinner tables. Indeed, one would have had to go back half a century to a landmark treatise on black–white relations, Gunnar Myrdal's *An American Dilemma*, to find a social science book that engendered a comparable buzz.

Even in retrospect, it is difficult to know fully what contributed to the notoriety surrounding *The Bell Curve*. None of the book's major arguments were new to the educated public. Herrnstein, a Harvard psychology professor, and Murray, an American Enterprise Institute political scientist, argued that intelligence is best thought of as a single property distributed within the general population along a bell-shaped curve. That is, comparatively few people have very high intelligence (say, IQ over 130), comparatively few have very low intelligence (IQ under 70), and most people are clumped together somewhere in between (IQ from 85 to 115). Moreover, the authors adduced evidence that intelligence is to a significant extent inherited—that is, within a defined population, the variation in measured intelligence is due primarily to the genetic contributions of one's biological parents.

These claims were fairly well known and hardly startling. But Herrnstein and Murray went further. They moved well beyond a discussion of measuring intelligence to claim that many of our current social ills are due to the behaviors and capacities of people with relatively low intelligence. The authors made considerable use of the National Longitudinal Survey of Youth, a rich data set of over 12,000 youths who have been followed since 1979. The population was selected in such a way as to include adequate representation from various social, ethnic, and racial groups; members of the group took a set of cognitive and aptitude measures under well controlled conditions. On the basis of these data, the authors presented evidence that those with low intelligence are more likely to be on welfare, to be involved in crime, to come from broken homes, to drop out of school, and to exhibit other forms of social pathology. And while they did not take an explicit stand on the well-known data showing higher IQs among whites than among blacks, they left the clear impression that these differences were difficult to change and, therefore, probably were a product of genetic factors.

I have labeled the form of argument in *The Bell Curve* "rhetorical brinkmanship." Instead of stating the unpalatable, the authors lead readers to a point where they are likely to draw a certain conclusion on their own. And so, while Herrnstein and Murray claimed to remain "resolutely neutral" on the sources of black–white differences in intelligence, the evidence they presented strongly suggests a genetic basis for the disparity. Similarly, while they did not recommend eugenic practices, they repeatedly used the following form of reasoning: Social pathology is due to low intelligence, and intelligence cannot be significantly changed through societal interventions. The reader is drawn, almost ineluctably, to conclude that "we" (the intelligent reader, of course) must find a way to reduce the number of "unintelligent" people.

The reviews of *The Bell Curve* were primarily negative, with the major exception of those in politically conservative publications. Scholars were extremely critical, particularly in regard to the alleged links between low intelligence and social pathology. Not surprisingly, the authors' conclusions about intelligence have been endorsed by many psychologists who specialize in measurement and on whose work much of the book was built.

Why the fuss over a book that offered few new ideas and dubious scholarship? I would not minimize the skill of the publisher, who kept the book under wraps from scholars while making sure that it got into the hands of people who would promote it or write at length about it. The application of seemingly scientific objectivity to racial issues on which many people hold private views may also have contributed to the book's success. But my own, admittedly more cynical, view is that a demand arises every twenty-five years or so for a restatement of the "nature," or hereditary explanation, of intelligence. Supporting this view is the fact that the *Harvard Educational Review* in 1969 published a controversial article titled "How much can we boost scholastic achievement?" The author, the psychologist Arthur Jensen, harshly criticized the effectiveness of early childhood intervention programs like Head Start. He said that such programs did not genuinely aid disadvantaged children and suggested that perhaps black children needed to be taught in a different way.

Just one year after the appearance of *The Bell Curve*, another book was published to even greater acclaim. In most respects, *Emotional Intelligence*, by the *New York Times* reporter and psychologist Daniel Goleman, could not have been more different from *The Bell Curve*. Issued by a mass-market trade publisher, Goleman's short book was filled with anecdotes and presented only a few scattered statistics. Moreover, in sharp contrast to *The Bell Curve*, *Emotional Intelligence* contained a dim view of the entire psychometric tradition, as indicated by its subtitle: *Why it can matter more than IQ*.

In *Emotional Intelligence*, Goleman argued that our world has largely ignored a tremendously significant set of skills and abilities—those dealing with people and emotions. In particular, Goleman wrote about the importance of recognizing one's own emotional life, regulating one's own feelings, understanding others' emotions, being able to work with others, and having empathy for others. He described ways of enhancing these capacities, particularly among children. More generally, he argued that the world could be more hospitable if we cultivated emotional intelligence as diligently as we now promote cognitive intelligence. *Emotional Intelligence* may well be the best-selling social science book ever published. By 1998, it had sold over 3 million copies worldwide, and in countries as diverse as Brazil and Taiwan it has remained on the best-seller list for unprecedented lengths of time. On the surface, it is easy to see why *Emotional Intelligence* is so appealing to readers. Its message is hopeful, and the author tells readers how to enhance their own emotional intelligence and that of others close to them. And—this is meant without disrespect—the message of the book is contained in its title and its subtitle.

I often wonder whether the readers of *The Bell Curve* have also read *Emotional Intelligence*. Can one be a fan of both books? There are probably gender and disciplinary differences in the audiences: To put it sharply, if not stereotypically, business people and tough-minded social scientists are probably more likely to gravitate toward *The Bell Curve*, while teachers, social workers, and parents are probably more likely to embrace *Emotional Intelligence*. (However, a successor volume, Goleman's *Working with Emotional Intelligence*, sought to attract the former audiences, too.) But I suspect that there is also some overlap. Clearly, educators, business people, parents, and many others realize that the concept of intelligence is important and that conceptualizations of it are changing more rapidly than ever before.

A BRIEF HISTORY OF PSYCHOMETRICS

By 1860 Charles Darwin had established the scientific case for the origin and evolution of all species. Darwin had also become curious about the origin and development of psychological traits, including intellectual and emotional ones. It did not take long before a wide range of scholars began to ponder the intellectual differences across the species, as well as within specific groups, such as infants, children, adults, or the "feeble-minded" and "eminent geniuses." Much of this pondering occurred in the armchair; it was far easier to speculate about differences in intellectual power among dogs, chimpanzees, and people of different cultures than to gather comparative data relevant to these putative differences. It is perhaps not a coincidence that Darwin's cousin, the polymath Francis Galton, was the first to establish an anthropometric laboratory for the purpose of assembling empirical evidence of people's intellectual differences.

Still, the honor of having fashioned the first intelligence test is usually awarded to Alfred Binet, a French psychologist particularly interested in children and education. In the early 1900s, families were flocking into Paris from the provinces and from far-flung French territories. Some of the children from these families were having great difficulty with schoolwork. In the early 1900s, Binet and his colleague

Théodore Simon were approached by the French Ministry of Education to help predict which children were at risk for school failure. Proceeding in a completely empirical fashion, Binet administered hundreds of test questions to these children. He wanted to identify a set of questions that were discriminating, that is, when passed, such items predicted success in school and when failed, the same items predicted difficulty in school.

Like Galton, Binet began with largely sensory-based items but soon discovered the superior predictive power of other, more "scholastic" questions. From Binet's time on, intelligence tests have been heavily weighted toward measuring verbal memory, verbal reasoning, numerical reasoning, appreciation of logical sequences, and ability to state how one would solve problems of daily living. Without fully realizing it, Binet had invented the first tests of intelligence.

A few years later, in 1912, the German psychologist Wilhelm Stern came up with the name and measure of the "intelligence quotient," or the ratio of one's mental age to one's chronological age, with the ratio to be multiplied by 100 (which is why it is better to have an IQ of 130 than one of 70).

Like many Parisian fashions of the day, the IQ test made its way across the Atlantic—with a vengeance—and became Americanized during the 1920s and 1930s. Whereas Binet's test had been administered one on one, American psychometricians—led by Stanford University psychologist Lewis Terman and the Harvard professor and army major Robert Yerkes—prepared paper-and-pencil (and, later, machine-scorable) versions that could be administered easily to many individuals. Since specific instructions were written out and norms were created, test takers could be examined under uniform conditions and their scores could be compared. Certain populations elicited special interest; much was written about the IQs of mentally deficient people, of putative young geniuses, U.S. Army recruits, members of different racial and ethnic groups, and immigrants from northern, central, and southern Europe, and by the mid-1920s, the intelligence test had become a fixture in educational practice in the United States and throughout much of western Europe.

Early intelligence tests were not without their critics. Many enduring concerns were first raised by the influential American journalist Walter Lippmann. In a series of debates with Lewis Terman, published in the *New Republic*, Lippmann criticized the test items' superficiality and possible cultural biases, and he noted the risks associated with assessing an individual's intellectual potential via a single, brief oral or paper-and-pencil method. IQ tests were also the subject of countless jokes and cartoons. Still, by sticking to their tests and their tables of norms, the psychometricians were able to defend their instruments, even as they made their way back and forth among the halls of academe; their testing cubicles in schools, hospitals, and employment agencies; and the vaults in their banks.

Surprisingly, the conceptualization of intelligence did not advance much in the decades following the pioneering contributions of Binet, Terman, Yerkes, and their American and western European colleagues. Intelligence testing came to be seen, rightly or wrongly, as a technology useful primarily in selecting people to fill academic or vocational niches. In one of the most famous—and also most cloying—quips about intelligence testing, the influential Harvard psychologist E. G. Boring declared, "Intelligence *is* what the tests test." So long as these tests continued to do what they were supposed to do—that is, yield reasonable predictions about people's success in school—it did not seem necessary or prudent to probe too deeply into their meanings or to explore alternative views of what intelligence is or how it might be assessed.

THREE KEY QUESTIONS ABOUT INTELLIGENCE

Over the decades, scholars and students of intelligence have continued to argue about three questions. The first: Is intelligence singular, or are there various, relatively independent intellectual faculties? Purists—from Charles Spearman, an English psychologist who conducted research in the early 1900s, to his latter-day disciples Herrnstein and Murray—have defended the notion of a single, supervening "general intelligence." Pluralists—from the University of Chicago's L. L. Thurstone, who in the 1930s posited seven "vectors of the mind," to the University of Southern California's J. P. Guilford, who discerned up to one hundred and fifty "factors of the intellect"—have construed intelligence to be composed of many dissociable components. In his much cited *The Mismeasure of Man*, the paleontologist Stephen Jay Gould argued that the conflicting conclusions reached on this issue simply reflect alternative assumptions about a particular statistical procedure ("factor analysis") rather than about "the way the mind really is." More specifically, depending upon the assumptions made, the procedure called "factor analysis" can yield different conclusions about the extent to which different test items do (or do not) correlate with one another. In the ongoing debate among psychologists about this issue, the psychometric majority favors a general intelligence perspective.

The general public, however, generally focus on a second, even more contentious question: Is intelligence (or are intelligences) predominantly inherited? Actually, this is by and large a Eurocentric question. In the Confucius-influenced societies of East Asia, it is widely assumed that individual differences in intellectual endowment are modest and that personal effort largely accounts for achievement level. Interestingly, Darwin was sympathetic to this viewpoint. He wrote to his cousin Galton, "I have always maintained that, excepting for fools, men did not differ much in intelligence, only in zeal and hard work."

In the West, however, there is more support for the view—first defended vocally by Galton and Terman, and echoed recently by Hernstein and Murray—that intelligence is inborn and that a person can do little to alter his or her quantitative intellectual birthright.

Studies of identical twins reared apart provide surprisingly strong support for the "heritability" of psychometric intelligence (the intelligence tapped in standard measures like an IQ test). That is, if one wants to predict someone's score on an intelligence test, it is on the average more relevant to know the identity of the biological parents (even if the individual has had no contact with them) than the identity of the adoptive parents. By the same token, the IQs of identical twins are more similar than the IQs of fraternal twins. And contrary to both common sense and political correctness, IQs of biologically related individuals actually grow more *similar*, rather than more different, after adolescence. (This trend could be a by-product of general healthiness, which aids performance on any mental or physical measure, rather than a direct result of native intellect reasserting itself.)

While the statistics point to significant heritability of IQs, many scholars still object to the suggestion that biological lineage largely determines intelligence. They argue, among other things:

- The science of behavioral genetics was developed to work with animals other than humans. In any event, it is a new science that is changing rapidly.
- Since researchers cannot conduct genuine experiments with human beings (such as randomly assigning identical and fraternal twins to different homes), behavioral genetic conclusions involve unwarranted extrapolations from necessarily messy data.
- Only people from certain environments—chiefly middle-class Americans—have been studied, so we cannot know about the

"elasticity" of human potential across more diverse environments.

- Because they look alike, identical twins are more likely to elicit similar responses from others in their environment.
- Generally, identical twins reared apart were placed in backgrounds similar to those of their biological parents, in terms of race, ethnicity, social class, and so forth.
- Identical twins reared apart did share one environment from conception to birth.

Even without such findings for support, many of the general public as well as scholars simply feel uncomfortable with the view that culture and child rearing are impotent when stacked against the powers of the gene. They point to the enormous differences between individuals raised in different cultural settings (or even different cultures within one country), and they cite the often impressive results of their own and others' efforts to rear children who exhibit certain traits and values. Of course, the resulting differences among children are not necessarily an argument against genetic factors. After all, different racial and ethnic groups may differ in respect to their genetic makeup, on intellectual as well as physical dimensions. And children with different genetic makeups may elicit different responses from their parents.

Most scholars agree that even if psychometric intelligence is largely inherited, it is not possible to pinpoint the reasons for differences in average IQ *between* groups. For instance, the fifteen-point difference typically observed in the United States between African-American and white populations cannot be readily explained, because it is not possible in our society to equate the contemporary (let alone the historical) experiences of these two groups. The conundrum: One could only ferret out genetic differences in intellect (if any) between black and white populations in a society that was literally color-blind.

A third question has intrigued observers: Are intelligence tests biased? In early intelligence tests, the cultural assumptions built into certain items are glaring. After all, who except the wealthy could draw on personal experiences to answer questions about polo or fine wines? And if a test question asks respondents whether they would turn over money found in the street to the police, might responses not differ for middle-class respondents and destitute ones? Would the responses not be shaped by the knowledge that the police force is known to be hostile to members of one's own ethnic or racial group? However, test scorers cannot consider such issues or nuances, and therefore score only orthodox responses as correct. Since these issues resurfaced in the 1960s, psychometricians have striven to remove the obviously biased items from intelligence measures.

It is far more difficult, though, to deal with biases built into the test situation. For example, personal background certainly figures into someone's reactions to being placed in an unfamiliar surrounding, instructed by an interrogator who is dressed in a certain way and speaks with a certain accent, and given a printed test booklet to fill out or a computer-based test to click. And as the Stanford psychologist Claude Steele has shown, the biases prove even more acute in cases when the test takers belong to a racial or ethnic group widely considered to be less smart than the dominant group (who are more likely to be the creators, administrators, and scorers of the test), and when these test takers *know* their intellect is being measured.

Talk of bias touches on the frequently held assumption that tests in general, and intelligence tests in particular, are inherently conservative instruments—tools of the establishment. Interestingly, some test pioneers thought of themselves as social progressives who were devising instruments that could reveal people of talent, even if they came from "remote and apparently inferior institutions" (to quote wording used in a catalogue for admission to Harvard College in the early 1960s).

And occasionally, the tests did reveal intellectual diamonds in the rough. More often, however, the tests indicated the promise of people from privileged backgrounds (as evidenced, for instance, in the correlation between wealthy areas' ZIP codes and high IQ scores). Despite the claims of Herrnstein and Murray, the nature of the causal relation between IQ and social privilege has not been settled; indeed, it continues to stimulate many dissertations in the social sciences.

Paradoxically, the extensive use of IQ scores has led to the tests not being widely administered anymore. There has been much legal wrangling about the propriety of making consequential decisions about education (or, indeed, life chances) on the basis of IQ scores; as a result, many public school officials have become test shy. (Independent schools are not under the same constraints and have remained friendly to IQ-style measurements—the larger the applicant pool, the friendlier the admissions office!) By and large, IQ testing in the schools is now restricted to cases in which there is a recognized problem (such as a suspected learning disability) or a selection procedure (such as determining eligibility for an enrichment program that serves gifted children). Nevertheless, intelligence testing—and, perhaps more importantly, the line of thinking that gives rise to it—have actually won the war. Many widely used scholastic measures are thinly disguised intelligence tests—almost clones thereof—that correlate highly with scores on standard psychometric instruments. Virtually no one raised in the developed world today has gone untouched by Binet's deceptively simple invention of a century ago.

ATTACKS ON THE INTELLIGENCE ESTABLISHMENT

Although securely ensconced in many corners of society, the concept of intelligence has in recent years undergone its most robust challenges since the days of Walter Lippmann and the *New Republic* crowd. People informed by psychology but not bound by psychometricians' assumptions have invaded this formerly sacrosanct territory. They have put forth their own conceptions about what intelligence is, how (and even whether) it should be measured, and which values should be invoked in shaping the human intellect. For the first time in many years, the intelligence establishment is clearly on the defensive, and it seems likely that the twenty-first century will usher in fresh ways of thinking about intelligence.

The history of science is a tricky business, and particularly so when one sits in the midst of it. The rethinking of intelligence has been affected especially by the perspectives of scholars who are not psychologists. For instance, anthropologists, who spend their lives immersed in cultures different from their own, have called attention to the parochialism of the Western view of intelligence. Some cultures do not even have a concept called intelligence, and others define intelligence in terms of traits that Westerners might consider odd—obedience or good listening skills or moral fiber, for example. These scholars also have pointed out the strong and typically unexamined assumption built into testing instruments: that performance on a set of unrelated items, mostly drawn from the world of schooling, can somehow be summed up to yield a single measure of intellect. From their perspective, it makes far more sense to look at a culture's popular theory of intellect and to devise measures or observations that catch such forms of thinking on the fly. As the cross-cultural investigator Patricia Greenfield has remarked, with respect to the typical Western testing instrument, "You can't take it with you."

Neuroscientists are equally suspicious of the psychologists' assumptions about intellect. Half a century ago, there were still neuroscientists who believed that the brain was an all-purpose machine and that any portion of the brain could subserve any human cognitive or perceptual function. However, this "equipotential" position (as it was called) is no longer tenable. All evidence now points to the brain as being a highly differentiated organ: Specific capacities, ranging from the perception of the angle of a line to the production of a particular linguistic sound, are linked to specific neural networks. From this perspective, it makes much more sense to think of the brain as harboring an indefinite number of intellectual capacities, whose relationship to one another needs to be clarified.

It is possible to acknowledge the brain's highly differentiated nature and still adhere to a more general view of intelligence. Some investigators believe that nervous systems differ from one another in the speed and efficiency of neural signaling, and that this characteristic may underlie differences in individuals' measured intelligence. Some empirical support exists for this position, though no one yet knows whether such differences in signaling efficiency are inborn or can be developed. Those partial to the general view of intelligence also point to the increasingly well-documented flexibility (or plasticity) of the human brain during the early years of life. This plasticity suggests that different parts of the brain can take over a given function, particularly when pathology arises. Still, noting that some flexibility exists in the organization of human capacities during early life is hardly tantamount to concluding that intelligence is a single property of a whole brain. And the early flexibility evidence runs counter to the frequently voiced argument of "generalists" that intelligence is fixed and unchangeable.

Finally, the trends in computer science and artificial intelligence also militate against the entrenched view of a single, general-purpose intellect. When artificial intelligence was first developed in the 1950s and 1960s, programmers generally viewed problem solving as a generic capacity and contended that a useful problem-solving program should be applicable to a variety of problems (for example, one should be able to use a single program to play chess, understand language, and recognize faces). The history of computer science has witnessed a steady accumulation of evidence against this "general problem-solver" tradition. Rather than setting up programs that embrace general heuristic strategies, scientists have found it far more productive to build specific kinds of knowledge into each program. So-called expert systems "know" a great deal about a certain domain (such as chemical spectrography, voice recognition, or chess moves) and essentially nothing about the other domains of experience. Development of a machine that is generally smart seems elusive—and is perhaps a fundamentally wrong-headed conceit.

Like neuroscientists, some computer scientists have retained a generic view of intelligence. They point to new parallel-distributed systems (PDPs) whose workings are more akin to the human brain's processes than the step-by-step procedures of earlier computational systems. Such PDPs do not need to have knowledge built into them; like most animals, they learn from accumulated experience, even experience unmediated by explicit symbols and rules. Still, such systems have not yet exhibited forms of thinking that cut across different content areas (as a general intelligence is supposed to do); if anything, their realms of expertise have thus far proved even more specific than those displayed by expert systems based on earlier computer models.

The insularity of most psychological discussions came home to me recently when I appeared on a panel devoted to the topic of intelligence. For a change, I was the only psychologist. An experimental physicist summarized what is known about the intelligence of different animals. A mathematical physicist discussed the nature of matter, as it allows for conscious and intelligent behavior. A computer scientist described the kinds of complex systems that can be built out of simple, nervelike units and sought to identify the point at which these systems begin to exhibit intelligent, and perhaps even creative, behavior. As I listened intently to these thoughtful scholars, I clearly realized that psychologists no longer own the term *intelligence*—if we ever did. What it means to be intelligent is a profound philosophical question, one that requires grounding in biological, physical, and mathematical knowledge. Correlations (or noncorrelations) among test scores mean little once one ventures beyond the campus of the Educational Testing Service.

THE RESTLESSNESS AMONG PSYCHOLOGISTS

Even some psychologists have been getting restless, and none more so than the Yale psychologist Robert Sternberg. Born in 1949, Sternberg has written dozens of books and several hundred articles, most focusing on intelligence in one way or another. Influenced by the new view of the mind as an "information-processing device," Sternberg began with the strategic goal of understanding the actual mental processes—the discrete mental steps—someone would employ when responding to standardized test items. He asked what happens—on a millisecond-by-millisecond basis—when one must solve analogies or indicate an understanding of vocabulary words. What does the mind do, step by step, as it completes the analogy "Lincoln : president :: Margaret Thatcher : ?" According to Sternberg, it is not sufficient to know whether someone could arrive at the correct answer. Rather, one should look at the test taker's actual mental steps in solving a problem, identify the difficulties encountered, and, to the extent possible, figure out how to help this person and others solve items of this sort.

Sternberg soon went beyond identifying the components of standard intelligence testing. First, he asked about the ways in which people actually order the components of reasoning: For example, how do they decide how much time to allot to a problem, and how do they know whether they've made a right choice? As a cognitive scientist might put it, he probed the microstructure of problem solving. Second, Sternberg began to examine two previously neglected forms of intelligence. He investigated the capacity of individuals to automatize familiar information or problems, so that they can be free to direct their attention to new and unfamiliar information. And he looked at how people deal practically with different kinds of contexts—how they know and use what is needed to behave intelligently at school, at work, on the streets, and even when one is in love. Sternberg noted that these latter forms of "practical intelligence" are extremely important for success in our society and yet are rarely, if ever, taught explicitly or tested systematically.

More so than many other critics of standard intelligence testing, Sternberg has sought to measure these newly recognized forms of intelligence through the kinds of pencil-and-paper laboratory methods favored by the profession. And he has found that people's ability to deal effectively with novel information or to adapt to diverse contexts can be differentiated from their success with standard IQ-test–style problems. (These findings should come as no surprise to those who have seen high-IQ people flounder outside of a school setting or those who, at a high school or college reunion, have found their academically average or below-average peers to be the richest or most powerful alumni at the event.) But Sternberg's efforts to create a new intelligence test have not been crowned with easy victory. Most psychometricians are conservative: They cling to their tried-and-true tests and believe any new tests to be marketed must correlate highly with existing instruments, such as the familiar Stanford-Binet or Wechsler tests.

Other psychologists have also called attention to neglected aspects of the terrain of intelligence. For example, David Olson of the University of Toronto has emphasized the importance of mastering different media (like computers) or symbol systems (like written or graphic materials) and has redefined *intelligence* as "skill in the use of a medium." The psychologists Gavriel Salomon and Roy Pea, both experts on technology and education, have noted the extent to which intelligence inheres in the resources to which a person has access, ranging from pencils to Rolodexes™ to libraries or computer networks. In their view, intelligence is better thought of as "distributed" in the world rather than concentrated "in the head." Similarly, the psychologist James Greeno and anthropologist Jean Lave have described intelligence as being "situated": By observing others, one learns to behave appropriately in situations and thereby appears intelligent. According to a strict situationalist perspective, it does not make sense to think of a separate capacity called intelligence that moves with a person from one place to another. And my colleague at Harvard, David Perkins, has stressed the extent to which intelligence is learnable: One can master various strategies, acquire different kinds of expertise, and learn to negotiate in varied settings.

Nearly every year ushers in a new set of books and a new ensemble of ideas about intelligence. On the heels of *The Bell Curve* and *Emotional Intelligence* came David Perkins's *Outsmarting IQ*, Stephen Ceci's *On Intelligence: More or Less*, Robert Sternberg's *Successful Intelligence*, and Robert Coles's *Moral Intelligence of Children*. Some of the authors sought to differentiate among different forms of intelligence, such as those dealing with novel, as opposed to "crystallized," information. Some sought to broaden the expanse of intelligence to include emotions, morality, creativity, or leadership. And others sought to bring intelligence wholly or partially outside the head, situating it in the group, the organization, the community, the media, or the symbol systems of a culture.

The different textures of these books are of interest chiefly to those within the trade of social scientists. Outsiders are well advised not to try to follow every new warp and woof, since many will soon unravel. However, the general message is clear: Intelligence, as a construct to be defined and a capacity to be measured, is no longer the property of a specific group of scholars who view it from a narrowly psychometric perspective. In the future, many disciplines will help define intelligence, and many more interest groups will participate in the measurement and uses of it.

Now I want to focus on the view of intelligence that, in my view, has the strongest scientific support and the greatest utility for the next millennium: the theory of multiple intelligences.

THE THEORY OF MULTIPLE INTELLIGENCES

A Personal Perspective

ORIGINS

Nothing in my youth foretold that I would become a student (and a theorist) of intelligence. As a child, I was a good student and a good test taker, so the issue of intelligence was relatively unproblematic for me. Indeed, in another life, I might have become a defender of the classical view of intelligence, like so many of my aging white male contemporaries.

The proverbial Jewish boy who hated the sight of blood, I (and many others in my world) expected that I would become a lawyer. Only in 1965, at the close of my undergraduate years at Harvard College, did I decide to pursue graduate studies in psychology. At first, like other adolescents, I was fascinated by the issues of psychology that intrigue the layperson: emotions, personality, and psychopathology. My heroes were Sigmund Freud and my own teacher, the psychoanalyst Erik Erikson, who had been analyzed by Freud's daughter, Anna. However, after meeting Jerome Bruner, a pioneering researcher of cognition and human development, and after reading the works of Bruner and his own master, the Swiss psychologist Jean Piaget, I decided instead to undertake graduate studies in cognitive-developmental psychology.

THE PATH INTO NEUROPSYCHOLOGY

Once I had begun my studies of developmental psychology, I was surprised by one phenomenon: Nearly all developmentalists assumed that scientific thought and the career of science represented the pinnacles or "end-states"of human cognitive development. That is, people with fully developed cognitive capacities would think like scientists— indeed, like the kind of people who studied developmental psychology or (even better!) particle physics or molecular biology. This is not the first time in the history of the academy that scholars looked into their disciplinary mirrors and saw their own reflections. In fact, it is this kind of egocentric thinking that led to the creation of the items on current intelligence tests.

In a way, I was no different. But there was one exception: When I was a youth, music in particular and the arts in general were important parts of my life. Therefore, when I began to think of what it meant to be "developed," when I asked myself what optimal human development is, I became convinced that developmentalists had to pay much more attention to the skills and capacities of painters, writers, musicians, dancers, and other artists. Stimulated (rather than intimidated) by the prospect of broadening the definition of *cognition*, I found it comfortable to deem the capacities of those in the arts as fully cognitive—no less cognitive than the skills of mathematicians and scientists, as viewed by my fellow developmental psychologists.

My early research career followed naturally from this train of reasoning. Piaget and his colleagues had illuminated children's cognitive development by tracing how youngsters became able to think like scientists. By a parallel line of reasoning, my colleagues and I studied how children became able to think and perform like artists. Thus we began to design experiments and observational studies that would illuminate the stages and phases of the development of artistry.

Through associations with the philosopher Nelson Goodman and with others interested in artistic thinking, development, and education, I was exposed to a wide range of contemporary thinking on the arts and, more broadly, on human symbolization. Much of this exposure occurred at Project Zero, a Harvard Graduate School of Education research group (with which I have been affiliated since its start in 1967). Without question, the epochal event for me was the almost chance opportunity in 1969 to hear a lecture at Project Zero by the already eminent neurologist Norman Geschwind. Before that, I had not thought much about the human brain—indeed, in the late 1960s few of my colleagues in human development thought much about the nervous system. Geschwind, however, not only had pored over the neuroscientific literature of the past century but also had studied many people affected by strokes or other kinds of brain damage. With his colleagues, he documented the amazing, counterintuitive patterns of spared and lost capacities resulting from such damage.

Almost immediately, I was transformed into a student of neuropsychology. Until then, I had been wrestling with the issues of how artists develop the capacities they exhibit and how they manage to create, perform, and critique at high levels. I was not making much progress, for any number of reasons. I myself was not in any real sense an artist; many artists are understandably reluctant to have their minds dissected by a graduate student in psychology; some of those willing to serve as guinea pigs have little insight into the workings of their own minds; and, in any event, artists' skills are typically so fluent that they prove difficult to dissect and analyze in context.

The ravages of brain damage change this picture. Every stroke represents an accident of nature from which the careful observer can learn
much. Suppose, for example, one wants to study the relation between
the ability to speak fluently and the ability to sing fluently. One can
mount arguments indefinitely about the relatedness or the independence of these faculties, but the facts of brain damage actually resolve
the debate. Human singing and human language are different faculties,
that can be independently damaged or spared. Paradoxically, however,
human *signing* and human speaking are similar faculties. Those parts
of the brain that subserve spoken language in hearing people are
(roughly speaking) the same parts of the brain that subserve sign language in deaf people. So here we encounter an underlying linguistic
faculty that cuts across sensory and motor modalities.

After learning a bit about neuropsychology, I realized I should join a
neurological unit and investigate in detail how the brain operates in
normal people and how it is impaired and sometimes retrained following injury to the nervous system. Thanks to the support of Geschwind
and his colleagues, I was able to do just that: I spent a good deal of
time (and continued for the next twenty years) working as an investigator at the Boston University Aphasia Research Center, part of the
Boston University School of Medicine and the Boston Veterans Administration Medical Center. Actually, this became part of my professional
dual track. Each morning I would journey to the Aphasia Research
Center, with its population of stroke victims suffering from impaired
language and other kinds of cognitive and emotional disorders. I
would try to understand each patient's pattern of abilities and also
carry out experiments with groups of patients. I was particularly interested in the fate of artistic capacities under conditions of brain damage,
but quite naturally, my inquiries spread out until they encompassed a
wide range of human problem-solving capacities. At noon or shortly
thereafter, I would visit my other laboratory, located at Harvard's Proj-

ect Zero, where I worked with ordinary and gifted children in an attempt to understand the development of human cognitive capacities. Again, I focused on artistic capacities (such as storytelling, drawing, and showing sensitivity to artistic style), but I gradually incorporated many other abilities seen as part of general cognition.

The daily opportunity to work with children and with brain-damaged adults impressed me with one brute fact of human nature: People have a wide range of capacities. A person's strength in one area of performance simply does not predict any comparable strengths in other areas.

More specifically, some children seem to be good at many things; others, very few. In most cases, however, strengths are distributed in a skewed fashion. For instance, a person may be skilled in acquiring foreign languages, yet be unable to find her way around an unfamiliar environment or learn a new song or figure out who occupies a position of power in a crowd of strangers. Likewise, weakness in learning foreign languages does not predict either success or failure with most other cognitive tasks.

I also came to appreciate the fact that skewed strengths are even more apparent after brain disease, especially in relation to the site of damage. If a right-handed person suffers damage to the central areas of his left cortex, for instance, he will almost certainly become aphasic, that is, have difficulty in speaking, comprehending, reading, and writing. (Aphasiologists can make more specific predictions, based on the precise location and depth of the cortical lesion.) Most other functions will remain reasonably intact. That same person, with damage in comparable parts of the right hemisphere, will have few, if any, of the aforementioned linguistic problems, yet will, depending on the site of the lesion, probably have difficulty in maintaining spatial orientation, singing a tune, or relating properly to other people. Strangely enough, the latter problems will not arise for most right-handers, following even significant injury to the left hemisphere. (I don't mean to slight left-handers. I was born left-handed but, like many other children of European background, was shifted to being a right-hander.) The organization of capacities in left-handers is less predictable. Some left-handers have cortical representation just like right-handers, some have the opposite pattern, and some are a curious hybrid.

Both of the populations I was working with were clueing me into the same message: that the human mind is better thought of as a series of relatively separate faculties, with only loose and nonpredictable relations with one another, than as a single, all-purpose machine that performs steadily at a certain horsepower, independent of content and context. On an intuitive level, I had embraced the view of the human brain and the human mind that is now called *modularity*: the view that, over hundreds of thousands of years, the human mind/brain has evolved a number of separate organs or information-processing devices. I had arrived at this insight by 1974, when I completed a book in neuropsychology, *The Shattered Mind*. Indeed, I have in my files a book outline dating from 1976 called *Kinds of Minds*, in which I planned to describe the various kinds of minds given to us by nature—how they develop in young children and how they decompose under various forms of brain damage.

However, I did not write that book, probably because I was not yet convinced that I knew exactly what those kinds of minds *were* and how they could best be described. The opportunity to tackle these questions head-on materialized in 1979, when a group of colleagues and I received a generous five-year grant from the Bernard Van Leer Foundation of the Netherlands. Under the grant, we were to produce a scholarly synthesis of what had been established in the biological, social, and cultural sciences about the "nature and realization of human potential." Given my own predilections, my assignment on the "Project on Human Potential" was straightforward, if a bit daunting: to write about recent advances in our understanding of the human mind.

THE DEFINITION AND CRITERIA
FOR MULTIPLE INTELLIGENCES

It took four years of research to proceed from the Van Leer invitation to the positing of the theory explored in the *Kinds of Minds* outline. I knew intuitively that I wanted to describe the human faculties, but I needed a method to determine those faculties as well as a way to write about them. I had always been intrigued by the challenge and promise of examining human cognition through a number of discrete disciplinary lenses. I enjoyed investigating psychology, neurology, biology, sociology, and anthropology as well as the arts and humanities. And so I began reading systematically in these areas in order to gain as much information as possible about the nature of various kinds of human faculties and the relationships among them.

At the same time, I pondered how best to write about my discoveries. I considered using the venerable scholarly term *human faculties*; psychologists' terms like *skills* or *capacities*; or lay terms like *gifts, talents*, or *abilities*. However, I realized that each of these words harbored pitfalls. I finally elected to take the bold step of appropriating a word from psychology and stretching it in new ways—that word, of course, was *intelligence*. I began by defining *an intelligence* as "the ability to solve problems or to create products that are valued within one or more cultural settings." I called attention to key facts about most theories of intelligence: namely, they looked only at problem solving and ignored the creation of products, and they assumed that intelligence would be evident and appreciated anywhere, regardless of what was (and was not) valued in particular cultures at particular times. This is the definition that I used in the 1983 book that grew out of the Van Leer project: *Frames of Mind: The Theory of Multiple Intelligences*.

Nearly two decades later, I offer a more refined definition. I now conceptualize an intelligence as *a biopsychological potential to process*

information that can be activated in a cultural setting to solve prob-
lems or create products that are of value in a culture. This modest
change in wording is important because it suggests that intelligences
are not things that can be seen or counted. Instead, they are potentials—presumably, neural ones—that will or will not be activated,
depending upon the values of a particular culture, the opportunities
available in that culture, and the personal decisions made by individuals and/or their families, schoolteachers, and others.

I have pondered what would have happened if I had written a book
called *Seven Human Gifts* or *The Seven Faculties of the Human Mind*.
My guess is that it would not have attracted much attention. It is
sobering to think that labeling can have much influence in the scholarly world, but I have little doubt that my decision to write about
"human intelligences" was a fateful one. Instead of producing a theory
(and a book) that simply catalogued things that people could excel in,
I was proposing an expansion of the term *intelligence* so that it would
encompass many capacities that had been considered outside its scope.
Moreover, in arguing that these faculties were relatively independent
of one another, I was challenging the widespread belief—one held by
many psychologists and entrenched in our many languages—that intelligence is a single faculty and that one is either "smart" or "stupid"
across the board.

I was by no means the first psychologist to posit relatively independent human faculties, though I may have been among the first persons
to violate the rules of English (and other Indo-European tongues) by
pluralizing the term *intelligence*. Indeed, a whole (if brief) history of
psychology could be written about taxonomies of human faculties, as
indicated in chapter 2 and discussed at length in the textbook *Intelligence: Multiple Perspectives*.

I did, however, pioneer ways of exploring the sources of evidence
that undergird my list of human intelligences. Other accounts of intelli-

gences came primarily out of the psychometric tradition. Psychologists administered tests or test items to people and examined the pattern of correlation among the resulting scores. If the scores correlated highly with one another, the psychologists assumed that they reflected the operation of a single, underlying general intelligence (the fabled "g"). If, however, the matrix of correlations appeared to have been spawned by a variety of factors, the psychologists endorsed the possibility of separate human faculties. In either case, the psychometric approach to intellectual plurality was (and still is) generally restricted to those faculties assessable through brief oral questions or paper-and-pencil instruments. Also, as stressed by Stephen Jay Gould, the psychometricians' conclusions reflected their particular statistical assumptions, ways of handling the data, and approaches to interpreting the results.

My approach was entirely different. Instead of relying primarily on the results of psychometric instruments, I laid out a set of eight separate criteria. I combed the relevant scientific literature for evidence on the existence of many candidate faculties. Indeed, like Galton and Binet, I started with faculties tied closely to particular sensory modalities (for example, a candidate "visual intelligence" and a candidate "tactile intelligence"). Of course, I found differing amounts and quality of research on the various candidate faculties. (Scientists know much more, for example, about the faculty of language than about the faculty of self-knowledge.) Still, accepting the available evidence, I asked myself whether a candidate faculty met the set of criteria reasonably well. If it did, I called it a human intelligence; if it did not, I either searched for another way of conceptualizing this ability or cast it aside.

The Criteria's Roots and Meanings

One way of introducing the criteria is to group them in terms of their disciplinary roots. From the biological sciences came two criteria:

1. *The potential of isolation by brain damage*—As a neuropsychologist, I was particularly interested in evidence that one candidate intelligence could be dissociated from others. Either patients exist who have this intelligence spared despite other damaged faculties, or there are patients in whom this faculty has been impaired while others have been spared. Either pattern increases the likelihood that an intelligence has been discovered. Thus, both the separation of language from other faculties and its essential similarity in oral, aural, written, and sign forms point to a separate linguistic intelligence.

2. *An evolutionary history and evolutionary plausibility*—Despite all its gaps, evidence about the evolution of our species is crucial to any discussion of the contemporary mind and brain. When I wrote *Frames of Mind*, most of the evidence came from either inferences about *Homo sapiens* and its predecessors or information about contemporary species. Thus, we can infer that early hominids had to be capable spatially of finding their way around diverse terrains, and we can study the highly developed spatial capacities of other mammalian species, like rats. More recently, the emerging field of evolutionary psychology has given students of human cognition new tools. Evolutionary psychologists engage in reverse engineering: from the contemporary operation of human capacities, they try to infer the selection pressures that led over many thousands of years to the development of a particular faculty. These studies give new plausibility to evolutionary accounts of such faculties as the intelligence that scrutinizes the world of plants and animals, or the intelligence that computes the motives of other members of the species.

Two other criteria emanate from logical analysis:

3. *An identifiable core operation or set of operations*—In the real world, specific intelligences operate in rich environments, typically in

conjunction with several other intelligences. For analytic purposes, however, it is important to tease out capacities that seem central or "core" to an intelligence. These capacities are likely to be mediated by specific neural mechanisms and triggered by relevant internal or external types of information. Analysis suggests that linguistic intelligence, for instance, includes core operations of phonemic discriminations, command of syntax, sensitivity to the pragmatic uses of language, and acquisition of word meanings. Other intelligences also have their component operations or processes, such as the sensitivity to large-scale, local, three-dimensional and two-dimensional spaces (spatial intelligence), or the aspects of musical processing that encompass pitch, rhythm, timbre, and harmony (musical intelligence).

The existence of what I've termed "intellectual cores" or "subintelligences" raises an important question: Are these "cores"—sometimes called "subintelligences"—closely enough linked to warrant their being grouped under seven to eight generic headings? I believe that, even if these "cores" or subintelligences are actually separate from one another, they tend to be used in conjunction with one another and so merit being grouped together. In other words, even if there were some scientific justification for disaggregating the "cores," there is much to be said for positing a small number of intelligences.

4. *Susceptibility to encoding in a symbol system*—Particularly at work and in school, we spend much of our time mastering and manipulating various kinds of symbol systems—spoken and written language, mathematical systems, charts, drawings, logical equations, and so on. Rather than occurring naturally, these systems have been developed—and are being developed—by people to convey culturally meaningful information systematically and accurately. Historically, symbol systems seem to have arisen precisely to code those meanings to which the human intelligences are most sensitive. Indeed, with respect to each

human intelligence, there are both societal and personal symbol systems that allow people to traffic in certain kinds of meanings. And so, because humans isolate events and draw inferences about them, we have developed linguistic and pictorial symbols that can handily capture the meanings of events. The human brain seems to have evolved to process certain kinds of symbols efficiently. Put differently, symbol systems may have been developed precisely because of their preexisting, ready fit with the relevant intelligence or intelligences.

Two of the criteria came from developmental psychology:

5. *A distinct developmental history, along with a definable set of expert "end-state" performances.* Individuals do not exhibit their intelligences "in the raw"; they do so by occupying certain relevant niches in their society, for which they must prepare by passing through an often lengthy developmental process. In a sense, intelligences have their own developmental histories. Thus, people who want to be mathematicians must develop their logical-mathematical abilities in certain ways. Other people must follow distinctive developmental paths to become, for instance, clinicians with well-developed interpersonal intelligence or musicians with well-developed musical intelligence.

As I elaborate in Chapter 6, there is an unfortunate tendency to confuse or conflate an intelligence with a societal domain. Ideally, we should speak of the development of a mathematician in the societal domain called mathematics, rather than the development of mathematical intelligence. If I were to rework this criterion today, I would speak about the development of end states that harness particular intelligences. Moreover, I would underscore the importance of assuming a *cross-cultural perspective,* since an intelligence may be revealingly corralled in cultures that exhibit very different roles and value systems. For example, both the clinician in American culture and the shaman in a tribal culture are using their interpersonal intelligences but in different ways and for somewhat different ends.

6. *The existence of idiot savants, prodigies, and other exceptional people.* As I have noted, in ordinary life, intelligences commingle freely, almost with abandon. Thus, it is particularly important for researchers to take advantage of those accidents in nature, such as trauma or strokes, that allow them to observe the identity and operations of a particular intelligence in sharp relief. Nature provides one other bounty to the student of multiple intelligences: people who, without any documented signs of brain injury, have unusual profiles of intelligence. One example is the *savant*, who exhibits an area of stunning strength along with other ordinary abilities or even marked deficits. Autistic people are an even clearer example, since many autistic children are outstanding at numerical calculation, musical performance or reproduction of melodies, or drawing. At the same time, they characteristically evince marked impairments in communication, language, and sensitivity to others. Indeed, researchers have recently proposed that autistic people—like individuals who suffer significant damage to the right hemisphere—may have an impairment in the brain area that governs the ability to understand other people's intentions.

More fortunate is the prodigy, the person who is outstanding in a specific performance area and talented, or at least average, in other areas. Like the autistic person, prodigies tend to emerge in domains that are rule governed and that require little life experience, such as chess, mathematics, representational drawing, and other forms of pattern recognition and creation. Often, prodigies have advantages and disadvantages that accompany their special status in life: They may be able to work effectively with much older people, but they may also have difficulty relating to their peers. Contrary to popular wisdom, most prodigies neither become great creators nor end up as broken people; rather, they become experts in an area that draws on one or more intelligences but are unlikely to leave a permanent mark on the world.

The final two criteria are drawn from traditional psychological research:

7. *Support from experimental psychological tasks.* Psychologists can tease out the extent to which two operations are related to each other by observing how well people can carry out two activities simultaneously. If one activity does not interfere with the other, researchers can assume that the activities draw on discrete brain and mental capacities. For example, most of us have no trouble walking or finding our way around while we are conversing; the intelligences involved are separate. On the other hand, we often find it very difficult to converse while we are working on a crossword puzzle or listening to a song with words; in these cases, two manifestations of linguistic intelligence are competing. Studies of transfer (usually a good thing) or of unwarranted interference (usually a bad thing) can help us to identify discrete intelligences.

8. *Support from psychometric findings.* Since multiple intelligences theory was devised as a reaction to psychometrics, it may seem odd to see psychometric evidence cited in this discussion of supporting criteria. And indeed, much psychometric evidence can be read as a criticism of multiple intelligences, because this evidence suggests the presence of a "positive manifold"—a correlation in scores among various tasks.

Nonetheless, it is prudent to take psychometric findings into account. Studies of spatial and linguistic intelligences, for example, have yielded persuasive evidence that these two faculties have at best a weak correlation. Moreover, as psychologists have broadened their definitions of intelligence and increased their tools for measuring intelligence, psychometric evidence in favor of multiple intelligences has accrued. Thus, for example, studies of social intelligence have revealed a set of capacities different from standard linguistic and logical intelligences. Similarly, investigations of the new construct of emotional intelligence—roughly an amalgam of the two personal intelligences—have indicated that this phenomenon may well be independent of how one scores on the traditional intelligence-testing items.

The criteria I presented in 1983 do not represent the last word in the identification of intelligences. Today I might define them differently, and I would stress much more the relevance of cross-cultural evidence. Still, taken together, they constitute a reasonable set of factors to be considered in the study of human cognition. Indeed, I consider the establishment of these criteria to be one of the enduring contributions of multiple intelligences theory. Thus I have been surprised that commentators—whether well- or ill-disposed to the theory—have rarely called attention to the criteria. Perhaps because the criteria draw self-consciously from a number of disciplines, they fall outside the purview of many critics' interests and expertise.

THE ORIGINAL SEVEN INTELLIGENCES

In *Frames of Mind,* I proposed the existence of seven separate human intelligences. The first two—*linguistic* and *logical-mathematical*—are the ones that have typically been valued in school. *Linguistic intelligence* involves sensitivity to spoken and written language, the ability to learn languages, and the capacity to use language to accomplish certain goals. Lawyers, speakers, writers, poets are among the people with high linguistic intelligence.

Logical-mathematical intelligence involves the capacity to analyze problems logically, carry out mathematical operations, and investigate issues scientifically. Mathematicians, logicians, and scientists exploit logical-mathematical intelligence. (Piaget claimed that he was studying all of intelligence, but I believe that he was actually focusing on logical-mathematical intelligence.) Having a blend of linguistic and logical-mathematical intelligence is no doubt a blessing for students and for anyone else who must take tests regularly. Indeed, the fact that most psychologists and most other academics exhibit a reasonable amalgam of linguistic and logical intelligence made it almost inevitable that those faculties would dominate tests of intelligence. I often wonder whether a different set of faculties would have been isolated if the test developers had been business people, politicians, entertainers, or military personnel.

The next three intelligences are particularly notable in the arts, though each can be put to many other uses. *Musical intelligence* entails skill in the performance, composition, and appreciation of musical patterns. In my view, musical intelligence is almost parallel structurally to linguistic intelligence, and it makes neither scientific nor logical sense to call one (usually linguistic) an intelligence and the other (usually musical) a talent. *Bodily-kinesthetic intelligence* entails the potential of using one's whole body or parts of the body (like the hand or the mouth) to solve problems or fashion products. Obviously, dancers, actors, and athletes foreground bodily-kinesthetic intelligence. However, this form of intelligence is also important for craftspersons, surgeons, bench-top scientists, mechanics, and many other technically oriented professionals. *Spatial intelligence* features the potential to recognize and manipulate the patterns of wide space (those used, for instance, by navigators and pilots) as well as the patterns of more confined areas (such as those of importance to sculptors, surgeons, chess players, graphic artists, or architects). The wide-ranging ways in which spatial intelligence is deployed in different cultures clearly show how a biopsychological potential can be harnessed by domains that have evolved for a variety of purposes.

In the original list, the final two intelligences, which I call the personal intelligences, raised the most eyebrows. *Interpersonal intelligence* denotes a person's capacity to understand the intentions, motivations, and desires of other people and, consequently, to work effectively with others. Salespeople, teachers, clinicians, religious leaders, political leaders, and actors all need acute interpersonal intelligence. Finally, *intrapersonal intelligence* involves the capacity to understand oneself, to have an effective working model of oneself—including one's own desires, fears, and capacities—and to use such information effectively in regulating one's own life.

In *Frames of Mind*, I devoted separate chapters to each of the first five intelligences, but I treated the personal intelligences in a single chapter, as if they were of a piece. I still believe it makes sense to speak of two forms of personal intelligence—and, indeed, recent evolutionary and psychological work has stressed the long history of interpersonal intelligence (as compared to the relatively recent emergence of intrapersonal intelligence, perhaps in conjunction with human consciousness). In the initial discussion of intrapersonal intelligence, I also stressed its origins in a person's emotional life and its strong alliance with affective factors. I continue to view emotional life as a key ingredient of intrapersonal intelligence, but now I stress the vital role of intrapersonal intelligence in a person's life-course decisions. Also, I now consider emotional facets of each intelligence rather than restrict emotions to one or two personal intelligences. In Chapters 11 and 12, I further discuss the growing importance of intrapersonal intelligence as the new millennium approaches.

From the first, I emphasized that the list of intelligences was provisional, that each of the intelligences housed its own area or subintelligences, and that the relative autonomy of each intelligence and the ways the intelligences interact needed further study. Since *Frames of Mind* appeared, I have carefully examined works that might ultimately influence the cartography of the various intelligences. In fact, Chapter 4 is focused on the question of whether additional intelligences exist.

TWO ESSENTIAL CLAIMS

I am amazed that even though the theory was promulgated in the early 1980s, and even though I have spoken about it hundreds of times since then, it was only around 1997 that I fully appreciated the exact nature of my two fundamental claims about multiple intelligences. This theory presents two complementary claims. First, the theory is an account of human cognition in its fullness—I put forth the intelligences as a new definition of human nature, cognitively speaking. Whereas Socrates saw man as the rational animal and Freud stressed the irrationality of human beings, I (with due tentativeness) have described human beings as those organisms who possess a basic set of seven, eight, or a dozen intelligences. Thanks to evolution, each of us is equipped with these intellectual potentials, which we can mobilize and connect according to our own inclinations and our culture's preferences.

Given this perspective, it is instructive to consider how intelligences in other species compare with our own. Rats, for example, might best us in spatial and bodily-kinesthetic intelligence, though it seems adventurous to attribute to them any intrapersonal intelligence. The profiles of other primates—particularly chimpanzees—would be much closer to our own. The exercise can also be carried out with respect to artificial intelligence. While artificial-intelligence programs can no doubt trounce us logically—and may soon surpass us in many spatial and linguistic feats—I view the notion of the interpersonal intelligences of a machine as a "category error."

A specieswide definition represents one essential claim about human intelligences; the existence of individual differences in the profile of intelligences marks the other. Although we all receive these intelligences as part of our birthright, no two people have exactly the same intelligences in the same combinations. After all, intelligences arise from the combination of a person's genetic heritage and life conditions in a given culture and era. While identical twins raised in the same womb and the same home obviously share much of an environment, they still differ from one another because of the facts of their lives, which ensure that neither their psyches nor their brains are identical. Many identical twins, indeed, strive valiantly to differentiate themselves. And if human clones eventually appear, they will have somewhat different intelligences from their donors, if only because of the different environments in which they develop.

The second claim—that we each have a unique blend of intelligences—leads to the most important implication of the theory for the next millennium. We can choose to ignore this uniqueness, strive to minimize it, or revel in it. Without in any sense wishing to embrace egocentrism or narcissism, I suggest that the big challenge facing the deployment of human resources is how best to take advantage of the uniqueness conferred on us as the species exhibiting several intelligences.

One final point, to which I shall return repeatedly: It is tempting to think of particular intelligences as good or bad, and it is undoubtedly better to have more of certain intelligences than to lack those intelligences largely or wholly. That said, however, I must stress that no intelligence is in itself moral or immoral. Intelligences are strictly amoral, and any intelligence can be put to a constructive or a destructive use. Both the poet Johann Wolfgang von Goethe and the propagandist Josef

Goebbels were masters of the German language; however, Goethe used the language to create great art, while Goebbels spawned hatred. Both Mahatma Gandhi and Niccolò Machiavelli stressed the importance of understanding other people; however, Gandhi encouraged empathic responses, while Machiavelli directed his wit toward the manipulation of others. Clearly, we must strive to nurture both intelligences and morality and, insofar as possible, yoke them together as virtues. But it is a grave error to confuse the two. Constructive and positive use of intelligences does not happen by accident. Deciding how to deploy one's intelligences is a question of values, not computational power.

4

ARE THERE ADDITIONAL
INTELLIGENCES?

IN THE FIRST edition of *Frames of Mind,* I listed seven intelligences largely because these intelligences best met my eight criteria, but I readily conceded that the decision to enumerate seven entailed neither logical nor scientific necessity. Since then, I have repeatedly been asked about any expansions of the list. At first, I gave a lighthearted response: "My students have often asked me whether there is a cooking intelligence, a humor intelligence, or a sexual intelligence. They have concluded that I can recognize only the intelligences that I myself possess." More seriously, I have contemplated a number of candidate additional intelligences but until recently have thought it prudent not to expand the list.

Here, I consider directly the evidence for three "new" candidate intelligences: a *naturalist intelligence*, a *spiritual intelligence*, and an *existential intelligence*. The strength of the evidence for these varies, and whether or not to declare a certain human capacity another type of intelligence is certainly a judgment call. My mission here is to explore anew the process of identifying an intelligence and to voice my reservations about extending the concept in less secure directions.

THE NATURALIST INTELLIGENCE

I generally introduce each intelligence in terms of an end state—a socially recognized and valued role that appears to rely heavily on a particular intellectual capacity. Thus, I designate a poet to denote linguistic intelligence, a computer scientist to represent logical-mathematical intelligence, and a salesperson or a clinical psychologist to exemplify interpersonal intelligence.

The very term *naturalist* combines a description of the core ability with a characterization of a role that many cultures value. A naturalist demonstrates expertise in the recognition and classification of the numerous species—the flora and fauna—of his or her environment. Every culture prizes people who not only can recognize members of a species that are especially valuable or notably dangerous but also can appropriately categorize new or unfamiliar organisms. In cultures without formal science, the naturalist is the person most skilled in applying the accepted "folk taxonomies"; in cultures with a scientific orientation, the naturalist is a biologist who recognizes and categorizes specimens in terms of accepted formal taxonomies, such as the botanical ones devised in the 1700s by the Swedish scientist Carolus Linnaeus.

In Western culture, the word *naturalist* is readily applied to those with extensive knowledge of the living world. The environmentalist Rachel Carson and the ornithologists John James Audubon and Roger Tory Peterson come to mind, as do others who have studied organisms for more theoretically oriented purposes, such as Charles Darwin, Louis Agassiz, Ernst Mayr, Stephen Jay Gould, or E. O. Wilson. Interestingly, Darwin said that he was "born a naturalist" and Wilson titled his 1994 autobiography *Naturalist*. My recognition that such individuals could not readily be classified in terms of the seven antecedent intelligences led me to consider this additional form of intelligence and to construe the scope of the naturalist's abilities more broadly.

The application of these abilities, in making and justifying distinctions, can occur through ordinary vision or under magnification—or by nonvisual means. For example, blind people can be acute in recognizing species, and the renowned twentieth-century Dutch naturalist Geermat Vermij depends on touch. Also, it seems reasonable to assume that a naturalist's capacities can be brought to bear on artificial items. The young child who can readily discriminate among plants or birds or dinosaurs is drawing on the same skills (or intelligence) when she classifies sneakers, cars, sound systems, or marbles.

Judged in terms of the eight criteria proposed in *Frames of Mind* (and discussed in chapter 3), the naturalist's intelligence proves as firmly entrenched as the other intelligences. There are, to begin with, the core capacities to recognize instances as members of a group (more formally, a species); to distinguish among members of a species; to recognize the existence of other, neighboring species; and to chart out the relations, formally or informally, among the several species. Clearly, the importance of a naturalistic intelligence is well established in evolutionary history, where the survival of an organism has depended on its ability to discriminate among similar species, avoiding some (predators) and ferreting out others (for prey or play). The naturalist's capacity presents itself not only in those primates evolutionarily closest to human beings; birds also can discern the differences among species of plants and animals (including ones not in their "normal," expected environment) and can even recognize which forms in photographs are humans.

Turning to the role of the naturalist in human culture, it is worth noting that a full-blown naturalist does much more than apply taxonomic capacities. Exhibiting what Wilson has termed "biophilia," the naturalist is comfortable in the world of organisms and may well possess the talent of caring for, taming, or interacting subtly with various living creatures. Such potentials exist not only with the end states I have already cited but also with many other roles, ranging from hunters to fishermen to farmers to gardeners to cooks. Even apparently remote capacities—such as recognizing automobiles from the sounds of the engines, or detecting novel patterns in a scientific laboratory, or discerning artistic styles—may exploit mechanisms that originally evolved because of their efficacy in distinguishing between, say, toxic and nontoxic ivies, snakes, or berries. Thus, it is possible that the pattern-recognizing talents of artists, poets, social scientists, and natural scientists are all built on the fundamental perceptual skills of naturalist intelligence.

Consistent with the developmental course of other intellectual capacities, a scale ranging from novice to expert can be stipulated for a budding naturalist. At the early stages, no formal instruction is necessary, but entire formal fields of study, such as botany or entomology, have arisen for the development and deployment of naturalists' skills.

An important source of information about the independence of an intelligence comes from studies that identify individuals who either excel at, or lack, a certain capacity, as well as "dedicated" neural regions that appear to subserve these capacities. Thus, the existence and independence of musical and linguistic intelligence is underscored by the identification of brain centers that mediate linguistic and musical processing as well as by individuals, ranging from prodigies to savants, who feature singular capacities that are either precocious or surprisingly lacking.

Just as most ordinary children readily master language at an early age, so too are most children predisposed to explore the world of nature. The popularity of dinosaurs among five-year-olds is no accident! However, certain young children unquestionably show a pronounced early interest in the natural world, plus acute capacities to identify and employ many distinctions. Biographies of biologists routinely document an early fascination with plants and animals and a drive to identify, classify, and interact with them; Darwin, Gould, and

Wilson are only the most visible members of this cohort. Interestingly, these patterns are not echoed in the lives of physical scientists, who, as children, more often explored the visible manifestations of invisible forces (like gravity or electricity) or played with mechanical or chemical systems. Similarly, social scientists in childhood more often pursued verbal activities, read nonfiction, or sought interactions with other people.

While certain individuals are gifted in recognizing naturalistic patterns, others are impaired in this respect. The most dramatic examples, widely reported in clinical and experimental studies, are of brain-damaged people who remain able to recognize and name inanimate objects but lose the capacity to identify living things, or individuals who exhibit the reverse problem of abilities and defects. Just which neural centers are involved in the capacities to recognize and name animate and inanimate entities has not been determined definitively. Species recognition may well be represented in different ways in different people, depending, for example, on whether the species are known primarily through drawings and photos or through direct interactions with the plants or animals in question. But because the human naturalistic capacity appears closely related to that of other animals, it should be possible to confirm which brain regions are crucial in naturalistic perception. The identification of neural networks involved in particular forms of recognition—such as face or paw recognition—may provide important clues for this undertaking.

The capacities of the naturalist have not been studied much by psychologists, who have traditionally used artificial stimuli (such as geometric forms) to assess pattern recognition. Thus, their studies have yielded little information on more natural forms of categorization. Similarly, test makers have rarely if ever included items that assess people's skills at categorizing species membership (or other skills of the naturalist). One important exception is the work on categorization by the psychologist Eleanor Rosch and her associates. Their research suggested the existence of special psychological mechanisms that identify "natural kinds" (for example, birds or trees) and that organize such concepts in terms of their resemblance to prototypes (for instance, how "birdlike" or "treelike" is the living being in question?). Much of children's early language learning and classification also seems to build upon these natural forms of categorization rather than those forms that have evolved (or have been recast) to deal with manufactured objects.

The final criterion for an intelligence is its susceptibility to encoding in a symbol system. The extensive linguistic and taxonomic systems that exist in every culture for the classifying of plants and animals testify to the universality of this feature. (In Western culture, we are especially indebted to Aristotle and Linnaeus for their pioneering taxonomies.) Works of art—from cave paintings to ritual dances to choreographers' notations—represent other ways of capturing the identifying features of phenomena of the naturalist's world. Much of religious and spiritual life, including sacred rites, also draws on the natural world and attempts to capture it or comment on it in ways valued within a culture.

My review process indicates that the naturalist's intelligence clearly merits addition to the list of the original seven intelligences. Those valued human cognitions that I previously had to ignore or smuggle in under spatial or logical-mathematical intelligence deserve to be gathered together under a single, recognized rubric. Eschewing formal ceremony, I have thus acknowledged an eighth intelligence by a simple performative speech act. My review process can later be used to consider and, if appropriate, incorporate additional capacities within the family of human intelligences.

THE VARIETIES OF SPIRITUAL LIFE

The realm of the naturalist seems straightforward. In contrast, even a hesitant entry into the world of spirituality reveals a far more complex picture. Any discussion of the spirit—whether cast as spiritual life, spiritual capacity, spiritual feeling, or a gift for religion, mysticism, or the transcendent—is controversial within the sciences, if not throughout the academic world. Language, music, space, nature, and even understanding of other people—all seem *comparatively* straightforward. Many of us do not recognize the spirit as we recognize the mind and the body, and many of us do not grant the same ontological status to the transcendent or the spiritual as we do to, say, the mathematical or the musical.

Even those who cannot identify with the spiritual realm or domain recognize its importance to most human beings—indeed, some might quip, its excessive importance. Presidents (and their spouses) consult astrologers rather than historians or clinicians; religions save thousands of lives but also contribute to many people's deaths; books about the spirit or the soul crowd out those about memory or perception on the psychology shelves of bookstores. Regrettably, the majority of scholars in the cognitive and biological sciences turn away from questions of a spiritual nature, consigning this realm chiefly to the true believers and the quacks.

Indeed, an *a priori* decision to eliminate spiritual intelligence from consideration is no more justifiable than a decision to admit it by fiat or on faith. After all, once one includes the understanding of the personal realm within a study of intelligence, such human proclivities as the spiritual must legitimately be considered. There certainly are no easy grounds for a decision, but several other intelligences deal with phenomena other than sheer physical matter. If the abstract realm of mathematics constitutes a reasonable area of intelligence (and few would challenge that judgment), why not the abstract realm of the spiritual?

Let us assume, then, that it is reasonable to inquire about a possible spiritual intelligence or a set of spirit-related intelligences. What are the capacities and traits that are evoked when one enters the realm of the spiritual? To approach this area, I propose three distinct senses of spiritual. And to aid in the discussion, I suggest that one keep in mind the difference between spiritual concerns that are approached through a traditional or organized means (such as participation in a formal religion) and spiritual concerns that are approached in a more personal, idiosyncratic, or creative manner.

Spiritual as Concern with Cosmic or Existential Issues

The first variety of spirituality reflects a desire to know about experiences and cosmic entities that are not readily apprehended in a material sense but that, nonetheless, seem important to human beings. If we humans can relate to the world of nature, we can also relate to the supernatural world—to the cosmos that extends beyond what we can perceive directly, to the mystery of our own existence, and to life-and-death experiences that transcend what we routinely encounter. And, indeed, the realms of mythology, religion, and art have perennially reflected our efforts to understand the ultimate questions, mysteries, and meanings of life: Who are we? Where do we come from? What does the future hold for us? Why do we exist? What is the meaning of life, of love, of tragic losses, of death? What is the nature of our relation to the wider world and to beings who lie beyond our comprehension, like our gods or our God?

While human beings may well puzzle over these questions on their own or in discussions with their neighbors, organized systems that deal with these issues have also been constructed over the centuries. In any culture, people may elect (or be compelled) to adopt an existing code or set of beliefs about these issues of ultimate concern. Some adopt a traditional version of spiritual knowledge while others create a personal (possibly idiosyncratic) blend of spiritual knowledge.

Stated in this way, the content of spiritual knowledge may seem relatively straightforward. In practice, however, identifying the content being mastered by the putatively spiritual knower—its realm, truth value, and limitations—is problematic and controversial. Indeed, having read numerous accounts of the spiritual realm, I am tempted to conclude that it refers to everything: mind, body, self, nature, the supernatural—and, sometimes, even to nothing! This conceptual sprawl contrasts sharply with the domains of science and math, which are relatively delimited and uncontroversial.

Spiritual as Achievement of a State of Being

In considering any intelligence, one must distinguish between the two classical senses of knowing: *knowing how* and *knowing that.* For other intelligences, this distinction is uncontroversial because the content of the intelligence is evident (for example, musical patterns or spatial arrays), and it is equally clear that people differ in their skills or expertise in dealing with the domain.

When it comes to the spiritual realm, however, the two forms of knowing must be more carefully distinguished. The first sense of spiritual delineates the realms of experience, or domains of existence, that people seek to understand. Of course, many communities recognize particular people as being more skilled at achieving certain psychological states or as having had certain phenomenal experiences deemed "spiritual." Within such communities, reasonable consensus exists on who has the know-how; some people are simply more skilled than others at meditating, achieving trance states, envisioning the transcendent, or being in touch with psychic, spiritual, or noetic phenomena. Indeed, some physiological and brain states may be correlated predictably with the achievement of such alterations of consciousness. Mystics, yogis, and meditators are those whose ability to achieve these states—and, perhaps, to enable others to achieve them—is noteworthy.

With respect to this second variety of spirituality, one may reinvoke a distinction introduced earlier. It is possible to achieve a state of spirituality by following a *traditional* route—for example, by executing a set of exercises suggested by a specific priest, mystic, or guru. But people also can achieve such an elaborated state through a more *personalized* form of control of consciousness—through stimulation by specific substances (such as hallucinogenic drugs) or sensory experiences (such as listening to music, hiking up mountains). A prudent observer might well concede that it is plausible to think of "a talent in achieving certain mental states" as lying within the realm of scientific analysis. Similarly, one might construe the "gymnastic" aspect of controlling mental states as a subspecies of bodily-kinesthetic intelligence.

But the believers or spokespersons for spirituality go further by claiming that spiritual concerns lead to an encounter with a deeper or higher truth. According to them, it is not merely the case—as some would claim, the uncontroversial case—that people need to locate themselves with respect to the cosmos and to the infinitesimal, nor even that some states of consciousness are universally desirable. Rather, enthusiasts argue, there is a specific content—a spiritual truth—to which only some or only those who have followed a certain path can have access. And this slippery slope leads all too often to a belief that the world can be divided between those who qualify on some spiritual, religious, or metaphysical ground and those who do not. Moreover, while the attainment of altered states of consciousness can be measured objectively, the same does not hold true for the attainment of a state of spiritual truth. Here, we have left the realm of intelligence and moved to the sphere of dogma.

Viewed from one perspective, these two forms of knowing—mastering a set of contents and mastering the craft of altering one's consciousness—can be seen as uses of the mind, whether one considers such uses profound or frivolous, inspired or misguided. But cognitively-based discussions of the spiritual can prove problematic, since interested observers see the essence of spirit as primarily phenomenological—the attainment of a certain state of being, what has been called a "feeling of surrender"—and not as a domain that involves any kind of problem solving or product making. In fact, some view spiritual concerns as primarily emotional or affective—as centered in a feeling of a certain tone or intensity—and hence, beyond the confines of a cognitive investigation.

Spiritual as Effect on Others

Certain people may be considered spiritual because of the effects they apparently exert on others, either through their activities or, perhaps even more, through their sheer being. For instance, knowing about Mother Teresa's life, being blessed by Pope John XXIII, or listening to Pablo Casals playing the Bach *Suites for Unaccompanied Cellos* makes some people feel more whole and more in touch with themselves, their God, and the cosmos. And though I prefer to cite benign instances of this phenomenon, it must be conceded that Adolf Hitler had this effect on many of his compatriots.

All three senses of the spiritual can be aroused. In some cases, spiritually potent figures drive people toward exploring cosmic issues. Sometimes, the spiritually effective figure evokes an altered state of consciousness. Occasionally, there is a contagion: People affected by a spiritual individual pass on a reflected spirituality to others. Indeed, many religions have spread by just such a charismatic process that circulates among, and is expanded by, disciples and disciples of disciples.

The great religious leaders—such as Buddha, Christ, Saint Joan, and

Confucius—are often seen as having attained a level of consciousness, a connectedness to the rest of the world, a deemphasis of self, that represent an exemplary spiritual existence. Clearly, it is the prospect of attaining such a state that motivates millions of people reflecting the spectrum of cultures to strive to achieve a state of spirituality or to heighten their personal spiritual aspects. Undoubtedly, certain individuals exude a feeling of spirituality, a sense of being in touch with the cosmos, and a capacity to make those around them feel that they themselves have been touched, made to feel more whole or more themselves, or led toward an enhanced relation to the transcendent. Whatever the mechanism—and the term *charisma* captures (though hardly explains) much of it—this "contact with the spiritual" constitutes an important ingredient in conveying to people the goal of their quest and, perhaps equally important, how they might embark upon the right pathway. But whatever intellectual powers may be reflected in the achievements of a Buddha or a Christ, it seems clear that "problem solving" or "product making" is not an appropriate description. Achievement of a certain "state of being" is more apt.

My brief survey confirms that the "words" and the "examples" of the spirit can cover a multitude of human capacities, inclinations, and achievements, at least some of which fall well outside the project of identifying additional human intelligences. For one thing, I have deliberately defined *intelligence* in amoral terms: No intelligence is in itself moral or immoral, and any intelligence can be put to prosocial or antisocial uses. Thus, it is not valid to delineate any particular form of spirituality as appropriate or inappropriate on the basis of adherence to a moral code. Just as personal intelligence cannot be limited to a particular political or social system, the attainment of a specific set of beliefs or a specific role within an organized religion cannot be deemed a demonstration of a particular intelligence. By the same token, the achievement of particular phenomenal states should not qualify an individual as realizing, or failing to realize, a particular intelligence. One can have high musical or mathematical intelligence without reporting any cognitive or affective state; similarly, the claim that someone "thinks mathematically" or "feels musical" has no meaning unless that person demonstrates an ability to solve problems or fashion products.

Finally, while the capacity to affect others may prove an effective means of inculcating an intelligence, it does not, strictly speaking, constitute an embodiment of an intelligence. For example, without possessing or exhibiting interpersonal intelligence myself, I might be able to stimulate the development of interpersonal understanding in others simply by behaving in unpredictable or antisocial ways. On the other hand, I might have outstanding mathematical intelligence but be unable to help anyone else master the mathematical sphere. My definition of intelligence is unduly stretched if it is expected to encompass an individual's effect (or lack of effect) on others.

In reflecting on the possibility of a spiritual intelligence, I am struck by the problematic nature of the "content" of spiritual intelligence, its possibly defining affective and phenomenological aspects, its often privileged but unsubstantiated claims with respect to truth value, and the need for it to be partially identified through its effect on other people. To deal with this important sphere of life, I find it more comfortable to talk about a potential to engage in thinking about cosmic issues, which might be motivated by pain, powerful personal or aesthetic experiences, or life in a community that highlights spiritual thinking and experience. I must be candid and concede that I am also somewhat alarmed by the prospect of being assimilated to the many fanatics and frauds who invoke spirituality as if it were a given, or a known truth, rather than a tremendously complex phenomenon that demands careful analysis and more than a touch of humility. Still, I do not want to risk prematurely eliminating a set of human capabilities worthy of consideration within a theory of intelligences. It seems more responsible to carve out that area of spirituality closest "in spirit" to the other intelligences and then, in the sympathetic manner applied to naturalist intelligence, ascertain how this candidate intelligence fares. In doing so, I think it best to put aside the term *spiritual,* with its manifest and problematic connotations, and to speak instead of an intelligence that explores the nature of existence in its multifarious guises. Thus, an explicit concern with spiritual or religious matters would be one variety—often the most important variety—of an existential intelligence.

EXISTENTIAL INTELLIGENCE AND THE EIGHT CRITERIA

Existential intelligence, or a concern with "ultimate" issues, seems the most unambiguously cognitive strand of the spiritual. That is because it does not include features that, according to my definition, are not germane to a consideration of intelligence. If this form qualifies, then we may legitimately speak of existential intelligence; if it does not, further consideration of the realm of spirituality is unnecessary.

Let me begin by proposing a core ability for a candidate existential intelligence: the capacity to locate oneself with respect to the furthest reaches of the cosmos—the infinite and the infinitesimal—and the related capacity to locate oneself with respect to such existential features of the human condition as the significance of life, the meaning of death, the ultimate fate of the physical and the psychological worlds, and such profound experiences as love of another person or total immersion in a work of art. Note that there is no stipulation here of attaining an ultimate truth, any more than the deployer of musical intelligence must produce or prefer certain kinds of music. Rather, there is a species potential to engage in transcendental concerns, a capacity that can be aroused and deployed under certain circumstances.

This capacity has been valued in every known human culture. Cultures devise religious, mystical, or metaphysical systems for dealing with existential issues; and in modern times or in secular settings, aesthetic, philosophical, and scientific works and systems also speak to this ensemble of human needs. Many of the most important and enduring sets of symbol systems (such as those featured in the Catholic liturgy) represent crystallizations of key ideas and experiences that have evolved within specific institutions. Moreover, in each of these culturally devised systems, there are clear stages of sophistication. One can be a novice in a religious system, in philosophy, or in the expressive arts, and one can work to achieve journeyman or expert status. (In his *Journal,* the future Pope John XXIII chronicled years of painstaking training of his spiritual or existential facets.) The greater the premium a society places on a particular vehicle of existential exploration and expression, the more firmly delineated are the steps en route to excellence. And there should be widespread consensus in most cases about the level of sophistication that is displayed by a learner, an apprentice, a committed student, and a budding master. Such assessments may go well beyond the cognitive, to include aspects of social, moral, or emotional existence; but that eclecticism can be equally true in the evolution of a musician, a poet, or even a scientist.

Particularly intriguing questions surround the identification, in the first years of life, of the future Dalai Lama (and of other lamas). If one does not believe in reincarnation, one must choose between the hypothesis that this individual is unusually gifted in the spiritual/existential sphere while a young child or that his early identification (on whatever dimension) leads to a self-fulfilling prophecy. According to a recent journalistic account, a candidate lama proves his mettle by correctly choosing articles that belonged to the recently deceased lama; success occurs because the lama can draw on memories of his earlier incarnation. A more secular hypothesis is that the future lama may stand out because of his capacity to discern certain patterns in the environment (a vestige of natural, rather than supernatural, intelligence). A better marker for later existential excellence might be an early-emerging concern for cosmic issues, of the sort reported for religious leaders like Gandhi or for physicists like Albert Einstein.

When one moves to the more biologically tinged facets of existential knowledge, evaluating the evidence proves less straightforward. While hints of ritualistic and symbolic experiences have been found in higher primates and in the precursors of modern humans (like a Neanderthal who marked a grave with flowers), explicit existential concerns probably gained ascendancy in the Stone Age. At this point in evolution humans clearly possessed a brain capable of imagining the infinite and the ineffable and of considering the cosmological issues central to existential intelligence. Indeed, I would go so far as to suggest that one of the major cognitive activities among early humans was a grappling with these existential issues and that much early art, dance, myth, and drama dealt implicitly or explicitly with cosmic themes.

Only with the advent of formal religions and systematic philosophy did direct linguistic-propositional accounts of the existential realm arise. (Myths and drama are better thought of as implicit investigations of the existential.) Like language, existential capacity is a distinctive trait of humans, a domain that separates us from other species. This capacity may have emerged from a conscious sense of—and impulse to struggle against—finite space and irreversible time. More generally, human consciousness in its fuller senses may presuppose a concern with existential issues.

There is little information on the physiological concomitants of knowledge about cosmic issues. Scattered evidence suggests that words from the religious sphere (such as terms referring to God or to ritual practices) may activate specific regions in the temporal lobe. But the most suggestive evidence may come from individuals with temporal-lobe epilepsy, who exhibit a predictable set of symptoms, including hyper-religiosity. They attach the greatest importance to the most minute objects and experiences, often using them as points of departure for the elaboration of extended introspective diary entries or flights of spiritual fancy. It is widely believed that certain artists, including Vincent Van Gogh and Fyodor Dostoyevsky, suffered from temporal-lobe epilepsy, yet channeled their symptoms and pain into powerful, dramatic works of art.

There is a growing body of evidence, based both on naturally occurring and artificially induced experiences, relevant to the phenomenal aspects of spiritual/religious concerns. For example, when people undergo tremendous pain—whether physical, psychic, or both—they feel estranged from their habitual world and experience an acute desire to go beyond the usual categories of experience, to refocus their attention (perhaps beyond bodily pain altogether), and reevaluate their relation to the external and the psychic worlds. Thoughts about existential issues may well have evolved as responses to necessarily occurring pain, perhaps as a way of reducing pain or of better equipping people to cope with it. It is thus at least imaginable that ultimate concerns have some adaptive significance.

Not surprisingly, people have learned to re-create these transcendent phenomenal experiences even in the absence of pain, through drugs and religious states (mystics and gurus who can control their psychic states are able to enter the realm of the transcendent voluntarily). The attainment of heightened attention, as in "flow states," is also within at least partial control of the experiencer. Under such highly desirable circumstances, people become so immersed in the execution of an activity that they lose all sense of time and space. Certain brain centers and neural transmitters are mobilized in these states, whether they are induced by the ingestion of substances, involvement in a hobby, or sheer control of the will.

The final line of evidence, gleaned from psychological investigations, presents a mixed picture. Some inventories of personality include dimensions of religiosity or spirituality, and these instruments yield consistency in scores; indeed, even identical twins reared apart show a strong link in degree of religiosity, thereby suggesting a possible heritable component in this capacity. Yet it remains unclear just what is being probed by such instruments and whether self-report is a reliable index of existential intelligence. I know of no attempts to relate psychometric intelligence to the capacity or inclination to activate existential intelligence, though the popularity of the movie *Forrest Gump* suggests a widely held popular conviction that these two capacities are remote from, if not antithetical to, each other.

Perhaps surprisingly, existential intelligence scores reasonably well on the eight criteria, and considering this a version of spiritual intelligence eliminates some of the problematic aspects that might otherwise have invalidated the quest. Although empirical psychological evidence is sparse, what exists certainly does not invalidate the construct. It may seem, then, that I have backed myself into an analytic corner. However, I conclude that the narrowly defined variety of spiritual intelligence here termed "existential" may well be admissible, while the more broadly defined "spiritual intelligence" is not.[1]

A PERSONAL PERSPECTIVE
ON SPIRITUAL INTELLIGENCE

Let me address this conundrum of spiritual intelligence from another, more personal level. As suggested earlier, I feel no personal

---

[1] For another view of the plausibility of spiritual intelligence, based on the several criteria, see R. Emmons, "Is Spirituality an Intelligence?" in *International Journal for Psychology of Religion*, 1999, in press; and see also my response, "A case against spiritual intelligenc," Ibid.

involvement in the realm of spirituality. I do not have a religious identity (though I have a cultural identity) as a Jewish person. And I am as much frightened as intrigued by people who see themselves (or who are seen by others) as spiritual individuals. I fear the strangeness of the beliefs to which they may subscribe, and I fear the effects that charismatic figures (in the style of Jim Jones or David Koresh) may exert on often hapless followers.

Yet in at least one sphere of my life, I undergo some of the experiences that others ascribe to spiritual matters—in the realm of music. Particularly when I listen to or perform certain kinds of music, I lose track of mundane concerns, alter my perceptions of space and time, and, occasionally, feel in touch with issues of cosmic import. I don't define these issues in terms of natural objects (such as mountains or seas) or specific cosmological issues (such as the meaning of life or death), kinds of associations often mentioned by music lovers and by certain composers, such as Ludwig van Beethoven and Gustav Mahler. But I do feel that I am encountering the formal aspects of these realms of existence, and I feel enriched, ennobled, and humbled by the encounter. I have similar, though less acute, reactions when I come into contact with works of visual art and architecture, with evocative dramatic performances, and with the work of certain very powerful writers. And, switching realms, I have some of these experiences when in contact with people I love, particularly at times of unbridled happiness or sadness.

My decision to speak of spiritual or existential intelligence entails a semantic judgment. I could say that my musical or linguistic or artistic intelligences have been stimulated and that, consequently, I have a heightened sensitivity to issues of the cosmos, just as I might be stimulated to hurt someone or to give my savings to a charitable cause. I could say that I am having a strong emotional reaction to a work. In such cases, I would not speak of either spiritual or existential intelligence. But I could with equal justification decide that I am, through intense engagements with art objects or with people I love, exercising my spiritual or existential intelligence, as I would if I were working with a guru. Thus, I experience certain triggering events, or "affecting" objects and experiences, that activate an existential intelligence. This point of view is powerfully conveyed in a passage from Marcel Proust:

> It is inconceivable that a piece of sculpture or a piece of music which gives us an emotion that we feel to be more exalted, more pure, more true, does not correspond to some definite spiritual reality, or life would be meaningless.

Despite the attractiveness of a ninth intelligence, however, I am not adding existential intelligence to the list. I find the phenomenon perplexing enough and the distance from the other intelligences vast enough to dictate prudence—at least for now. At most, I am willing, Fellini-style, to joke about "8$^{1}/_{2}$ intelligences."

A FINAL STOCK-TAKING

Of course, I cannot claim exclusive ownership of the concept of multiple intelligences, although I assume responsibility for having developed the idea. As in the case of the original list of intelligences, readers are welcome to examine my criteria and reach their own conclusions about whether or not natural, spiritual, or existential intelligences (or others) "truly" qualify. But I feel strongly that judgments should be based on careful application of the set of criteria. If decisions about intelligences are to be taken seriously, they must rest on a fair-minded examination of the available data, an undertaking that I began in *Frames of Mind* and am revisiting here.

5

IS THERE A
MORAL INTELLIGENCE?

ONCE WE PURSUE the idea of multiple intelligences, it is only a matter of time before someone nominates a "moral intelligence." And, indeed, if we broaden the standard notion of intelligence to include knowledge of human beings, an intelligence in the moral realm is plausible. But unless we can establish with some precision the relation among knowledge, actions, and values, recognizing a moral intelligence harbors significant risk.

When I developed the original list of intelligences, I did not seriously consider the possibility of a moral intelligence. As noted earlier, I adhered to the long-standing disjunction between description and prescription and, therefore, regarded intelligences as decidedly "morally neutral" or "value free."* Adding an explicitly moral intelligence also would have entailed delineating a distinctive realm called "the moral," within which individuals display readily measurable skills. As far as I was concerned, morals represented a subspecies of a cultural value system. People master the value system of their culture through linguistic,

---

*Of course, I deem as intelligences those abilities that are valued within a culture, but I do not myself pass judgment on the validity of those evaluations.

logical, and personal intelligences. Whether they then adhere to that value system or go on to revise it in positive or destructive ways is a personal decision, not an exercise of that computational system I call (an) intelligence. This division between the "true" and the "good" has been entrenched in Western civilization; the fact that many other cultures meld the realms of knowledge and virtue leaves most contemporary Westerners untouched, if not bewildered. Like character, morality may be important—indeed, more important than intelligence—but it should not be confused or confounded with intelligence.

CLUES FROM SPIRITUAL
AND EMOTIONAL INTELLIGENCES

My recent survey of candidate intelligences, in the light of the aforementioned criteria, has turned up one clear additional intelligence—that of the naturalist—and has shown the possibility of a "spiritual intelligence" to be problematic. Indeed, only one connotation of spirituality seems congruent with other intelligences: the capacity to think about cosmic and existential issues—from our existence and role in the universe to the nature of life, death, bliss, and tragedy. In most societies, organized religious, mythical, or philosophical systems deal with these issues, but people may also develop their own unique existential or spiritual frameworks. While I am not yet ready to proclaim a ninth intelligence, I am willing to accept the possibility that a proclivity for pondering ultimate cosmic or existential concerns constitutes a distinctive human intellectual capacity.

How does the positing of an existential intelligence affect the case for a moral intelligence? From one point of view, acknowledgment of an existential intelligence might appear to smooth the way. After all, if the realm of the moral seems vaguely noncognitive, then certainly an existential (and, most certainly, a spiritual) form of intelligence would be similarly characterized. Yet, from another vantage point, an existential intelligence does not advance the plausibility of a moral intelligence. Existential intelligence can be manifested by anyone who exhibits facility, clarity, or depth in thinking about "ultimate" issues, whether the thoughts are positive or negative, moral or immoral, open ended or conclusive. For every Saint Joan or Father Pierre Teilhard de Chardin, there is a David Koresh or a Gregory Rasputin who can also lay claim to being "existential."

The key is whether one can think of skill in the moral realm, independent of the particular uses to which that skill might be put. The recent example of "emotional intelligence" is instructive. In his book *Emotional Intelligence*, Daniel Goleman describes a collection of capacities having to do with knowledge of emotions, control of emotions, and sensitivity to one's own or others' emotional states. This characterization fits comfortably with my own sense of interpersonal and intrapersonal intelligences. But when Goleman speaks about emotional intelligence as if it entails a certain set of recommended behaviors—empathy, considerateness, or working toward a more smoothly functioning family or community—he leaves the realm of intelligence, in a strictly scholarly sense, and enters the separate spheres of values and social policy.

DELINEATING THE MORAL DOMAIN

The existence of a moral intelligence rests on the existence of an identifiable moral domain. That domain must, on the one hand, extend beyond the usual spheres of intrapersonal and interpersonal intelligences and, on the other hand, not coincide with any set of mandated moral behaviors or attitudes. In attempting to delineate a moral domain, scholars have debated a number of vexing issues, including the relation between moral action and moral judgment; the possibility of a universal moral code; and the role of such key virtues as justice, truth, and caring. Given the myriad philosophical stances and the abundant social-scientific research data related to such issues, it is hardly surprising that no single delineation of "the moral" satisfies all parties. Fortunately, however, my enterprise here hinges not on a consensual definition but on a conception that accomplishes two goals: first, encompassing the themes that scholars in this area have highlighted; and second, permitting further exploration of the relations between intelligence (in a broader sense) and morality.

Central to a moral domain is a concern with those rules, behaviors, and attitudes that govern the sanctity of life—in particular, the sanctity of human life and, in many cases, the sanctity of any other living creatures and the world they inhabit. A moral sense entails the capacity to recognize and make judgments about such issues. Clearly, many aspects of life fall outside the domain of morality: Every society features innumerable practices and conventions that facilitate daily living without touching on what is sacred or privileged about human existence. But when one encroaches on the treatment of other human beings, on their own chances to live and, by extension, to live decently, one has entered the moral domain. All societies recognize in some manner the difference between a traffic code and a list like the Ten Commandments; differences among societies inhere in *where* one draws the lines that separate the pragmatic, the social, and the moral.

Adopting this definition, we can begin to discern what people with strengths in moral intelligence might display:

- Ready recognition of issues related to the sanctity of life in its diverse facets
- Facility in mastering traditional symbolic renderings and codifications that deal with sacred issues
- Enduring commitment to reflecting on such issues
- Potential for going beyond the conventional approaches to cre-

ate new forms or processes that regulate the sacrosanct facets of human interactions.

As was the case with other faculties, individuals differ from one another in the extent to which they display early signs of these capacities, and they also differ in the extent to which, and the facility with which, they develop these skills and sensitivities to the fullest. In all likelihood, the ambient culture plays a determining role: It is hard to imagine how an individual could develop strengths in the moral domain, in the absence of a culture where such issues are prominent.

Empirical Considerations

On some criteria, ability or skill in the moral domain seems to qualify as an intelligence. By the age of two, most children have developed some sense of right and wrong, and throughout childhood, this moral sense undergoes a characteristic developmental trajectory. As shown by a considerable body of research, some cognitive features accompany moral judgment and action, but a moral sense cannot be reduced to a general cognitive sophistication. Without question, societies have developed symbolic systems that encode moral considerations, and most societies designate certain individuals, such as judges or elders, as especially qualified in the moral domain. Evidence about the evolution of a moral sense and about its possible representation in the human brain is more speculative, but it is becoming clear that primates have an incipient sense of right and wrong. Moreover, evolutionary psychologists have come to believe that a sense of fairness is a product of natural selection in the human species. Evidence is also accruing that some kinds of psychopathy and sociopathy are associated with a weakened sense of right and wrong or with a disconnecting of that sense from emotional consequences.

Another way to approach a candidate moral intelligence is to consider the moral dimensions of individuals who have accomplished extraordinary cognitive feats. I have studied some thirty outstanding creators and leaders with respect to their extraordinariness, but without specific regard to their concern for moral issues. (In-depth profiles appeared in my books *Creating Minds* and *Leading Minds*; in chapter 8 I consider how intelligences relate to such people's lives.) Viewed through a moral lens, the lives of these individuals prove instructive. With the possible exception of Mahatma Gandhi, none of the creators of the modern era whom I studied can in any sense be thought of as moral exemplars in their personal lives. Indeed, for Pablo Picasso, Igor Stravinsky, T. S. Eliot, Martha Graham, Sigmund Freud, and even Albert Einstein, it would prove as easy to author a moral "pathography" as a moral hagiography. Alas, all of these men and women showed moral insensitivity in many aspects of their personal lives.

Yet, it is simplistic to dismiss any of these individuals as remote from the moral sphere. They associated themselves with certain moral causes, ranging from Einstein's support of pacifism and Zionism to Picasso's embracing of communist and pacifist ideologies. Moreover, as Mihaly Csikszentmihalyi has pointed out, eminent creators often display a keen sense—one that borders on the moralistic, if not the moral—of how work in a particular domain should be carried out. Thus, Martha Graham insisted on perfectly executed dances, T. S. Eliot applied strict principles in an admirably fair-minded manner when evaluating the poetry of others, Igor Stravinsky tenaciously policed "intrusive" reinterpretations of his own and others' scores, and Einstein so embraced an aesthetic of simplicity and beauty in his own work that he closed his eyes to empirical findings that appeared to violate this harmony.

Turning to those who eventually became leaders in a more conventional sense, one finds certain markers of concern with moral issues. At an early age, this concern typically coincides with an interest in religious issues, either through organized religion or by virtue of a more personalized ethic. Some, like Martin Luther King, Jr., and Robert Maynard Hutchins, came from a line of ministers and absorbed an interest in moral issues as part of their family environment. Others, like J. Robert Oppenheimer and Mahatma Gandhi, displayed a precocious concern with the treatment of others and with the consequences of violating one's moral code. Even in people who eventually embrace a totalitarian approach to politics and morality, one can sometimes identify an early "hurt" that they were motivated to alleviate, whether their backgrounds were relatively privileged, as with V. I. Lenin and Mao Zedong, or impoverished, as with Adolf Hitler and Josef Stalin. Various studies have also revealed that gifted children are more likely than their peers to raise issues of a moral nature, though this concern does not necessarily result in adherence to the code of the surrounding society.

Probably the most explicit form of concern with morality came in the training (and self-training) received by Angelo Roncalli, the future Pope John XXIII. Roncalli sought to master all of the precepts of his religion and to enact them in his daily life, imposing the most severe forms of self-castigation on those occasions when he violated explicit moral precepts. On the single recorded occasion when he was tempted to "test" the limits of the Catholic moral code, he was severely reprimanded by his supervisor. Thereafter, Roncalli resolved to keep doubts strictly to himself. He did so successfully for many years, until he was placed in a position where he was authorized to put forth his personal set of moral concerns.

Most outstanding creators have a strongly developed sense of propriety about permissible and impermissible moves within their domain. This terrain is not, strictly speaking, moral in the sense currently under discussion. Yet the sense of inviolateness with respect to the world of work is sometimes reflected in stances taken toward other human beings. Creators differ widely from one another, however, in whether the strong beliefs they bring to their work reappear in their relation to broader human or societal concerns. In most cases, such coupling is intermittent at best. Among those whose eventual expertise centers on the treatment of other human beings, one is more likely to encounter precocious concern with moral issues. With some people, such as Gandhi, this concern seems to reflect a heightened attention to the effects of one's actions on others. In other, less happy cases, the concern may reflect a person's feeling of having been treated unfairly, either as an individual or as part of a particular group. In this case, the leading figure may feel impelled to make amends for the perceived injustice; the examples of Hitler and Stalin come readily to mind.

A Framework for the Consideration of Moral Concerns

The foregoing review suggests that we can speak of a domain of existence—the moral domain—that is separate from the physical domain (laws that govern physical objects and the relations among them), the biological domain (laws that govern the fundamental physiological processes in living entities), the social domain (laws governing the full play of activities and relations among human beings), and the psychological domain (laws governing the thoughts, behaviors, feelings, and actions of individual persons). People enter the moral domain when they consider principles that pertain specifically to respect for human life (or all forms of life) in its various potentials. Indeed, just as the existential sphere pertains to the essential nature of the cosmos, the moral sphere pertains to the essential nature and quality of human life. Key to this concern is a delineation of what is proper or improper, right or wrong, or just or unjust, with respect to the sanctity of human life (or, by possible extension, to all forms of life). Taking this view, certain moral aspects appear relatively uncontroversial—for example, virtually all societies condemn the wanton taking of human life or of highly valued personal property. On the other hand, activities like abortion, euthanasia, and mortal combat represent terrains that are associated with deep and sometimes irreconcilable differences between individuals (or groups or cultures) who may otherwise share a depth of moral concern.

But even if we acknowledge a moral domain, should we speak of individuals as being more or less morally intelligent? If so, on what basis can we make such evaluations?

Here, the problems of construing the moral domain in cognitive terms come to the fore. With the seven original intelligences, the ability to judge people's possession of intelligences proved relatively uncontroversial. Irrespective of the kind of mathematical system elaborated within a culture, for instance, people can readily be arrayed with respect to their computational powers. As discussed earlier, similar judgments regarding the personal intelligences and naturalist intelligence may seem more vexing but still rest on obtainable, reliable data. Such evidence is not yet available, however, even for existential intelligence, the most plausible aspect of spirituality I closely examined. To evaluate moral intelligence, I must again narrow the focus.

I do not find the term *moral intelligence* acceptable as long as it connotes the adoption of any specific moral code. Such a move places us squarely in the realm of values. But we can restrict the term to those capacities or proclivities that pertain to the sanctity of human life and people's own stance with regard to this sanctity—however positive or negative these capacities might seem to us. For example, many societies (such as Nazi Germany) narrowly define "fully human," and they may even deny the humanity of certain individuals or groups. Others favor a broad definition that encompasses not only the body but also the feelings and thoughts of all people. (A few societies or subcultures also define the treatment of animals, and I recently heard experts in robotics speak of the moral rights and obligations of robots and other embodiments of artificial intelligence—shades of the science writer Isaac Asimov's laws that govern the treatment of robots.) By the same token, the societal or personal codes governing morality are as varied as the mythologies, philosophies, and religions that have emerged and evolved in diverse cultures over the millennia.

Even an implicit recognition of moral intelligence raises a new set of issues. Does it really make sense to draw a sharp line between cosmic issues—the nature of existence, time, life, and death—and issues concerning the sanctity of human life—how people should treat one another, what rules should govern communal harmony and discord, and so on? Might it not make more sense to speak of a general "philosophical intelligence," and not disaggregate it by trying to pinpoint the spiritual, the transcendental, the emotional, the moral, the cosmic, and the religious?

CONCLUSION: ON THE RELATION BETWEEN THE INTELLECTUAL AND THE MORAL REALMS

It makes sense to think of a realm as "intellectual," as the seat of an "intelligence," only after that realm's essence has successfully been captured. I do not believe that I (or others) have yet captured the essence of the moral domain as an instance of human intelligence. It is possible to focus principally on moral *judgments*, as the psychologists Lawrence Kohlberg and Carol Gilligan have done; in such investigations, one asks individuals what they would do in certain hypothetical situations (for instance, should one steal a drug to save the life of a sick person?). Such speculation remains at the level of philosophical understanding, and the distinctiveness of the moral domain is attenuated. In contrast, one can focus on moral *behaviors* (for instance, does a person do the right thing when he or she has the opportunity to shield an individual who is being unfairly pursued?), but in so doing, one bypasses the way in which the person conceptualizes his or her actions. One might be dealing with well-entrenched habits rather than with a separate intellectual sphere.

As I construe it, the central component in the moral realm or domain is a sense of personal agency and personal stake, a realization that one has an irreducible role with respect to other people and that one's behaviors toward others must reflect the results of contextualized analysis and the exercise of one's will. We do not think of Gandhi as a moral person just because of the sophistication of his philosophy or the praiseworthiness of his behaviors. Rather, we think of Gandhi (or of Mother Teresa, or Nelson Mandela, or Andrei Sakharov) as moral persons because of the central roles they have been willing to play in the realm of human affairs. The fulfillment of key roles certainly requires a range of human intelligences—including personal, linguistic, logical, and perhaps existential—but it is fundamentally a statement about the *kind of person* that one is or, more properly, about the kind of person that one has developed to be. It is not, in itself, an intelligence. "Morality" is then properly a statement about personality, individuality, will, character—and, in the happiest cases, about the highest realization of human nature.

MYTHS AND REALITIES ABOUT MULTIPLE INTELLIGENCES

SINCE *Frames of Mind* was published, I have heard, read, and seen several hundred different interpretations of what multiple intelligences (MI) theory is and how it can be applied in schools (see Appendix B for a sampling). For over a decade, I was content to let MI theory take on a life of its own. I had issued an ensemble of ideas (or "memes") to the world, and I was inclined to let those memes fend for themselves. But in light of my reading and observations, I gradually came to the conclusion that this laissez-faire policy was inadequate.

One strong spur to action came when I learned that an entire state in Australia had adopted an educational program based in part on MI theory. The more I heard about this program, the less comfortable I was. While parts of the program were reasonable and based on research, much of it was simply a mishmash of practices, with neither scientific foundation nor clinical warrant. Left-brain and right-brain contrasts, sensory-based learning styles, "neurolinguistic programming," and MI approaches were commingled with dazzling promiscuity. Clearly, no one had separated out the curricular wheat from the extracurricular chaff.

My boiling point was reached when I saw a list of the ethnic and racial groups in Australia, each aligned with a particular intelligence (as well as a corresponding area of intellectual weakness). This blatant racial and ethnic stereotyping went directly against my scientific knowledge and offended my personal ethic. Along with other critics, I appeared on a television news show and denounced the educational program. I am relieved to note that shortly afterward, the program was dropped from the state curriculum.

Thus spurred, I identified a number of myths about multiple intelligences, listed below along with the corresponding realities and some further commentary.

MYTH 1

Now that eight or nine intelligences have been identified, researchers can—and perhaps should—create a variety of tests and secure the associated scores.

REALITY 1

MI theory represents a critique of the standard psychometric approach, wherein researchers identify a construct (such as extroversion or gullibility) and then create a test to assess its incidence. Accordingly, having a battery of MI tests is not consistent with the major tenets of the theory.

COMMENT

My concept of intelligences is an outgrowth of accumulating knowledge about the human brain and about human cultures, not the result of *a priori* definitions or factor analyses of a set of test scores. Therefore, intelligences *must* be assessed in ways that are "intelligence fair"— that is, in ways that examine the intelligences directly rather than through the lenses of linguistic or logical intelligences (as ordinary paper-and-pencil instruments do). Thus, for example, if one wants to assess spatial intelligence, one should allow people to explore a terrain for a while and see whether they can find their way around it reliably, perhaps even when they have to enter or exit at an unfamiliar point. Or, if one wants to examine musical intelligence, one should expose people to a new melody in a reasonably familiar idiom and determine how readily they can learn to sing it, recognize it, transform it, and so on.

Assessment of multiple intelligences is needed only when one has a strong reason for it, such as establishing whether a child has a cognitive impairment that inhibits a certain kind of learning. When an assessment becomes advisable, it is best to administer it in a comfortable setting with materials (and cultural roles) that are familiar to the individual. These conditions clash with our general conception of testing as a decontextualized undertaking carved out in a neutral environment, using materials designed to be unfamiliar to the test takers. I am more comfortable assessing a child's intelligences by observing him in a children's museum for several hours than by giving him a standardized test battery.

In principle, an "intelligence-fair" set of MI measures could be devised, and we have sought to do this in Project Spectrum (an assessment-and-curriculum program for preschool children) with inviting materials that children find familiar and comfortable to play with. For example, we sample children's musical intelligence by letting them explore melodies on attractive Montessori bells and by having them learn new songs. Children's logical, spatial, and bodily-kinesthetic capacities are assessed by having them take apart and reassemble familiar household objects, like a pencil sharpener or a doorknob.

I am often asked to comment on measures of multiple intelligences that other investigators have devised. On principle, I demur from specific critiques of particular instruments. Instead, I stress several general points that any test developer should bear in mind: the importance of the distinction between individuals' *preferences* for materials/intelligences and their *capacities* in these spheres, the risks of relying on purely verbal measures of ability, and the importance of drawing on observations of actual skills and on the testimony of people familiar with the individuals being assessed. More generally, I would recommend that any intelligence be assessed by a number of complementary approaches that consider the several core components of an intelligence. Thus, for example, spatial intelligence might be assessed by asking people to find their way around an unfamiliar terrain, to solve an abstract jigsaw puzzle, and to construct a three-dimensional model of their home.

MYTH 2

An intelligence is the same as a domain or a discipline.

REALITY 2

An intelligence is a new kind of construct, one that draws on biological and psychological potentials and capacities. It should not be confused with domains or disciplines, which are socially constructed human endeavors.

COMMENT

I must shoulder a fair part of the blame for propagation of the second myth. In writing *Frames of Mind*, I was not as careful as I should have been in distinguishing intelligences from other related concepts. As I have now come to understand, particularly through my collaborations with Mihaly Csikszentmihalyi and David Feldman, an *intelligence* is a biopsychological potential that is ours by virtue of our species membership. That potential can be realized to a greater or lesser extent as a consequence of the experiential, cultural, and motivational factors that affect a person.

In contrast, a domain is an organized set of activities within a culture, one typically characterized by a specific symbol system and its attendant operations. Any cultural activity in which individuals participate on more than a casual basis, and in which degrees of expertise can be identified and nurtured, should be considered a domain. Thus physics, cooking, chess, constitutional law, and rap music are all domains in contemporary Western culture. For each of these domains, one can isolate particular symbol systems (for instance, numerical, musical) as well as operations relevant to those symbol systems (such as replaying a chess game that has been notated, or making changes in a recipe). Any domain can be realized through the use of several intelligences. The domain of musical performance, for example, involves bodily-kinesthetic, personal, and musical intelligences. By the same token, a particular intelligence, like spatial intelligence, can be applied in a myriad of domains, from sculpture to sailing to surgery. Some have suggested that MI theory is tautologous—that is, people are strong in an area and therefore exhibit that intelligence. Once again, this assertion is based on a simple confusion between "intelligence" and "domain." A person can be strong in an area without necessarily exhibiting the intelligence most commonly associated with such proficiency. By the same token, a person can show a strong intelligence without necessarily mastering domains with a similar name.

I am often asked whether an intelligence is the same thing as a talent or an ability. While I love to achieve conceptual clarity, I do not love terminological discussions, for they are often inconclusive, or even counterproductive. I have no objection if one speaks about eight or nine talents or abilities, but I *do* object when an analyst calls some abilities (like language) intelligences, and others (like music) "mere" talents. All should be called either intelligences or talents; an unwarranted hierarchy among the capacities must be avoided.

MYTH 3
An intelligence is the same as a learning style, a cognitive style, or a working style.
REALITY 3
The concept of style designates a general approach that an individ-

ual can apply equally to an indefinite range of content. In contrast, an intelligence is a capacity, with its component computational processes, that is geared to a specific content in the world. These contents (with their yoked intelligences) range from the sounds of lanaguge to the sounds of music to the objects of the natural or the man-made world.

COMMENT

To get at the difference between an intelligence and a style, consider this contrast. If a person is said to have a "reflective" or an "intuitive" style, we assume that he will be reflective or intuitive with all manner of content, from language to music to social analysis. However, this assumption needs to be investigated. That person might well be reflective with music but not so in a domain that requires mathematical or spatial thinking; another person might be highly intuitive in the social domain but not in the least so with mathematics or mechanics. In fairness, the same point ought to be made with reference to the intelligences. Someone who is good at writing in her native language will not necessarily excel at public speaking or at learning foreign languages. And people who have difficulty leading others will not necessarily have difficulty understanding the motivations of those with whom they come into contact.

In my view, the relation between my concept of intelligence and the various conceptions of style needs to be worked out empirically, on a style-by-style basis. We cannot assume that *style* means the same thing to all who have used the term, such as the psychologists Carl Jung and Jerome Kagan or the educators Tony Gregorc and Bernice McCarthy. Little evidence exists that a person who evinces a style in one milieu or with one content or test will necessarily do so with other diverse contents. And even less basis exists for equating style with intelligences.

Recently, the educator Harvey Silver made an intriguing proposal about a possible relationship between intelligence and style: that people with strengths in particular intelligences must still decide how to exploit these strengths. For example, someone gifted with linguistic intelligence might decide to write poetry or screenplays, engage in debates, master foreign languages, or enter crossword puzzle contests. Perhaps the decision about *how* to use one's favored intelligences reflects one's preferred style. Thus, for example, introverted people would be more likely to write poetry or do crossword puzzles, whereas extroverted ones would be drawn to public speaking, debating, or television talk shows.

MYTH 4

MI theory is not empirical. (A variant of this myth alleges that MI theory *is* empirical but has been disproved.)

REALITY 4

MI theory is based wholly on empirical evidence and can be revised on the basis of new empirical findings.

COMMENT

In fact, hundreds of studies were reviewed in *Frames of Mind*, and the actual intelligences were identified and delineated on the basis of empirical findings from brain science, psychology, anthropology, and other relevant disciplines. The intelligences described in *Frames of Mind* represented my best-faith effort to identify mental abilities of a scale that could be readily discussed and critiqued. Since the publication of that book, I have remained open to the possibility of additional intelligences. As we have seen, evidence now exists for the positing of an eighth and, possibly, a ninth intelligence.

I have been gratified by the empirical work of other scholars, which bolsters the claim of specific intelligences. This work has been particularly dramatic in the case of the personal intelligences, since many studies have shown that intelligence about the human sphere is independent from intelligence with respect to other realms of experience. Of particular relevance are studies in children of the development of a "theory of mind." By the age of four or so, most children appreciate that other individuals have minds and that these "other minds" may not be privy to the information that the children themselves possess. The apparent absence of "theory of mind" in autistic children provides another line of evidence about the autonomy of this ability. The accumulated work on so-called emotional intelligence draws on and is congenial to my own claims about intrapersonal and interpersonal intelligences (as I suggested in chapter 3).

I have watched with interest the recent efforts to relate musical intelligence to other cognitive domains, especially in the studies begun by the psychologist Frances Rauscher, the physicist Gordon Shaw, and their colleagues. On the basis of patterns of maturation in the nervous system, these researchers (who collaborated at the University of California at Irvine) speculated that musical and spatial capacities may be closely allied in human cognition. They secured evidence that adults who listen to classical music show a transient superiority on spatial tasks requiring them to rotate objects, or geometric figures, in their imagination. And in a parallel line of investigation, Rauscher, Shaw, and colleagues found that young children who study a keyboard instrument perform better than various control groups on tasks requiring spatial-temporal operations. Still, it would be premature to remake the cartography of human faculties by collapsing musical with spatial abilities, or perhaps aligning certain spatial and certain musical abilities. Many more studies, with appropriate controls, need to be undertaken. However, if musical (or spatial) intelligence turns out to be primary and to stimulate the development of other intelligences, I would certainly reconfigure my list of intelligences.

Indeed, no empirically based theory is ever established permanently. All claims are perpetually "at risk" in the light of new findings, and properly so. The questions to ask of a new theory are whether it stimulates important questions and investigations, and whether its initial delineation of factors appears to be on the right track. A search for multiple intelligences represents an effort to cut nature at its proper joints, and only empirical evidence can determine the effectiveness of such intellectual surgery.

MYTH 5

MI theory is incompatible with *g* (the term used by psychometricians to designate the existence of general intelligence), with hereditarian accounts, and/or with environmental accounts of the nature and causes of intelligence.

REALITY 5

MI theory questions not the existence but the province and explanatory power of *g*. By the same token, MI theory is neutral on the question of the heritability of specific intelligences, instead underscoring the centrality of genetic and environmental interactions.

COMMENT

Interest in *g* comes chiefly from those who probe scholastic intelligence and those who study the correlations between test scores. Recently, investigators have become intrigued by the possible neurophysiological underpinnings of *g*. I have long contended that much of the research in this tradition overlooks too many important ingredients of human intellect. But I do not consider the study of *g* to be scientifically suspect, and I am willing to accept the utility of *g* for certain theoretical purposes. My interest, obviously, centers on those intelligences and those intellectual processes that are not subsumed under *g*.

On the question of MI theory's supposed incompatibility with hereditarian and environmental views, I reject the "nature–nurture" dichotomy, as do most other biologically informed scientists. Instead, I stress the constant and dynamic interaction, from the moment of conception, between genetic and environmental factors. On the one hand, I do not doubt that human abilities—and human differences—have a genetic base. As the human genome project (which seeks to map all of the genes on every human chromosome) nears completion, can any contemporary scientist question the existence of genes and gene complexes that are relevant to intellectual strengths or defects? Does it make sense to ignore or attempt to explain away the behavioral genetic studies, particularly those of identical twins reared apart, that document the significant heritability of most human capacities and traits? If tests were devised for the various human intelligences, I have little doubt that each intelligence would have a significant heritability. In all probability, heritabilities would vary. I speculate that mathematical, spatial, and musical intelligences would have higher heritabilities than linguistic, naturalist, and personal intelligences.

On the other hand, environmental factors obviously come into play at birth—indeed, there is increasing evidence that they come into play *before* birth. Even people who seem gifted in a particular intelligence or domain will accomplish little if they are not exposed to materials that engage the intelligence. By the same token, as demonstrated vividly by such programs as the Suzuki Music Talent Education Program, shrewd environmental interventions can convert ordinary people into highly proficient performers or experts. Indeed, the "smarter" the environment and the more powerful the interventions and the available resources, the more proficient people will become, and the less important will be their particular genetic inheritance.

MYTH 6

By broadening the term *intelligence* to include a broad spectrum of psychological constructs, MI theory renders the term and its typical connotations useless.

REALITY 6

This criticism is simply wrong. On the contrary, the standard definition of *intelligence* narrowly constricts our view by treating a certain form of scholastic performance as if it encompassed the range of human capacities and by engendering disdain for those who happen not to score well on a particular psychometric instrument.

COMMENT

MI theory is about the intellect, the human mind in its cognitive aspects. I believe that conceptualizing a number of semi-independent intelligences presents a more sustainable view of human cognition than does positing a single bell curve of intellectual potency. Note, however, that MI theory makes no claims to deal with issues beyond the intellect. It is not about personality, character, will, morality, attention, motivation, or any other psychological constructs. Nor is it connected to any set of morals or values.

MYTH 7

There is a single "approved" educational approach based on MI theory.

REALITY 7

MI theory is in no way an educational prescription. There is always a gulf between scientific claims about how the mind works and actual classroom practices. Educators are in the best position to determine whether and to what extent MI theory should guide their practice.

COMMENT

Contrary to much that has been written, MI theory does not incorporate a position on tracking, gifted education, interdisciplinary curricula, the schedule of the school day, the length of the school year, or other hot-button educational issues. In general, my advice has echoed the traditional Chinese adage: "Let a hundred flowers bloom." (I discuss MI theory and schools further in chapter 9.) Nonetheless, many hours of visiting MI classrooms (or viewing them on videotape) have sensitized me to possible superficial applications of the theory. In particular, I am leery of implementations such as the following:

- Attempting to teach all concepts of subjects using all of the intelligences. To be sure, most topics can be approached in varied ways, but applying a scattershot approach to each topic is a waste of effort and time.

- Believing that going through certain motions activates or exercises specific intelligences. I have seen classes in which children were encouraged to move their arms or run around, on the assumption that such exercise enhances bodily-kinesthetic intelligence. It does not, any more than babbling enhances linguistic or musical intelligence. I don't mean that exercise is a bad thing, only that random muscular movements have nothing to do with cultivation of the mind, or even the body.

- Using intelligences primarily as mnemonic devices. It may well be easier to remember a list if one sings it (or dances to it). However, these uses of the "materials" of an intelligence are essentially trivial. What is not trivial is the capacity to think musically—for example, to draw on some of the structural features of the classical sonata form to illuminate aspects of concepts like biological evolution or historical cycles.

- Conflating intelligences with other desired outcomes. This practice proves particularly notorious when it comes to the personal intelligences. Interpersonal intelligence, the understanding of other people, is often distorted as a program for cooperative learning or as a playground for extroverts. Intrapersonal intelligence, the understanding of oneself, is often misused as a rationale for self-esteem programs or is attributed to introverts. These distortions and misapplications suggest a shallow (or nonexistent) understanding of my writings on intelligence.

- Labeling people in terms of "their" intelligences. For many people, tossing around the terminology of different intelligences is an enjoyable parlor game. I have nothing against someone speaking of himself informally as being "highly linguistic" or "spatially impaired." However, when these labels become shorthand references for educators, they carry considerable risk. People so labeled may then be seen as capable of working or learning only in certain ways, a characterization that is almost never true. Even if it has a certain rough-and-ready validity, such labeling can impede efforts to provide the best educational interventions for success with a wide range of children.

For these reasons, I am loath to issue any imperatives for so-called MI schools. Instead, I regard MI theory as a ringing endorsement of three key propositions: We are not all the same; we do not all have the same kinds of minds (that is, we are not all distinct points on a single bell curve); and education works most effectively if these differences are taken into account rather than denied or ignored. Taking human differences seriously lies at the heart of the MI perspective. At the theoretical level, this means that all individuals cannot be profitably arrayed on a single intellectual dimension. At the practical level, it suggests that *any* uniform educational approach is likely to serve only a small percentage of children optimally.

When visiting a so-called MI school, I look for signs of personalization: evidence that all involved in the educational encounters take differences among human beings seriously and that they construct curricula, pedagogy, and assessment in the light of these differences. Overt attention to MI theory and to my efforts means little if the children are treated in a homogenized way. By the same token, whether or not staff members have ever heard of MI theory, I would happily send my children to a school that takes differences among children seriously, that shares knowledge about differences with children and parents, that encourages children to assume responsiblity for their own learning, and that presents materials in such a way that each child has the maximum opportunity to master those materials and to show others and themselves what they have learned and understood.

Indeed, in education, the challenge of the next millennium consists precisely in this: Now that we know about the enormous differences in how people acquire and represent knowledge, can we make these differences central to teaching and learning? Or will we instead continue to treat everyone in a uniform way? If we ignore these differences, we are destined to perpetuate a system that caters to an elite—typically those who learn best in a certain, usually linguistic or logical-mathematical manner. On the other hand, if we take these differences seriously, each person may be able to develop his or her intellectual and social potential much more fully.

I cherish an educational setting in which discussions and applications of MI theory have catalyzed a more fundamental consideration of schooling—its overarching purposes, its conception of a productive life in the future, its pedagogical methods, and its educational outcomes, particularly in the context of a community's values. Visits to other schools and extended forms of networking among MI enthusiasts (and critics) constitute important parts of this building process. If a more personalized education results from these discussions and experiments, the heart of MI theory has been embodied. And if personalization is fused with a commitment to achieving educational understandings for all children, then the cornerstone for a powerful education has indeed been laid. The burgeoning of communities that take MI issues seriously is not only a source of pride to me but also the best guarantor that the theory will continue to evolve productively.

ISSUES AND ANSWERS REGARDING MULTIPLE INTELLIGENCES

EVERY WEEK, sometimes every day, I receive questions about multiple intelligences theory. Some of the questions concern the theory itself, though many more deal with recommended practices or with questionable applications. The questions come from scholars, teachers, parents, college students, high school students, and elementary school students; they emanate from many states and many lands. The questions used to arrive primarily by letter and phone; now, of course, they arrive as well by fax and e-mail. And whenever I speak publicly about the theory, whether in person or on radio or television, a new set of questions greets me afterward at my office.

At first I tried to answer each question individually. More recently, however, it has become impossible to do so, even with staff help. I have drafted generic letters that answer the most frequent questions—for example, "Is there a test for multiple intelligences?" (Answer: "Not one that I endorse") and "Are there MI-focused high schools?" (Answer: "A few so far"). And when an interesting and novel question arises, I sometimes write a lengthy answer and may even paraphrase it in a publication.

In 1992, when I was preparing to issue *Multiple Intelligences: The*

Theory in Practice, I culled the twenty most frequently asked sets of questions and provided targeted responses in the book. When possible, I have appropriated those questions and answers and treated them in an updated fashion elsewhere in this volume. However, some of the questions still crop up regularly, new questions arise, and others require a new and different response than in the early 1990s. Moreover, as MI theory has become better known, lengthier and harsher critiques of the theory have appeared in both the popular and the scholarly presses (see Appendix B). In the pages that follow, I present an updated set of responses to questions that are still raised frequently. Some of these answers were initially developed with my long-time colleague at Project Zero, Joseph Walters.

TERMINOLOGY

Q. I am confused by terminology. Is intelligence a product, a process, a content, a style, or all of the above?

A. I wish this were a simple matter. Fundamentally, an intelligence refers to a biopsychological potential of our species to process certain kinds of information in certain kinds of ways. As such, it clearly involves processes that are carried out by dedicated neural networks. No doubt each of the intelligences has its characteristic neural processes, with most of them similar across human beings. Some of the processes might prove to be more customized to an individual.

The intelligence itself is not a content, but it is geared to specific contents. For instance, linguistic intelligence is activated when people encounter the sounds of language or when they wish to communicate something verbally to others. However, linguistic intelligence is not dedicated only to sound. It can be mobilized as well by visual information, when an individual decodes written text; and in deaf individuals, linguistic intelligence is mobilized by signs (including syntactically arranged sets of signs) that are seen or felt.

From an evolutionary point of view, each intelligence probably evolved to deal with certain kinds of contents in a predictable world. However, once such a capacity has emerged, there is nothing that mandates that it must remain tied to the original inspiring content. In different terms, the capacity can be *exapted* for other purposes. I assume, for example, that mechanisms related to the recognition of species in nature are now regularly used in recognizing commercial products. Also, some of the most powerful human systems—like written language—came about not directly through evolution but through the yoking of visual-spatial and linguistic capacities that had evolved for different purposes.

Speaking more loosely, we can describe certain products—for example, maps, drawings, and architectural plans—as involving a particular intelligence: in this case, spatial intelligence. However, the identification of a specific intelligence entails an inference on the part of an observer. After all, someone could complete maps, drawings, or architectural plans by using a nonspatial set of intelligences—for example, combining linguistic with bodily intelligences. Until it becomes possible to designate neural circuitry as representing one or another intelligence in action, we cannot know for sure which intelligence or intelligences are being invoked on a specific occasion.

Q. Isn't it odd to speak of skill in a gym or on a playing field as an intelligence? If not, wouldn't this mean that people with physical defects are mentally deficient?

A. I don't find it odd to speak of the bodily skill used by, say, an athlete, a dancer, or a surgeon as embodying intelligence. The performances of these individuals are valued in many societies, and they involve an enormous amount of computation, practice, and expertise. Snobbishness about use of the body reflects the Cartesian split between mind and body, and a concomitant degradation of processes that seem nonmental, or less mental than others. However, contemporary neuroscience has sought to bridge this gap and to document the cognition involved in action (and, for that matter, in emotion).

As for the characterization of "cognitive deficiency," it is true that the loss of a certain physical capacity could cause an individual to have problems in the bodily-kinesthetic area, just as the loss of hearing or sight could cause problems with linguistic or spatial capacities. In such cases, therapists are challenged to substitute other systems, whether adapted bodily mechanisms or prostheses.

Indeed, computer scientists have already produced robots to carry out physical actions such as lifting or sorting or navigating, as well as prostheses that can substitute for impaired sensory or motor capacities in people. In the future, these devices will help people with impairments to carry out actions that unimpaired people execute with their bodies. The once notable gap between physically impaired and unimpaired may disappear.

Should one still use the term *intelligence* in such cases? That depends on the role played by the person. If the machine simply substitutes for the person, then it is the machine, not the person, that is displaying intelligence. But if the person programs the machine or makes consequential decisions, then he or she is exercising a particular intelligence and using the computer as a tool. (The same line of reasoning can be invoked with respect to music. Composition used to presuppose instrumental and notational skills; now computers can substitute for both. The analyst must locate the source of the intelligence: Does it inhere in the programmer, the program, or the user of the program?)

THE THEORY

Q. Is multiple intelligences really a theory? Could it be confirmed or disconfirmed by experiment?

A. The term *theory* has two different meanings. Among physical scientists, it is reserved for an explicit set of propositions linked conceptually and having individual and joint validity that can be assessed through systematic experimentation. Laypeople use the term more loosely, to refer to any set of ideas put forth orally or in writing. As the man on the corner says, "I've got a theory about that." The MI theory falls somewhere between these two uses. There is no systematic set of propositions that could be voted up or down by a board of scientists, but the theory is not simply a set of notions I dreamed up one day. Rather, I offer a definition, a set of criteria for what counts as an intelligence, data that speak to the plausibility of each individual intelligence, and methods for revising the formulation.

In many sciences, theories occupy this intermediary status. Certainly, theories in the social sciences attempt to be as systematic as possible, yet they are rarely proved or disproved decisively. And broad theories in the natural sciences, like evolution or plate tectonics, are similarly immune from a single, simple test. Rather, they gain or lose plausibility on the basis of many, accumulated findings over a lengthy period. This is how I think about MI theory. I've presented a candidate set of intelligences, said to have their own characteristic processes and to be reasonably independent of one another. Over time, the particular intelligences nominated and their degree of dependence or independence from one another will be more firmly established.

People in search of a decisive thumbs-up or thumbs-down vote on any theory of intelligence are naïve. Still, it is important to indicate the kinds of considerations that would lend greater or lesser plausibility to the theory. Suppose that researchers discovered, for example, that a certain brain region in fact subserved more than one intelligence, or that people who were strong in one intelligence were invariably impaired in another intelligence, or that symbol systems ostensibly associated with one intelligence actually drew on the same cognitive processes as another intelligence. Each of these lines of evidence would cast doubt on the validity of the overall theory, although the theory might continue to be valid if appropriately revised. We do not reject Jean Piaget's overall theory of cognitive development, for instance, just because some of its specific claims have been undermined by subsequent research.

I once thought it possible to create a set of tests of each intelligence—an intelligence-fair version, to be sure—and then simply to determine the correlation between the scores on the several tests. I now believe that this could only be accomplished if someone developed several measures for each intelligence and then made sure that people were comfortable in dealing with the materials and methods used to measure each intelligence. And so, as I've suggested, a person's spatial intelligence would be assessed through performance in such activities as navigating an unfamiliar terrain, playing chess, interpreting blueprints, and remembering the arrangement of objects in a recently vacated room. If such measurements of intelligences were developed, the findings would be of scientific interest—at least to me! However, one reason I have moved away from creating these measures is that they may lead to new forms of labeling and stigmatization. As I stress, the intelligences should be mobilized to help people learn important content and not used as a way of categorizing individuals. To use the language of one of my critics, I do not want to inspire the creation of a new set of "losers."

Q. Does brain research continue to support your theory?

A. In brain sciences, a decade is a long time, and the theory of multiple intelligences was developed two decades ago. We now know much more about the functioning and development of the nervous system, and we have powerful new machinery for monitoring cortical processes while they are actually occurring. The accumulating neurological evidence is amazingly supportive of the general thrust of MI theory. Research supports the particular intelligences that I have described and provides elegant evidence of the fine structure of such capacities as linguistic, mathematical, and musical processing. At the same time, this research calls into some question an effort to localize each intelligence at a specific point in the brain. It makes more sense now to speak of several brain areas involved in any complex intellectual activity, and to highlight the extent to which different individuals may carry out a certain function using different portions of their respective brains.

It is sometimes argued that MI theory is questionable because the brain is a very flexible organ subject to the events of early experience. This remark is not pertinent, since "neural plasticity" is independent of the issue of different intelligences. MI theory demands that linguistic processing, for example, occur via a different set of neural mechanisms than does spatial or interpersonal processing. The fact that the processing may occur in somewhat different regions of the brain for different people, because of their early experiences, is interesting but irrelevant to the identification of intelligences *per se*. Indeed, suppose that, in one person, musical processing occurred in region A and spatial processing in region B. Suppose, further, that these representations were reversed in another person. MI theory would not thereby be affected. Even if musical intelligences were represented in regions A, B, and C in one person, and regions D, E, and F in a second person, that fact still would not affect the theory. If, however, musical and spatial processing were identically represented in a population, that fact would suggest the presence of one intelligence, not two separate intelligences.

Q. What do other scholars think of MI theory?

A. A wide spectrum of opinion exists, both within psychology and across the biological and behavioral sciences. Psychometricians are almost always critical of the theory, whereas other psychologists generally are open to the expansion of the concept and measurement of intelligence. Still, psychologists like neat measures of their constructs, and many are frustrated that the "new" intelligences are not as readily measured as the standard "generalized" intelligence.

Scholars are not known for responding generously to new theories, and so I have not been surprised at the considerable criticism leveled at MI theory. Perhaps a more reliable index of acceptance is the extent to which the theory has been cited in scholarly articles and textbooks. Over the years, the theory has been mentioned in innumerable articles and in most texts that touch on issues of intelligence. These references have generally been respectful. Most gratifying has been the response by scholars in the "hard" sciences (such as biology) and in nonscientific fields (such as the arts and humanities). The idea of multiple intelligences has considerable appeal across the disciplines, and my particular choice of intelligences is often endorsed. Of course, one could argue that scholars in other fields are not expert in the psychology of intelligence, but it is also true that they have less of an ax to grind.

Q. Is a rapprochement possible between MI theory and competing theories?

A. To some extent. Aspects of the theory are compatible with propositions advanced by other theorists (as mentioned in chapter 2). I am comfortable with the biocultural approach defended by Stephen Ceci, the emphasis on media and symbol systems adopted by David Olson, the cultural sensitivity emphasized by Patricia Greenfield, and the multifactorial stance of earlier scholars like L. L. Thurstone. More broadly speaking, the modular approach* put forth by psychologists like Steven Pinker, linguists like Noam Chomsky, and anthropologists like Stephen Mithen is consonant with the recognition of distinct intelligences.

Recently, the most widely discussed approach to intelligence has been Robert Sternberg's "triarchic" model (see chapter 2). Sternberg and I agree more on our criticism of standard intelligence theory than on the directions that new theoretical work should follow. That is, we reject the focus on a single scholastic intelligence that is measured by a certain kind of short-answer test. Sternberg proposes three different facets of intelligence—which he calls the componential, the experiential, and the contextual—and has devised measures for each. Along with most other theorists in this area, Sternberg does not attend to the particular contents with which intelligence operates. That is, it is immaterial to his theory whether a person is processing words, pictures, bodily information, or material from the personal or natural worlds. Rather, Sternberg, being more sympathetic to a "horizontal" view of mind, assumes that the same components will operate, whatever the kind of material being processed. Here our intuitions and claims differ fundamentally.

I applaud Sternberg's effort to develop new measures of intelligence, which clearly can help broaden our notions of human capacities. I wish, however, that his new measures were more adventurous. Sternberg adheres too closely to the kinds of linguistic and logical items that have traditionally dominated intelligence testing; and I predict his new measures will end up correlating highly with standard tests and with one another. In these emphases, Sternberg reveals that he is much more

---

*As noted in chapter 3, the modular approach is the view of the human mind as having evolved many separate information-processing devices.

of a psychologist and a psychometrician than I am. And this may explain why his work has been of greater interest to psychologists, while mine has captured the interest of educators and the general public.

THE STRUCTURE OF INTELLIGENCES
AND THEIR COMBINATION

Q. Need the intelligences be entirely independent?

A. The theory is simpler, both conceptually and biologically, if the intelligences are totally independent of one another. Yet each intelligence does not have to be independent of the others, and it may turn out empirically that certain intelligences are more closely tied together than are others, at least in particular cultural settings. The independence of intelligences makes a good working hypothesis. It can be tested only by using appropriate measures in different cultural settings; otherwise we might prematurely conclude that two intelligences are tied together, when in fact the apparent correlation is an artifact of a particular measure in a particular culture.

The reason for underscoring independence is to reemphasize that strength in one area does not necessarily signal strength in other areas—as is equally true for weaknesses. At a practical level, people will show pairs or trios of strengths and weaknesses. For example, some mathematicians will become involved with music, thus suggesting a link between musical and logical-mathematical intelligence. Life is interesting, however, because these pairs are no more predictable than the romantic attraction (or aversion) between two people.

Q. How do you know that the intelligences represent the right-sized unit of analysis? Can't each of the intelligences be broken down indefinitely, for example?

A. I doubt that there is a single, uniquely correct unit of analysis in an area as complex as intelligence. For certain purposes—for example, determining whether a mentally retarded person can benefit from schooling—a single measure like IQ *might* suffice. But if one wants to represent what is involved in particular musical tasks, like conducting, performing, or composing music, a single construct of "musical intelligence" is far too gross.

In writing about multiple intelligences, I have always noted that each intelligence comprises constituent units. There are several musical, linguistic, and spatial "subintelligences"; and for certain analytic or training purposes, it may be important to dissect intelligence at this level. I justify my small set of intelligences on the basis of parsimony and usefulness. If I were to write about dozens of subintelligences, I might be more accurate scientifically, but the construct would then be unwieldy for educational uses. Moreover, there is evidence to suggest that the subintelligences often work together and support one another, and for that reason, too, it makes sense to speak of eight or nine intelligences rather than one or a hundred.

Q. How do you view the often-noted connection between mathematical and musical intelligences?

A. Undoubtedly, mathematically talented people often show an interest in music. I think this linkage occurs because mathematicians are interested in patterns, and music is a gold mine of harmonic, metric, and compositional patterns. Interest, however, is not the same as skill or talent; a mathematician's interest in music does not predict that he or she will necessarily play well or be an astute critic of the performances of others. It's important to note that the imputed link rarely works the other way. We do not expect randomly chosen musicians to be interested, let alone skilled, in mathematics. There may also be a bias in the kind of music at issue. Those involved with classical music are far more likely to be oriented toward science and mathematics than those engaged in jazz, rock, rap, and other popular forms.

These observations suggest another factor: Certain families, and perhaps also certain ethnic groups, strongly emphasize scholastic and artistic accomplishment, expecting their children to do well in school and to perform creditably on musical instruments. These twin goals yield a population with many children who stand out in both math and music. There may be other common underlying factors, such as willingness to drill regularly, an inclination toward precision in dealing with marks on paper, and a desire to attain high standards. One would have to sample a wide variety of skills—from being punctual to writing cogent essays—before jumping to the conclusion that a privileged connection exists between musical and mathematical intelligence.

Q. What about capacities that cut across the different intelligences, such as memory?

A. I am skeptical about the existence of horizontal faculties—ones such as memory or attention or perception that are alleged to operate equivalently across all manner of content. One of the most important discoveries in the cognitive and brain sciences is that the mind is better viewed in a vertical way, as a set of faculties geared to particular contents in the external world and in human phenomenal experience.

Looking more specifically at memory, considerable neuropsychological evidence documents different kinds of memory: immediate memory, short-term memory, long-term memory, semantic (or generic) memory, episodic memory (memory for particular events), procedural memory (knowing how), and propositional memory (knowing that). These memories reflect different psychological processes and are served by different neural centers. There is convincing neuropsychological evidence that linguistic memory can be separated from musical memory as well as memory for shapes, faces, bodily movements, and the like. The notion of a single unitary memory falls apart under closer inspection. In this connection, it is instructive to consider what we mean when we speak of someone having a "good memory." Usually this means that the person has a good *linguistic* memory—he or she can remember names, dates, and definitions. We typically do not know, however, whether that person is equally facile at remembering visual patterns, musical patterns, and bodily movements, or what that person (or others) felt at a recent social event. Each of these skills may have its own mnemonic process, quite unrelated to the others.

Q. How can diverse and possibly independent intelligences function effectively without a leader or an executive?

A. A theory that does not posit an executive function has certain advantages over one that does. It is simpler, and it avoids the specter of infinite regression—the "homunculus" question of who or what is in charge of the executive. Nor does effective work require an executive. Many groups—whether artistic or athletic—perform well without a designated leader, and an increasing number of work teams are organized around patterns other than hierarchical ones.

The question of an executive—what I have sometimes called a Central Intelligences Agency—needs to be considered on theoretical and practical planes. On the theoretical level, the question is whether behavior is better modeled as the result of positing an executive function. That executive function could be "smart," intentionally making well-motivated decisions, or "dumb," simply ensuring that two antagonistic processes are not going off simultaneously. Considerable evidence suggests that such executive functions are handled by structures in the frontal lobe. The "modeler" must then decide whether to consider this a separate intelligence, or an entity that emerges from other intelligences, such as the intrapersonal intelligence. At present, I lean toward the latter alternative.

At a practical level, we need to ask how people can best organize their activities and their lives, given vast and interesting individual differences. Some people are reflective and "metacognitive"; they are immersed in self-conscious planning, which can be very helpful in accomplishing goals. Others are more intuitive: They know what they want to do, and they accomplish their business when they find themselves in the appropriate contexts. It is said that Dante and Shakespeare had minds so fine that they were never violated by a thought. If this statement has meaning, it suggests that neither craftsman devoted much time to obsessing about what to do, when to do it, and how to do it; he just waited until he was prepared to commence his creations, and then did his job as well as he could.

Ultimately, I have no objection if people find it helpful to invoke some kind of executive function. For modeling purposes, it is useful to see whether one can explain human behavior in the absence of such hierarchical considerations, or whether the hierarchy can emerge naturally, as part of everyday functioning, rather than by invoking a separate executive intelligence.

Q. What of a general capacity called critical thinking? Isn't this important in today's society? Shouldn't we have courses that help youngsters develop this faculty?

A. As with the executive function, I am not irredeemably opposed to the notion of critical thinking. Indeed, I would like myself, my children, my students, and my friends to think critically, and anything that can aid in that process should be encouraged. But I doubt that there is a particular form of thinking called critical thinking. As I've suggested with reference to memory and other putative "across-the-board" capacities, closer analysis calls their existence into question. Particular domains seem to entail their own idiosyncratic forms of thinking and critique. Musicians, historians, taxonomic biologists, choreographers, computer programmers, and literary critics all value critical thinking. But the *kind* of thinking required to analyze a fugue is fundamentally of a different order from that involved in observing and categorizing different species, editing a poem, debugging a computer program, or creating and revising a new dance. There is little reason to think that training of critical thinking in one of these domains is the same as training of critical thinking in another domain, and I do not think appreciable "savings" or "transfers" occur when someone broaches a new domain, because each domain exhibits its own particular objects, moves, and logic of implications.

To be sure, there may be certain habits of thought that are useful across domains. One can benefit from so-called weak moves like taking one's time, considering alternatives, brainstorming, eliciting critical feedback from sympathetic peers, putting work aside for a while when a snag appears, and so forth. Such habits of mind ought to be cultivated early and widely. But even these must be practiced explicitly in every domain where they are applicable; indeed, they are called weak precisely because they do not in themselves get one very far. It is unrealistic to expect that the individual who takes her time when completing her homework will necessarily do so when investing in the stock market or falling in love.

For these reasons, I do not place much stock in courses that feature critical thinking per se. I much prefer that critical thinking be featured in each and every course or activity where it can prove valuable. Courses that help people draw on these lessons can be helpful; courses that are expected to substitute for, or render unnecessary, the modeling of critical thinking in particular domains strike me as a waste of time. Ultimately, the surest road to across-the-board critical thought is a regimen in which critical thinking is inculcated in one discipline and domain after another. And so, for example, if one wants individuals to be able to offer cogent explanations, it makes sense to introduce the kinds of explanations needed for historical argument, scientific demonstrations, or literary interpretations. Perhaps, if each of these forms of critical thinking is mastered, a student will find it easier in the future to offer cogent explanations in a legal procedure or a coaching session.

I encounter the greatest resistance to this perspective when I speak to mathematicians or logicians. To them, thinking *is* thinking: If one knows how to be logical, one should be able to apply logic everywhere. Mathematics and logic undoubtedly merit our admiration precisely because they involve a quest for the greatest generality for the propositions and patterns they feature. However, such people often do not epitomize what they espouse. Often they prove to be impractical or illogical in their personal lives, or they seek to apply logic to inappropriate activities, such as pursuing love relationships or dealing with difficult people. "Psycho-logic" turns out to be quite different from mathematical logic.

Q. Is there an artistic intelligence?

A. Strictly speaking, no artistic intelligence exists. Rather, intelligences function artistically—or nonartistically—to the extent that they exploit certain properties of a symbol system. When someone uses language in an ordinary expository way, as I am doing here, he is not using linguistic intelligence aesthetically. If, however, language is used metaphorically, expressively, or in ways that call attention to its formal or sensuous properties, then it is being used artistically. By the same token, spatial intelligence can be exploited aesthetically by a sculptor or painter and nonaesthetically by a geometer or a surgeon. Even musical intelligence can function nonaesthetically; consider the bugle call that summons soldiers to a meal or to a flag raising. Conversely, patterns designed by mathematicians for mathematical purposes have ended up on display in art galleries; consider the enigmatic drawings of M. C. Escher.

Whether an intelligence is deployed for aesthetic purposes represents personal and cultural decisions. For instance, a person can apply linguistic intelligence as a lawyer, a salesperson, a poet, or an orator. However, cultures also highlight or thwart artistic uses of intelligences. In some cultures, almost everyone writes poetry, dances, or plays an instrument; in contrast, Plato sought to eliminate poetry from his Republic, while Stalin scrutinized every poem as if it were a diplomatic missive.

Of course, informally, it is perfectly all right to speak of artistic intelligences. I do this, particularly as a shorthand for intelligences that are frequently mobilized for artistic ends. In this context, it is worth noting that MI ideas have grown comfortably in schools that highlight the arts, while MI ideas seem an uncomfortable stretch in schools where the arts have been minimalized or marginalized.

GROUP DIFFERENCES

Q. Are intelligences the same in quality or quantity across groups? For instance, are men's profiles of intelligence different from women's? And how about different racial or ethnic groups?

A. These are potentially explosive questions. I suspect that if intelligence-fair tests were developed, they would reveal differences across gender and other readily identifiable groups. But if such differences were found, how to interpret them would not be clear. Women might

perform worse than men on spatial tasks in the West; in an environment where spatial orientation was important for survival (as among
the Eskimos), such differences might disappear or even be reversed. By
the same token, the gender difference regularly found in mathematics
scores on standardized tests in the United States is reduced in Asian
populations; indeed, Asian women often score better than Americans.

There is also the intriguing question of whether men and women use
their intelligences in identical ways. According to various studies, spatial orientation among lower mammals is mediated by landmarks for
females and by body position for males, and a similar difference may
well exist among humans. And there is the question of whether men
and women prioritize intelligences in the same way. Carol Gilligan's
pioneering work on moral judgments suggests that women place a
higher premium on interpersonal considerations, while men are more
likely to draw on logical-mathematical thinking.

In my own work, I have elected not to pursue this question. Apparent group differences have been exploited for politically dubious ends,
as in the Australian case mentioned in chapter 6, and I prefer not to
provide additional ammunition for such efforts. In any event, should
investigations demonstrate replicable differences among groups, I
would regard these differences as starting points for imaginative
efforts at remediation, rather than proof of inherent limitations within
a group.

Q. Does MI theory apply to other species and to artificial intelligence?

A. This is an intriguing question. My list of intelligences is one way
of characterizing human intellect, but it also offers a set of categories
that can be applied to other entities that might be deemed intelligent.
An inventory of intelligences applied to other organisms might reveal

that rodents have considerable spatial intelligence, that primates have superior bodily-kinesthetic intelligence, and that birds exhibit musical intelligence. Perhaps some species—such as bats or dolphins—exhibit intelligences unknown or undeveloped in humans. And certain intelligences, such as intrapersonal or existential, may be the exclusive purview of humans.

Already, highly intelligent computer programs have been created that compose music, complete complex calculations, and defeat chess champions in mind-to-mind combat, among other things. Whether computers can also develop personal intelligences is a subject of considerable dispute. Many experts in artificial intelligence believe that it is just a matter of time before computers exhibit intelligence about human entities. As I've already noted, I feel that this is a category error: One cannot have conceptions of persons in the absence of membership in a community with certain values, and it seems an undue stretch to attribute such a status to computers. However, in the future, both humans and computers may chuckle at my shortsightedness.

INTELLIGENCE AND THE LIFE COURSE

Q. What happens to multiple intelligences during later life?

A. In many ways, the multiple intelligences seem a particular gift of childhood. While observing children, we can readily see them using their several intelligences. Indeed, one of the reasons for my enthusiasm about children's museums is their evident cultivation of a plethora of intelligences. Nowadays, the average children's museum simply has a better fit with the minds of children than does the average school (see chapters 9 and 11).

It could be that multiple intelligences decline in importance as well as in visibility, but I believe that the opposite is true. As we age, our intelligences simply become internalized. We continue to think differently from one another—indeed, differences in modes of mental representation are likely to increase throughout active life—but the differences among older people are simply less manifest to observers.

Consider, for example, what happens in a lecture hall. If the speaker lectures, members of the audience sit and either take notes or just focus on the speaker. An observer might easily infer that no processing is going on or that the processing is entirely linguistic. However, once it comes to representing the contents of the lecture, the individual—lecturer no less than listener—is free to make use of whatever representational capacities she has at her disposal. A lecture on physics might be represented in language, in logical propositions, in graphic form, through some kind of kinetic imagery (that is how Einstein thought about physics), or even in some kind of musical format (the Greeks stressed the parallels between musical and mathematical forces). People may also take notes and use disparate aids to study and recall.

The recesses of our minds remain private, and no one can tell the mind exactly what to do. The challenge to the mind is to make sense of experience, whether on the street or in the classroom. The mind maximally uses the resources at its disposal—namely, our intelligences.

Q. I've heard it said there is no proof that MI-focused schools work. What's the evidence on that?

A. There is much evidence that schools influenced by MI theory are effective. The testimonials from satisfied administrators, parents, students, and teachers are legion. And many of the classes and schools claim that students are more likely to come to school, to like school, to complete school, and to do well in assessments. Of course, this evidence is almost entirely based on self-reports and is thus skewed in favor of MI advocates, who are more likely to report their reactions than are MI critics. Even if these claims could be independently substantiated, however, we could not be sure which effects were due to MI theory. Schools are incredibly complex institutions, located in incredibly complex environments (a topic explored further in chapter 9). When test scores or other performance measures go up or down, it is easy to attribute these "highs" or "lows" to one's favorite hero or villain. But without the kind of controlled studies that are almost impossible to mount outside of medical settings, it is simply not possible to *prove* that it was MI, and MI alone, that did the trick.

For these reasons, I have been reluctant to claim that application of MI theory definitely changes schools. I had anticipated admiration for this reticence, but, instead, my silence has been perceived in many quarters as a sign that MI theory does not work or that I disapprove of what is being done in MI-focused schools. Thus, I am most pleased that the educational researcher Mindy Kornhaber and her colleagues at Harvard's Project Zero have undertaken the SUMIT (Schools Using Multiple Intelligences Theory) project. The research team has been studying forty-one schools around the United States that have been applying MI theory for at least three years. The results from these schools are encouraging: 78 percent of the schools reported positive standardized test outcomes, with 63 percent of these attributing the improvement to practices inspired by MI theory. Seventy-eight percent reported improved performances by students with learning difficulties. Eighty percent reported improvement in parent participation, with 75 percent of these attributing the increase to MI theory; and 81 percent reported improved student discipline, with 67 percent of these attributing the improvement to MI theory. Even though these figures may reflect a positive spin, they are based on empirical data, which an impartial party cannot dismiss.

Q. Granted that some MI schools report improved academic outcomes, isn't the MI approach really a way to celebrate differences among students, without any particular focus on their learning?

A. Nothing could be further from the truth. In my own teaching and writing, I have always placed at the center of education the mastery of basic skills and the achievement of understanding within and across the disciplines. I am relentlessly focused on genuine learning and insistent on high standards for all those involved in the education process. And I strongly support the use of regular and appropriate assessments.

I part company from certain critics on the nature of academic content. I value conceptual understanding over accumulation of facts. I place little stock in a canon or a required core curriculum; I believe that understanding can be achieved from a variety of materials and depends upon in-depth exploration of a limited number of topics rather than on breadth of coverage. By the same token, I have a low regard for the use of standardized short-answer machine-scored instruments. I much prefer occasions where students can perform their understandings publicly, receive relevant critiques, and go on to enhance their performances and their understandings.

Some individuals and some schools may wave the banner of MI as a rationale for nonacademic goals, or they may use MI as an excuse to avoid skills and academic demands. However, I have seen few such mindless examples myself; they usually appear in the writings of conservatively oriented critics whose prejudices are stronger than their observational skills. In any event, it is hardly appropriate to blame the theory (or the theorist) for such abuses; any psychological perspective can be implemented in a constructive way or thoughtlessly abused. In chapters 9 and 10, I describe in some detail my own current thoughts regarding "MI in the schools."

Informally I have often described our work at Harvard Project Zero in this way: "We try to develop good ideas and give them a nudge in the right direction." That has been and will continue to be my stance toward MI theory.

8

THE INTELLIGENCES OF
CREATORS AND LEADERS

WORK IN MULTIPLE intelligences theory represents an effort at pluralization and at disaggregation. It means taking the once unitary notion of intelligence and fractionating it (one hopes) along the lines that nature intended. For this effort to be successful, however, requires that intelligence not be confounded with other virtues. In Chapter 5 I discussed, as an example, the importance of not conflating intelligence with morality.

But what about other valued human traits, particularly ones in the intellectual realm, such as creativity and leadership? Are creators or leaders intelligent? If so, in which ways? In this chapter, I examine such questions.

People are not created equal, nor are all intelligences. One of the most frequent observations across cultures is that some young children excel in certain pursuits. There are children who, at an earlier age than their peers, learn to speak, to sing or remember songs, to find their way around unfamiliar terrain, to master and win at physical or cerebral games, and so on. When such children stand out, we call them talented or gifted; and when they are truly precocious, performing at an adult level when they are still in rompers, we call them prodigies.

Prodigies are wondrous to behold, and they serve as a revealing "proof" of the separateness of intelligences. But it is important to note that gifted children and prodigies are precocious experts; they excel at precisely those activities that more ordinary adults can carry out. We expect violinists in a symphony orchestra to perform with technical virtuosity; we expect mathematicians teaching at universities to have mastered the important proofs in their subdisciplines; we expect chess masters to win handily in most tournaments. In each of these areas, prodigies are young people whose intelligences have unfolded with sufficient speed that they can hold their own with adult experts. Eventually, though, other youngsters catch up with prodigies, who then no longer stand out. Adult experts—former prodigies or not—who can perform or create distinctively receive our accolades. In proposing this distinction, I move toward a further delineation of the territory of creativity.

CONCEPTUALIZING CREATIVITY, TALENT, AND PRODIGIOUSNESS

My definition of *creativity* has revealing parallels with, and differences from, my definition of *intelligence*. People are creative when they can solve problems, create products, or raise issues *in a domain* in a way that is initially novel but is eventually accepted in one or more cultural settings. Similarly, a work is creative if it stands out at first in terms of its novelty but ultimately comes to be accepted within a domain. The acid test of creativity is simple: In the wake of a putatively creative work, has the domain subsequently been changed?

Let me underscore the relationship between my definitions of intelligence and creativity. Both involve solving problems and creating products. Creativity includes the additional category of asking new questions—

something that is not expected of someone who is "merely" intelligent, in my terms. Creativity differs from intelligence in two additional respects. First, the creative person is always operating in a domain or discipline or craft. One is not creative or noncreative in general; even Leonardo da Vinci, perhaps the Western world's ultimate Renaissance man (after all, the term was probably coined with him in mind), was creative in certain domains, like painting and invention, and not nearly as creative in others. Most creators stand out in one domain or, at most, in two. Second, the creative individual does something that is initially novel, but the contribution does not end with novelty—it is all too easy to do something merely different. Rather, what defines the creative act or actor is the ultimate acceptance of that novelty; and again, the acid test of creativity is its documented effect on the relevant domain or domains.

My definition focuses on what my students have dubbed "Big C Creativity"—creativity that affects a domain. No doubt, there are many cases of small-scale creativity—in novelties that bring delight and, perhaps, affect a domain minimally. And clearly, some people engage in mid-scale creativity, with results like the tune that never makes the Top Forty, the book that summarizes a new area of study for laypeople, the chess opening that works well in certain contexts. However, to understand the concept of creativity in its full-blown sense, one must look at people who have clearly affected domains: composers like Richard Wagner and John Lennon, writers like Johann Wolfgang von Goethe and Virginia Woolf, scientists like Marie Curie and Niels Bohr, moviemakers like Ingmar Bergman and Steven Spielberg.

In the social sciences, we do not expect major breakthroughs like the ones in theoretical physics or molecular biology. Much of the creativity is modest; mid-scale creators are the rule. However, I maintain that distinct progress occurred in the social science domain when the psychologist Mihaly Csikszentmihalyi proposed that we should not ask who or what is creative but, instead, ask where creativity is. In Csik-szentmihalyi's elegant formulation, creativity results from an interaction among three separate elements: (1) an individual (potential) creator, with his or her talents, ambitions, and personal foibles; (2) a domain of accomplishment that exists in the culture; and (3) the field, a set of individuals or institutions that judge the quality of works produced in the culture. During any historical period, many people are either producing fledgling works in a particular domain, or mastering it, typically in a currently favored symbol system. Of the many resulting works, the field picks a few that stand out. Ultimately, a very few of these distinctive works actually alter the structure or content of a domain, and it is these works and the individuals who have fashioned them that can be considered creative, in the major sense.

By describing creativity in this way, Csikszentmihalyi removes creativity from the individual's psyche—an entity emanating from the mind or the brain of the individual. Of course, this is not to deny that individuals are indispensable to creativity—at least, in the age before the smart machine. Rather, it is to call attention to the fact that "creativity" essentially and inevitably represents a communal judgment. The only way that we can reliably ascertain whether a person is creative is by observing the ultimate fate of the work(s) he or she has fashioned. The concept of the "field" calls attention to the fact that "creativity" essentially and inevitably represents a communal judgment.

Here, then, is a crucial difference between intelligence and creativity. Intelligence may reflect what is valued in a community, but ultimately it entails the smooth and skilled operation of one or more "computers" in the mind or brain of the individual. Creativity is different. It is obviously desirable to have a well-designed and well-performing cognitive computer (or two or more such neural machines). However, even the best designed computer does not promise creativity.

Some people are incensed by this view of creativity. They say that "feeling creative" or being deeply involved in an activity (as when a child is drawing) constitutes doing creative work. Other critics focus on artists, writers, scientists, and others who were ignored in their day, only to be recognized posthumously—indicating, say the critics, the stupidity or ineptness of the communal judges, the field.

Granted, the field—the institutions and individuals who are knowledgeable about the domain—is not fair, and it certainly is unreliable in the short run. But it is the only mechanism that we have for making legitimate judgments about works. And so, like it or not, we must rely on the evaluations and reevaluations of the fields over the years. Emily Dickinson or Vincent van Gogh may not have been appreciated in their day, but at least the field has come to the rescue in our day. And if someone does not like the field—as, for example, Freud did not like his fellow psychologists—he can always attempt to create a new domain and a new field. This is precisely what Freud did by founding the domain of psychoanalysis. He then invested its concomitant field—which he headed—with the authority to render decisions about work created in that domain.

Creative Personalities

In a rare instance of agreement among social scientists, most students of creativity concur that it takes about a decade for people to master a domain and up to an additional decade for them to fashion work that is creative enough to alter that domain. Mastery requires thousands of domain-specific work hours—in solving mathematical problems, practicing difficult passages on the violin, keeping journals, or working in a biological or chemical laboratory. This work, involving one or more intelligences, is cognitive in the finest sense of that term.

Mastery, however, is not equivalent to creativity. Studies of highly creative people have suggested that they are more likely to stand out in terms of personality configurations rather than sheer intellectual power. By the time they are capable of carrying out work that will be judged as creative, they already differ from their peers in ambition, self-confidence, passion about their work, tough skins, and, to put it bluntly, the desire to be creative, to leave a mark on the world. The difference between the intelligent person and the potentially creative person makes intuitive sense. We all know people who are highly skilled, quick, and likely to arrive first at the answer to a puzzle. They are intelligent in a traditional sense, but many of them are content just to learn more things or to engage in increasingly demanding efforts to solve other people's puzzles.

In contrast, there are other people who do not stand out in terms of quickness or general intellectual appetite, but who move away from the problems others are pondering. They are more likely to immerse themselves deeply in an area and to discover certain anomalies or puzzles themselves. They may at first try to sweep these anomalies out of the way, as did Freud when as a student he first heard about the sexual causes of hysteria, or Darwin, when he first sensed that species evolved over eons as a result of natural selection, or Picasso, when he found that his friend Gertrude Stein could not be rendered to his satisfaction by ordinary portraiture. These anomalies do not go away by themselves, and the potential creators eventually elect to spend their energies on figuring out what is actually going on. Of course, far more people hope to be creative than actually succeed: The proposed solution may not be satisfying, or it may satisfy the creator but elude the field that renders judgment.

I have taken care not to claim that the personality traits of creators are inborn. In fact, I doubt that some people are born as more ambitious, more tough-skinned, more prone to immersion in a domain for many years, or more committed to leaving a mark on the world. At most, these proclivities may correlate with certain inborn temperaments—for example, being energetic and tolerant of stress rather than shy and retiring. If this is so, why, by the age of ten or twenty, do some people seem to have the temperament and personality of the future expert, while others seem to have the characteristics we associate with creativity? My informed guess is that we are dealing with the coincidence of many different factors that, taken together, predispose some people to be aspiring creators. Among the factors, I would suggest the following:

- Early exposure to other people who are comfortable with taking chances and who do not easily admit failure. (It helps to be born in Renaissance Florence, for example.)
- The opportunity to excel in at least one pursuit when young
- Sufficient discipline so that a domain can be more or less mastered in youth
- An environment that constantly stretches the young person, so that triumph remains within grasp without being too easily achieved
- Peers who also are willing to experiment and who are not deterred by failure
- Late birth order or an unusual family configuration that encourages or at least tolerates rebellion
- Some kind of physical, psychic, or social obstacle or anomaly that makes a person marginal within his or her group.

This list is speculative. No doubt there are creative types who don't match the criteria and noncreative types who do. For instance, I have yet to discover a theory of creativity that explains the emergence of the world's most remarkable physicist, Isaac Newton, from obscure origins in seventeenth-century England.

In contrast, it is instructive to consider the likelihood of creativity for a twin or a sibling separated at birth who is exposed to the opposite set of conditions:

- No contact with people who ever take chances
- No encouragement to excel at a pursuit
- No opportunity to master a domain
- The absence of parents or coaches who constantly, but carefully, up the ante
- The absence of peers who are likely to join in experimentation
- Being a first-born, or part of a family constellation that quells signs of rebellion
- Total normality (averageness) with respect to one's community
- Removal to a milieu where efforts to stretch intellectually are ignored or actively squelched

Admittedly, it is difficult to imagine an environment that is so unconducive to the creative spirit. Yet, sketching it at least reminds us that the right set of genes hardly suffices to yield a creator.

Kinds of Creativity and Kinds of Intelligence

We now have a definition of creativity and a sense of the kinds of individuals likely to become major creators. But how does intelligence actually interact with creativity?

I first thought that the kinds of creativity followed directly from the kinds of intelligence: Writers are creative in language, mathematicians deploy logical-mathematical intelligence, and so on. As a first approximation, this equation is not wholly wrong. However, the relation between intelligence and creativity proves more complex and more intriguing.

It is true that creative people stand out in terms of certain intelligences, but in most cases they exhibit an amalgam of at least two intelligences, at least one of which proves to be somewhat unusual for that domain. Like most physicists, Einstein had outstanding logical-mathematical intelligence, but his spatial capacities were extraordinary even among physicists.* Freud saw himself as a scientist and had adequate logical-mathematical capacities, but his greater genius lay in the linguistic and personal intelligences. That fact contributed to his tremendous success with the public but also engendered long-simmering tension with more conventionally trained scientists. Stravinsky's musical intelligence was excellent, but he also stood out in other artistic intelligences, and perhaps this explains why he proved to be an outstanding composer of ballets, could skillfully set texts to music, and became one of the more trenchant artistic commentators of his era.

Although outstanding creators have notable amalgams of intelligences, they typically exhibit intellectual weaknesses as well. Freud, for example, lacked musical intelligence, while Picasso was a very poor student and hardly mastered the basic literacies. But creators are not defeated by these intellectual weaknesses; they learn to ignore them and to seek help in domains where they are deficient. Creative individuals come to know their strengths and recognize their cognitive or cultural niches, and they pursue these with full knowledge of their competitive advantage. They do not waste precious minutes, let alone months or years, lamenting what others can do better.

Different creative people are attracted to different kinds of activities, as reflected in one important dichotomy. Some find themselves working primarily in the world of *persons*: either as introspectors exploring their own minds (like Virginia Woolf or Sigmund Freud) or as influ-

---

*Recent studies of Einstein's brain by neuropsychologist Sandra Witelson confirm this speculation.

encers attempting to change the others' behaviors (like Winston Churchill or Mao Zedong). Other creative people are more attracted to the worlds of *objects*, *symbols*, and *ideas*—the inanimate, impersonal realm. They are more likely to become unsurpassed masters in a domain (like Mozart or Shakespeare), or to emerge as makers (like Darwin or Picasso), who change the fundamental constitution of the domain.

One can also distinguish creators by the types of work they do. Some (like James Watson and Francis Crick, the discoverers of DNA) solve problems that their colleagues have also puzzled over; some (like Einstein or Freud) create entirely new explanatory frameworks; some (like Picasso or Stravinsky) create permanent works in a genre; some (like the dancer Martha Graham or the actor Laurence Olivier) excel in ritualized performances; and some, like Gandhi, create while engaging in high-stakes, nonscripted performances (an unarmed Gandhi having to confront a battalion of armed troops).

We do not know enough about creativity to be sure what predisposes one creator to become an influencer and another a maker, or why some solve problems, others create new theories, and still others become performers of a ritualized or high-stakes, nonritualized form. I suspect that there is a connection between intellectual strength and mode of creativity. For example, those with an affinity for interpersonal intelligence are more likely to become influencers or performers. Those with strong logical-mathematical intelligence are more likely to become masters and theory builders. More complex interactions may occur between intellectual strength and personality types. Consider, for example, a set of people with linguistic intelligence. Those who are shy are more likely to become poets; others with equal linguistic intelligence but a more outgoing personality are likely to become comedians or political leaders.

DISCIPLINARY PERSPECTIVES ON LEADERSHIP

The leader seems to emerge from one kind of world and those who stand out in intelligence or creativity from quite another planet. Leaders deal primarily in power, persuasion, and policy. They gain a position of authority and then use those niches to carry out policies, either by force or, preferably, through persuasion. Leaders may need a modicum of intelligence; but, if anything, intelligence can get in their way if they want to connect with the public. As for creativity, that is the province of artists and scholars, not of those who would succeed in the "real" world.

Even those who analyze leadership from a psychological perspective seem remote from the kind of analysis proposed here. To the extent that psychologists have concerned themselves with leadership, they have tended to focus on the personality of the leader and on who becomes a follower. They see leaders as people with strong motives to gain ascendancy, to dominate, and to impose their will upon others. This motive is often tied to the relationship (or lack of relationship) with one's father; to feelings of inferiority, which must be compensated; to rivalry with siblings; or to early, charged experiences in a dominance hierarchy. Everyone is a follower in some portion of their life, but those most prone to fall sway to a leader are those with low status. I do not reject these views of leadership. Clearly, much of leadership falls within the province of political scientists, historians, and sociologists. And clearly, human personality and temperament strongly influence the psyches of leaders and followers. But I believe the cognitive facets of leadership have been underplayed, and my own analyses address this lack.

A COGNITIVE VIEW OF LEADERSHIP

Traditionally, leaders are people who can change the thoughts, feelings, and/ or behaviors of a significant number of other people. They
may bring about changes coercively, as in the case of a tyrant or an
authoritarian regime. But in these instances, the leadership is only as
effective as the force that grasps the trigger, and once the coercion has
been removed, the leader's effectiveness wanes. Alas, the history of this
century—from Hitler to Ceausescu to Milosevic—has been dominated
by coercive leaders and by the events they directly or indirectly precip-
itated.

I focus instead on those leaders I call voluntary—the men and
women who succeed in making changes without coercion. Leaders
achieve effects primarily by telling stories and by embodying those stories in their own lives.

First, storytelling. The goal of leaders is to change others' behavior
and thus frame events and possibilities so as to help their followers
think differently about the world and their places in it. (Managers
have no such passion; they maintain the status quo.) Leaders sense that
a story—unlike a mere slogan or message or even a vision—is a dramatic vehicle that features a protagonist, a set of goals, obstacles that
may thwart the goals, and a set of strategies by which to achieve the
goals. In telling stories, leaders create dramatic narratives about themselves, their families, their people, and their nations. Such narratives
can be compelling, for they draw listeners into the sweep of history,
causing them to identify with and make common cause with the leader.

Consider Margaret Thatcher, the British prime minister from 1979
to 1990. Thatcher's story during her initial campaign for election as
Conservative party leader was simple but compelling; in the words of
her campaign slogan: "Britain has lost its way." Since the end of World
War II, Britain had in effect been governed by a bipartisan coalition

that embraced a socialized state, nationalized industries, and powerful unions, resulting in a second-class economic and military status for Britain. Thatcher challenged the prevailing orthodoxy and harkened back to the Britain of an earlier era—a nation proud, independent, patriotic, and capable of acting on its own energies and values. She looked forward as well to a time when Britain could again take its place as a leader in the political and commercial world. Margaret Thatcher would help Britain find the proper way.

But Thatcher did not just tell a story well; she embodied the story. The daughter of a grocer, she and her family had lived atop her father's store. With wits, ambition, and much hard work, she had pursued higher education, including degrees in chemistry and law. She had married and raised two children. She had run for political office and achieved a series of firsts, including the first shadow prime minister and first female prime minister in British history. She also proved courageous, by taking a risky course in the 1982 Falkland-Malvinas War and by surviving a terrorist bomb attack at the 1984 Conservative party congress in Brighton. As the contemporary phrasemakers put it, she "walked the talk."

For every Margaret Thatcher who successfully creates and "sells" a new story, though, there are hundreds of orators standing atop egg crates in London's Hyde Park who are ignored except for a few, true, dedicated, equally benighted followers. Why? From an early age, we hear and view many stories, some of which congeal rapidly. The mind of the four- or five-year-old is well stocked with stories about heroes, villains, and the regularities and oddities of daily life. If a would-be leader tells a story that is too familiar, the followers assimilate it automatically into the ones they already know and see no special significance. If, on the other hand, the story is too removed from ordinary experiences, it is ignored or quickly forgotten—as most revolutionaries find out.

The art of the leader is to create and refine a story so that it engages the attention and commitment of followers, thereby changing their views of who they are, what they are committed to, and what they want to achieve and why. Effective leaders pay careful attention to the reactions of their early audiences and constantly refine their stories. Successful campaigners like Franklin Roosevelt, Ronald Reagan, and Bill Clinton learned to do this during their apprenticeship years. Still, it is risky to craft a story simply to satisfy an audience; leaders who do so are likely to be seen as inauthentic or, worse, hypocritical. Despite the rise of spin doctors, pollsters, and propagandists, an inherent public bias toward authenticity determines the long-term effectiveness of a leader.

THE INTELLIGENCES OF LEADERS

Which intelligences are crucial to leaders? First, they are gifted in language; they can tell effective stories and often can write skillfully, too. Second, they display strong interpersonal skills; they understand the aspirations and fears of other persons, whom they can influence. Third, they have a good intrapersonal sense—a keen awareness of their own strengths, weaknesses, and goals—and they are prepared to reflect regularly on their personal course. Finally, the most effective leaders are able to address existential questions: They help audiences understand their own life situations, clarify their goals, and feel engaged in a meaningful quest.

Of course, just as lawyers or scientists or architects differ from one another, leaders have different styles and strengths. President Bill Clinton is a brilliant storyteller, but he tends to tell too many stories, and it is not clear which ones he truly believes and genuinely embodies. Military leaders, like General George Marshall, have less need for a fresh story; instead, they superlatively embody a story that is already well known to troops on the field—and troops back home. Some leaders, like the biblical Moses or the twentieth-century statesman Jean Monnet, do not speak effectively and therefore must rely on spokespersons. Lyndon Johnson was accomplished at influencing individual legislators or journalists, but he lacked complementary interpersonal skills when he had to address larger and more distant groups, as when speaking on television.

Such diverse profiles are evident in the world of business, as well. Henry Ford was a clever inventor and visionary thinker, but he lacked insight into other people and himself; in the end, this interpersonal and intrapersonal obtuseness proved costly for his company. Ford's successor, Robert McNamara, was a strategic, logical-mathematical wizard, but he was less effective at addressing his employees' existential questions. Bill Gates's utopian vision and awkward persona appealed to other techies with a "nerdy" past and dreams of inheriting cyberspace. When Louis Gerstner first took the helm at IBM, he declared, "The last thing IBM needs now is a vision; it needs lower costs and better market focus in every division." But a year later, Gerstner acknowledged the importance of narratives and of interpersonal considerations: "[Changing a culture] is not something that you do by writing memos. You've got to buy in with their hearts and their beliefs, not just the minds." And so, armed with a new story about "market, execution, and teamwork," he toured the country and told his employees a new "identity story": "I'm one of us now." The message has worked well so far.

LEADERS AND CREATORS

I was originally drawn to the study of leadership because Mahatma Gandhi, a creator with superlative interpersonal intelligence, seemed to differ so markedly from other creators of the modern era. Thus, when I began my studies of leadership (as explored in my book *Leading Minds*), I assumed that leaders and creators were drawn from different populations.

I soon discovered I was wrong. Indeed, creators and leaders are remarkably similar. Both groups seek to influence the thoughts and behaviors of other people. Both are, accordingly, engaged in the enterprise of persuasion. Moreover, each leader or creator has a story to tell: A creator is contributing to the story of a chosen domain; a leader is creating a story about his group. Finally, embodiment is important for both groups: A leader must embody her stories in her daily life; a creator must embody his story by carrying out work in his domain. The difference lies in the *directness* of the influence. Conventional business and political leaders lead *directly*, by speaking (or, occasionally, writing) to their audiences and thereby seeking to bring about changes. Creators, in contrast, lead *indirectly*, through symbolic products—the works of art, the works of science, or the scientific or academic theories they produce. If such work is effective, it ends up changing the way people behave in arts, science, or scholarship and reshaping the stories they tell about who they are and how they go about their work. But on the issue of influence, it does not matter what kinds of persons Einstein or Picasso or T. S. Eliot or George Eliot were or whether they treated their families well or poorly. What matters enormously is the kind of work they carried out and how they carried it out, for that is the arena in which their ultimate contributions lie.

There are further parallels. An intriguing early marker of leaders is that when young, they often challenge people in authority—not necessarily through overt confrontation, but at least through trenchant analyses. The clear message: They could have weighed the alternatives and faced the challenges as competently as the leaders. General of the Army George C. Marshall provides a striking example of this trait. Not a particularly assertive or confrontational person, Marshall nonetheless challenged General John J. Pershing, the commander in chief of the Allied Expeditionary Forces, on their first meeting in October 1917. Risking a repetition of history, Marshall later as a cabinet officer publicly challenged his commander in chief, President Franklin D. Roosevelt, on their first meeting in November 1938. Happily for Marshall, in each case he was listened to rather than reprimanded by the two powerful people with whom he eventually joined forces.

I had initially thought that such public confrontation was a trait of leaders, not creators, since I had found few comparable stories in the lives of most notable creators. However, I had been looking in the wrong place. Future creators challenge their teachers and mentors all the time, but rarely through face-to-face criticism. Rather, they challenge through the iconoclastic works they create. Einstein had little use for his teachers, but he did not waste time arguing with them. Instead, he carried out scientific analyses and wrote papers that made their work irrelevant. It was the same story with Igor Stravinsky (who totally reconfigured the contributions of his teacher Nikolay Rimsky-Korsakoff) and with Pablo Picasso (whose Cubist works were meaningless to his artist father).

There is one crucial difference between creators and leaders. Because leaders speak directly to audiences, which are typically heterogeneous and often not well informed, their stories need to be simple, if not simplistic. In contrast, creators typically address people who know a great deal about the domain and who regularly read scientific literature or encounter novel works of art. And so they can assume a mind that is informed—one that has been schooled and that has attained at least some degree of expertise in the relevant domain.

CREATIVITY, LEADERSHIP, MORALITY, AND WISDOM

Although intelligences are not in themselves moral or immoral, there is some consensus about which individuals use their intelligences in prosocial or antisocial ways. But there are disagreements as well. Clearly, Ezra Pound had a high degree of linguistic intelligence; but whether this poet, who made Fascist broadcasts during World War II, used that intelligence constructively was fiercely debated when he was awarded the first Bollingen Prize for poetry under the auspices of the Library of Congress in 1949. Exactly the same issue can—and should— be raised about creativity and leadership. Creative individuals change domains, but they can do so in moral or immoral ways. The master documentarian Leni Riefenstahl influenced filmmaking in the mid- 1900s, but few who saw her paeans to Nazi superiority would argue that she used her talent in a moral, or even morally neutral, way. The same is true of leaders. Certainly—and here I strive to be bipartisan—John F. Kennedy, Lyndon Johnson, Richard Nixon, Ronald Reagan, and Bill Clinton were effective leaders, but historians will be arguing about their morality or immorality for decades, if not centuries.

As I have stressed in earlier chapters, sheer intellectual power and the uses of that power are two distinct considerations. As we move from intelligence to creativity to leadership, we steadily increase the scope of power: from people with their own expertise, to those who change a domain, to those whose decisions and actions affect the lives of thousands, or even millions, of people. And yet, the abyss between skill and morality cannot simply be ignored. In the final pages of this book, I put forth some ideas about how to reconcile these important human spheres. At this point, it is appropriate to introduce a consider- ation that may help in an ultimate effort at synthesis.

We intuitively know there is a difference between intelligence, cre- ativity, and leadership, even if we cannot put it into words or test it through social-scientific research. And we acknowledge a difference between moral and immoral creators, leaders, and intellectuals. In making the link to morality, we are placing a value judgment on their work: There must be standards for what counts as moral or immoral.

We also must acknowledge that people or works may score much higher on intelligence or creativity than on morality, or conversely, that they may be exemplary along the moral dimension but unremarkable in intellect or creativity.

Drawing a line between morality and wisdom is trickier. We hesitate to consider something wise if it is immoral, and we are more likely to consider something wise if it is also deemed moral. And yet, morality and wisdom also inhabit different terrains. The defining characteristic of wisdom is the breadth of considerations taken into account when rendering a judgment or recommending a course of action. Breadth of consideration benefits from long and varied experiences, and that is why we generally consider wisdom a sign of age. But wisdom is not a predictable feature of aging; many old people do not show particular range in reaching their judgments, and certainly some young people are wise beyond their years. The historian George Kennan and the philosopher Isaiah Berlin did not suddenly become wise when they entered their eighth or ninth decade, and, fortunately for them and us, their skill at synthesizing did not decline noticeably with age.

Armed with this glimpse at wisdom, we can revisit our core concepts one last time. A person who can use several intelligences together appropriately is more likely to be wise, because a greater number of faculties and factors will have entered into the equation. Hence, we look to the military leader who is also schooled in the arts and in diplomacy, as opposed to one who has mastered only wide-ranging battle plans. The chess champion Gary Kasparov (ignoring a possible category error) ascribed his defeat by the IBM Computer Deep Blue to the computer's greater interpersonal intelligence.

People who not only accomplish something novel but also relate their breakthrough to the efforts of others, both present and past, are more likely to be considered wise. We also attribute wisdom to creators when they experience a second breakthrough, which ties the initial radical breakthrough more integrally to established traditions—a so-called neoclassical period.

We treasure leaders who are both effective and wise, those who have lived through a great deal, have drawn lessons from their experiences, and know how to use these lessons. Of the various stories at their disposal, they can assemble the one that makes the most sense to the most people in the present moment. They can speak to individuals at the deepest level, and are most likely to speak to a variety of people, including those of different backgrounds and beliefs. Nelson Mandela's enormous authority in recent years is a tribute to his remarkable ability to communicate across multiple barriers.

A crucial point about wisdom is its modesty, its humility. Neither intelligence nor creativity nor leadership reserves a place for silence, for quiet, for resignation. And morality may also carry a shrillness or an unwarranted self-confidence. Youth, perhaps fortunately, knows no limits. The wise person knows when to say nothing, and when to step down and make room for someone else. The wise adult knows about the frailty of humanity and the difficulty of bringing about enduring changes.

MULTIPLE INTELLIGENCES IN THE SCHOOLS

WHEN PEOPLE HEAR about multiple intelligences, they sooner or later (usually sooner) ask, "How do you measure the intelligences?" Among policymakers and practitioners, it's almost a reflex. In fact, within a few years of the publication of *Frames of Mind*, several of the leading testing and publishing companies approached me to develop an instrument to assess intelligences. In many ways, this request was perfectly reasonable. Since I had introduced a collection of new intelligences, at the same time critiquing the standard view of intelligence, I was implying that one could measure intelligences. After all, for most of us in Western society, intelligence is a construct or capacity that can be measured by a set of short questions and answers, presented orally or in writing. Could not the same method be used to assess a new ensemble of intelligences?

ASSESSMENT: THE FIRST REFLEX

On the question of assessment, entrenched habits of thought can become dangerous. Like others influenced by contemporary practices in psychological measurement, I too began to think about assessment possibilities. But it soon became evident that the standard technology could not be applied appropriately to several of the intelligences. For instance, how do you measure someone's understanding of himself, or of other people, using a short-answer instrument? What would be an appropriate short-answer measure of an individual's bodily-kinesthetic intelligence?

Psychologists had more of a track record in assessing certain of the intelligences (as noted in chapter 2). In particular, linguistic and logical intelligences were the coin of the realm in intelligence testing. Some intelligence tests also plumb the regions of spatial reasoning, and there are certainly instruments that purport to assess musical potential. (Many of us who are middle-aged remember taking the Seashore tests of pitch and rhythmic and tonal sensitivity.) Even here, however, I remained a skeptic. I realized that certain aspects of these intelligences can be measured quickly and easily but that many others cannot. How does a person learn a new tune? How well does she remember an old one? Can a person find his way around a new territory or remember his way around a place he visited a while ago? Can a person express herself effectively in a group? Faced with an important decision, can a person reflect appropriately on previous dilemmas and make a judicious decision? All of these capacities are central to intelligences and yet clearly do not lend themselves to brief assessments.

In collaboration with colleagues David Feldman, Mara Krechevsky, and others, in the mid-1980s I hit on a different approach to assessment. Rather than devising yet another test battery, we created a rich environment—one we called the "Spectrum classroom"—in which children would be comfortable. Our initial Spectrum site, a preschool, was well stocked with materials to activate the different intelligences, including specimens of nature, board games, artistic and musical materials, and areas for exercise, dance, and building. We assumed that children would find these materials inviting, that they would interact with them regularly, and that they would reveal to us, by the richness and sophistication of their interactions, their particular array of intelligences. Hence the title "Spectrum."

After some years of experimentation, Spectrum worked out as we had hoped. We eventually identified materials that appealed not just to us but to children of different ages, inclinations, and social class backgrounds. Most children found it comfortable and inviting to explore the range of materials, and over the course of a year or more, they became more sophisticated with these materials. In cases where children avoided certain materials, we devised "bridging" activities. So, for example, if a child didn't want to tell stories about a picture, we gave her props and encouraged her to build a diorama. Using the diorama as a bridge, we then asked her to tell us what had happened to the people or animals in the diorama.

Our approach rested on an important principle. Rather than bringing the children to the assessment, as psychometricians have done (often, to be sure, for understandable reasons), we took the assessments to the children. We created an environment with inviting resources and let the children demonstrate their spectra of intelligences in as natural a fashion as possible.

Spectrum was initially used for children aged four to seven, but the approach could be adapted for any age. Indeed, a good measurement of intelligences at any age is provided when someone is parachuted into a new territory. If you were to drop me into three areas of Australia—the outback, the Great Barrier Reef, and a coastal city—and observe me for a day or two in each region, you would learn a great deal about my intelligences—as well as my multiple stupidities!

For most children, unfettered exploration in a Spectrum classroom or in a children's museum is enough to give a rough-and-ready picture of their intelligences at a given moment in their lives. Nothing more is needed, and as their intelligences are likely to evolve, it is important not to place too much weight on a single profile obtained at a single moment. For research purposes, or occasionally for clinical purposes, it may be useful to obtain a more targeted description of a child's profile of intelligences. And in such cases, it is possible to observe children at play (or at work) systematically and to arrive at a quantitative description of their intelligences. We have done such inventories on various occasions and have written about those efforts in books on Project Spectrum.

The Perils of Assessment

One of the unanticipated consequences of any theory is the ways in which it can be abused. There are several batteries of short tests that claim to measure the intelligences, but these tend to be strongly linguistic and often confound an *interest* in an intelligence with a demonstrated *skill* in that intelligence. These tests simply multiply by seven or eight the sins of original intelligence tests (or the original sin of intelligence testing).

Another risk in the "assessment mentality" is the tendency to label children (and others) as "linguistic" or "spatial" or "not at all musical" or even "interpersonally challenged." This is not wholly a bad thing. Children are attracted to the idea of multiple intelligences, which involves fun activities and looks far beyond the idea of a single intelligence. (Here, children are savvier than test givers.) Also, categorical systems provide a way for people to engage in personal reflection, which can be productive.

But the risks of labeling are patent. Labels can be stimulating, but also confining. No one likes to be called "stupid" because of low IQ scores, but the label "spatial but not linguistic" can be debilitating as well. Also, labeling intelligences involves two erroneous assumptions:

(1) We know exactly how to assess intelligences, and (2) The determination of an intelligence represents a lasting judgment. If I were asked to assess someone's intelligences, I would not be satisfied until I had observed him solving problems and fashioning products in a number of settings. This is usually not practical. And even then, I would have no guarantee that the intelligences profile would remain the same a year or two later. Indeed, shifting a person's daily routine dramatically can alter his or her profile of intelligences: That is what methods like the Suzuki Music Talent Education Program or (less pleasantly) military boot camp achieve. But labels tend to stick, and few people go back later to document a shifting profile of intelligences.

THE RORSCHACH TEST AND BEYOND

The educators who first learned about MI theory created a range of applications. At the Key School in Indianapolis, under the leadership of principal Patricia Bolanos, the teachers wanted to ensure that children had each intelligence stimulated each day and therefore created a rich curriculum. In addition to the staple "three R's" of the elementary years, every child studied a musical instrument, a foreign language, and physical education. Each day children also visited a "flow room" where they could pursue their own interests—ranging from chess to rocket ships—at their own pace over as many days as they wished. They enrolled in "pods"—interest groups where children of different ages could explore a common interest in greater depth. Pods have included topics like sign language, making money, or staging a play. And at a number of specified times each year, all the students in the school created projects around a common theme—such as patterns or the rain forest—which allowed them to foreground particular intelligences. As the first and probably best known of the so-called MI schools, the Key School (now called the Key Learning Community) has had wide influence both in the United States and abroad. But that school's approach to multiple intelligences is by no means the only one.

Working in the elementary grades in the Seattle area, classroom teacher Bruce Campbell created a set of learning centers through which students circulate regularly, sometimes daily. These learning centers are physically demarcated regions of the classroom that contain elements and displays designed, respectively, to engage each of the several intelligences. It is not uncommon for children to pursue a particular interest (such as flying kites) or a particular classroom assignment (such as adding fractions, understanding the solar system) across several of these learning centers. In variation of Campbell's approach, some teachers have adapted their standard curriculum so that it can be presented through several intelligences; others have chosen to focus directly on particular intelligences and have sought to reconfigure the curriculum so that it enhances particular intelligences.

Let me mention a few specific innovations that have proved fruitful. In one school, students write about people who exemplify a particular intelligence, then they try to re-create their exemplar's intelligence in a classroom presentation. In another school, the intelligences have become an organizing principle for the after-school program; children have the option to engage in activities designed to nourish and nurture particular intelligences. In still another school, older students teach particular concepts (like the principles that govern the functioning of a lever) to younger students, using a range of intelligences. It is particularly instructive to observe efforts to teach that circumvent the usual linguistic channel and depend instead on pantomime or graphic depiction.

Particular intelligences can also become the focal point for activities. Principal Tom Hoerr and his associates at the New City School in St. Louis have focused on the personal intelligences. They have developed numerous lessons that help students understand their own strengths and weaknesses better, as well as complementary lessons that aid students in understanding and working with others in the school. New York–based master teacher Naaz Hosseni has as her goal the incorporation of bodily-kinesthetic intelligence across the curriculum. And so she attempts to introduce science, social studies, and mathematical concepts through dance, gymnastics, and other bodily activities.

In the hands of educators, MI theory resembles a Rorschach test. When two people look at an inkblot, they may see very different things: One says, "Oh, it's a mother hugging her child," while another says, "Looks like a husband strangling his wife." The difference is not in the inkblot but in the "set" or "predisposition" of the observer. Thus, advocates of MI theory discern their own favored rationales for assessing, designing curricula, and identifying particular strengths or weaknesses—indeed, for approaching a whole gamut of educational problems and possibilities.

At first, I was intrigued by these initial entry points. I spent much time trying to understand why some educators were attracted to one implication of the theory (say, a new mode for describing their students), while others chose to stress another application (perhaps new ways to teach standard subjects or introduce electives). With time, however, I came to realize that the initial applications were less critical than the sequels stemming from them.

Any new idea or theory must first be assimilated into a preexisting set of assumptions and practices. (Note the similarity to the situation faced by leaders, who must engage the stories already mastered by their audiences). The established approach cannot (and perhaps should not) be changed immediately. Educators may say they are "doing multiple intelligences" when, in fact, they are largely continuing with their earlier practices while beginning to think about them in new ways. There also may be lamentable confusions in the early stages. I once watched a series of videos about multiple intelligences in the schools. In one video after another I saw youngsters crawling across the floor, with the superimposed legend "Bodily-Kinesthetic Intelligence." I said, "That is not bodily-kinesthetic intelligence; that is kids crawling across the floor. And I feel like crawling up the wall." And indeed, the flexing of one's body is not the enactment of an intelligence; a yawn is just a yawn. We use an intelligence when we actively solve a problem or fashion a product valued in society.

Mindy Kornhaber, my long-time colleague and a thoughtful researcher on multiple intelligences, once quipped, "Multiple intelligences is a way of saying that you are doing something new, so that you don't *really* have to do anything new." This observation may be unduly cynical, but it does convey an important point: Claiming to use MI theory can suggest that one is in tune with the latest educational thinking. But instituting a new practice in any domain is hard work, and the process of bringing about fundamental changes in educational practice takes years.

DEEPER INTO MULTIPLE INTELLIGENCES:
MI THEORY AS A TOOL

A generative question to ask about the introduction of MI ideas and practices in a school is: If one returns to the school three years later, what will one see? Perhaps MI theory will long since have been forgotten. Schools in the United States, in particular, have an unsettling track record of embracing practices for a short period of time and then dropping them. I can already hear the decisive declaration: "Oh, Multiple Intelligences. We used to do that." Or MI ideas may have become institutionalized without having undergone fundamental change in the interim. For instance, a school might have begun by performing an inventory on each child and continues to carry out such inventories without making use of the information. Or teachers might have assigned the students a project in which they were free to use whatever intelligences they preferred, and this "project practice" has endured. These practices may be beneficial, but applying MI thinking makes the most sense if it brings about deeper, more fundamental changes in the life of the school.

When people tell me, "We have a multiple intelligences school" or "We are using multiple intelligences in our elementary school," I wonder about the purposes for which they are using these new ideas about the human mind. After all, MI ideas and practices cannot be an end in themselves; they cannot serve as a goal for a school or an educational system. Rather, every educational institution must reflect on its goals, mission, and purposes continuously and, at least at times, explicitly. Only after such reflection can MI ideas be usefully implemented.

In fact, determining one's educational goals is so important and difficult an endeavor that, paradoxically, most institutions avoid explicitly doing it. They pay lip service to certain ideals—such as having well-rounded children and literate adolescents—and they carry on well-established practices, from conducting spelling bees to dissecting earthworms to assigning a Dickens novel. Their hesitation reflects our underlying fear that, if stated explicitly, each of us might find our own goals to be disparate from those of our fellow citizens.

Let me mention just a few of the educational values on which people are likely to differ, often profoundly: How important is the attainment of creativity? How important are the arts? Should technological proficiency be a high priority? Should schools be involved in religious education, moral education, civic education, health education, and sex education? Is it more important to master a lot of facts or to secure a deeper understanding of a limited number of disciplinary topics? Should one emphasize the more holistic aspects of language use or the drill-focused aspects of reading, writing, and spelling? Is mathematical problem solving or pattern recognition more important than the mastery of number facts? And, more broadly, do we want students who are well rounded or those who specialize in one or two areas?

One might think that multiple intelligences would appeal only to those who take certain clear-cut positions on these topics. Indeed, those who are partial to the arts also like multiple intelligences, perhaps because musical, bodily-kinesthetic, and other intelligences so readily suggest artistic priorities. Yet, in fact, MI theory could be made consistent—or inconsistent—with a myriad of practices, goals, and values. Let us say, for example, that one is devoted to a curriculum that focuses on the traditional subjects and that features regular tests. At first, this kind of program might seem to clash directly with the spirit of multiple intelligences. But because MI theory stipulates neither what to teach nor how to teach it, one could teach English literature or the theory of mechanics by using a number of different lesson plans or by giving students software that draws on their various intelligences. One could mobilize MI theory for more traditional ends by testing students' understanding of the plot of a Shakespeare play or of the "plot" involved when a spaceship is heading toward the moon.

The point is that there is no direct tie between a scientific theory and a set of educational moves. Whether one believes in one intelligence or twenty, and whether one thinks early experiences are more important than later ones, or the reverse, one is still free to implement any number of educational approaches. Indeed, in an art like teaching, the proof comes down to whether an approach works; it matters little whether the theory was correct. And, conversely, even if the theory is both correct and elegant, if it cannot be mobilized for concrete educational consequences, the theory matters not a whit to the educators.

Let us say that one has in fact identified a set of goals acceptable to the educational community. This is when one can indeed go "deeper into multiple intelligences" and declare: "We now have goals A, B, C, and D. How can we use this new theory of human mental representation to achieve these goals? And how will we know whether or not we have been successful?" At this point one stops being a visionary and begins to become a strategist. The vision having been stated, one can recommend specific practices, spell out a rationale, and hypothesize why these practices might indeed lead to the desired goal. And, going one step further, one can then begin to lay out criteria that will determine whether a practice inspired by multiple intelligences has led to a desired effect.

STEPS FOR ESTABLISHING AN MI ENVIRONMENT

There are many ways to proceed from goal to strategy to evaluation, and none is inherently superior. Here are some practices that have been effective in probing deeper into multiple intelligences.

1. *Learn more about MI theory and practices.* There is now a sizeable literature in English, plus a growing amount in other languages (see the appendices). The literature is theoretical and practical, visionary and realistic. There are also videos and CD-ROMS that illustrate MI practices.
2. *Form study groups.* Many people find it most comfortable to explore new ideas with others. A group that meets weekly or biweekly to reflect upon MI-related themes, with a particular eye to the needs of a certain school or of educational institutions in one locale, often makes fairly rapid progress.
3. *Visit institutions that are implementing MI ideas.* Interacting with teachers, staff, parents, and children at an MI site provides invaluable insights, raises questions, and triggers ideas one can implement locally.

4. *Attend conferences that feature MI ideas.* In many countries
    now, those involved in MI work hold workshops, symposia,
    and conferences. Project Zero, at the Harvard Graduate
    School of Education, holds an institute each summer; many
    graduates return, some serving as mentors to new attendees.
    At their best, these meetings demonstrate effective practices
    and introduce outstanding presenters. Even when the actual
    content of the meetings is less than stellar, one has the oppor-
    tunity to meet and begin to network with people more than
    casually interested in MI theory.

5. *Join a network of schools.* There are now explicit MI net-
    works—such as the one coordinated by New City School head
    Thomas Hoerr for the Association of Supervision and Cur-
    riculum Development—that provide up-to-date information
    and regular access to others devoted to exploring the educa-
    tional implications of MI theory.

6. *Plan and launch activities, practices, or programs that grow
    out of immersion in the world of MI theory and approaches.*
    It is important to be courageous but reasonable and to build
    in time for reflection. Also, having indices of effectiveness for
    a new activity will be necessary for determining whether to
    continue it. Yet, because most experimentation does not work
    well at first, it is important to be flexible and, as appropriate,
    either continue for a while, even in the absence of firm results,
    or change course and rethink the work.

These practices may seem self-evident, but when teachers become
interested in MI ideas, they often make unnecessary errors. They try
out recommended activities without understanding (and questioning)
their rationale; they are too ambitious and then become discouraged
when immediate, earth-shaking results do not occur; or, most com-

monly, they judge success completely on anecdotal evidence and never pose the difficult question of what data might convince a skeptical parent or school board.

I am pleased that my own impressions about the "conditions that are hospitable to MI theory" have recently been reinforced by the findings of Mindy Kornhaber and colleagues on the SUMIT project (see chapter 7). Based on its investigations of forty-one schools, the SUMIT team has identified a set of markers—the Compass Points Practices©— that characterize schools with some proven success in implementing MI-inspired practices:

- *Readiness*. It is important to launch processes that build awareness about the MI ideas and how they might be implemented. Such processes could include a faculty seminar, a parent awareness night, or a visit to other MI schools. This process of building awareness can be lengthy if the school does not already have beliefs and practices that are at least loosely aligned with the themes and spirit of MI.
- *Culture*. MI practices are most likely to emerge in settings that support diverse learners and encourage steady, hard work.
- *Collaboration*. There should be ample opportunities for formal and informal exchanges, both within the school and with others who share experiences and concerns. These exchanges remain crucial once the processes of change have begun, because there are always problems to discuss and decisions to make.
- *Choice*. The school should offer meaningful options for curriculum as well as for assessment of student growth and learning. The options should make sense both to the students and to the wider community. An "MI setting" can be undone if the curriculum is too rigid or if there is but a single form of assessment (which all too often is a short-answer standardized test).

- *Tool.* Multiple intelligences should be used as a means of fostering high-quality student work. In the last analysis, it is the students' work and their understanding of it that are the hallmarks of good schooling. MI approaches work best when integrally yoked to outcomes that everyone cares about strongly.
- *Arts.* A program rich in the arts should assume a significant role in the school. Otherwise, it will be difficult to address the range of intelligences exhibited by students and teachers.

Even when practices work, especially in the United States, justifying new practices is a political imperative. Since most schooling is supported by public funding, and private schooling relies on parental buyins, it is necessary to convince others that what one has undertaken is in fact worthwhile. Occasionally, a program has so obviously succeeded—or failed—that a keen political sense is not needed. In most cases, however, continuation of a program rests on proof of its superiority, as compared to competing programs. Justification, in turn, requires persuasive speaking, writing, and aggregation of data—but skill at persuasion is not intimately tied to skill at implementing a program. Sometimes, programs that are shoddy or that have little evidence in their favor continue because they have been eloquently defended. Some critics charge that this is what has happened in the United States with such long-running, mandated programs as Head Start, Chapter I bilingual education, and Chapter I funding for disadvantaged students. Conversely, even well-executed, clearly effective programs are sometimes abandoned because their advocates do not know how to make a strong case for them.

From my observations of community organizers like Ernesto Cortes, Jr., head of the Alliance Schools Network in Texas, I have learned much about what it takes to convince others of a program's viability. One has to be very precise about how the program works: its goals, the signs that it is working—"hard" (test scores) and "soft" (parental support), and the signs that it could be working even better. It is important to make the case cogently and concisely and to respond persuasively, though not defensively, when the program is criticized. Any new program will be challenged by those interests that feel threatened by the competition.

MI theory has become well enough known that it has been critiqued from nearly every political and pedagogical point of view. It has been disparaged as multicultural (because it is open to different learning approaches) and as racist and elitist (because it uses the word *intelligence* and because I, as its original proponent, happen to be affiliated with Harvard University). It has been seen as too flexible and loose (because it countenances activities in the arts) and as too rigid (because it holds that everything should be taught in varied ways). It has been seen as against standards and as imposing too many standards.

In any context, one needs to know what the most likely criticisms are going to be, and one has to have reasonable answers. One need not seize the defensive; indeed, one should listen carefully to criticisms, see where they may be on the mark, and attempt to learn from them. Yet, it is important to be prepared to draw a firm chalk line on the floor of the school auditorium. Some criticism is legitimate; some is based on reasonable uncertainty or ignorance. Some criticism, however, represents a mean-spirited determination to destroy MI efforts, no matter what the facts. Once one has given critics the benefit of the doubt, while they have steadfastly refused to reciprocate, then the time for charity is at an end. One must be prepared not only to emphasize the facts in the matter but also to unmask motives and hidden agendas (which might be to destroy public education, to favor an already entrenched elite, to eliminate the arts, or to discourage individual expression or initiative). At least, then, the contest will again become a fair one.

INDIVIDUALLY CONFIGURED EDUCATION:
THE KEY EDUCATIONAL IMPERATIVE
OF MULTIPLE INTELLIGENCES

As I have made clear, almost any number of educational programs can be crafted in the shadow of MI theory. However, there is one form of education that is antagonistic in spirit to MI—the uniform school. Unfortunately, throughout human history, the schooling of choice has been uniform, and so it is necessary to understand its power as well as its fundamental flaws.

The essence of uniform schooling is the belief that every individual should be treated in the same way: study the same subjects in the same way and be assessed in the same way. At first, this seems fair: No one has special advantages. And yet, a moment's thought reveals the essential inequity in the uniform school. The uniform school is based on the assumption that all individuals are the same and, therefore, that uniform schooling reaches all individuals equally and equitably. But we obviously look different from one another and have different personalities and temperaments. Most important, we also have different kinds of minds. Indeed, if we follow the line of reasoning in this book, no two people have exactly the same kinds of minds, since we each assemble our intelligences in unique configurations.

As educators, we face a stark choice: ignore these differences or acknowledge them. Sometimes, they are ignored out of ignorance; sometimes they are ignored because educators are either frustrated by the differences, or convinced that individuals are more likely to become members of a community if they can learn to be more alike. But those who ignore the differences are not being fair—and are typically focusing only on the language-logic mind (as perhaps most perfectly embodied in the mind of the law professor). To the extent that the student and the teacher share that focus, the student will do well and consider herself smart. But if the student has a fundamentally different kind of mind, she is likely to feel stupid—at least while attending that school.

What is the alternative? One possibility is *individually configured education*—an education that takes individual differences seriously and, insofar as possible, crafts practices that serve different kinds of minds equally well. Because it is not an educational goal in the sense I have been discussing, individually configured education can fit comfortably with a variety of goals: a traditional or experimental curriculum, an education aimed at breadth or depth, an education that seeks to develop liberal arts sensitivity, or an education oriented to the world of practice, vocations, or civic-mindedness. The crucial ingredient is a commitment to knowing the minds—the persons—of individual students. This means learning about each student's background, strengths, interests, preferences, anxieties, experiences, and goals, not to stereotype or to preordain but rather to ensure that educational decisions are made on the basis of an up-to-date profile of the student.

It is not necessary to move directly from this goal to a formal assessment of intelligence. Whatever their philosophies, good teachers, tutors, and coaches have always sought to know their students well. And these pedagogues have rarely used formal instruments to identify individuating features; they have observed, reflected, and spoken to the students and those close to them. The theory of multiple intelligences can be helpful because, as Mindy Kornhaber has pointed out, it is a good initial organizer. If one wants to know students well, it is helpful to have a set of categories by which one can describe their strengths and weaknesses, bearing in mind my cautions about labeling. One needs to go well beyond the eight intelligences, because they represent, at most, a first cut. And one must be prepared to update the descriptions regularly, because, happily, the minds of students—and, indeed, even the minds of their elders—are subject to change.

Knowing the minds of students represents but the first step. Crucial, thereafter, is an effort to draw on this knowledge in making decisions about curriculum, pedagogy, and assessment. Of course, if one chooses to have a curriculum rich in electives (or choices), then the role of MI ideas becomes clear. One can designate subjects (disciplines), teaching methods, hardware, software, and means of assessment that honor the particular cluster of intelligences of students under one's charge. But individually configured education is also compatible with a required standard curriculum. All young people should study the history of their country, the principles of algebra and geometry, and basic laws that govern living and nonliving objects. A commitment to some common knowledge does not mean that everyone must study these things in the same way and be assessed in the same way.

MI theory makes its most important contribution to education on this point. The theory stimulates teachers and students to be imaginative in selecting curricula, deciding how the curricula are to be taught or "delivered," and determining how student knowledge is to be demonstrated. Sometimes, all students will be exposed to a variety of curricula or assessments. At other times, certain students will learn and be assessed in one way, while other students—or even an individual student—will be instructed and assessed in other, more appropriate ways. These practices have been routine in some endeavors: for example, individual arts or sports coaching, academic tutoring, and "special education" for students with learning problems or disabilities. These students typically have difficulty mastering a subject, such as reading or mathematics, because they cannot learn in the "uniform way" available in their schools. The only choices are to give up, assuming that the students are ineducable, or to teach in another way. As we would now put it, the learning specialist must mobilize the students' spared intelligences so that they can learn, and can demonstrate that learning in ways that make sense to them.

Even those sympathetic to individually configured education doubt that it can be mobilized on a wide scale. This vision may be right, they say, but it can be provided only to those who are wealthy or to those who qualify for special government-funded programs. (Indeed, in my community, some parents seek out a "learning-disabled" label just so their children can qualify for tutoring.) It may be hard to think of individually configured education in a classroom with thirty or more students, not all of them as docile or motivated as one might like, but it is not impossible. Among the possible strategies are the following:

- Cull as much data as possible about how a particular child learns and share that knowledge with the teacher and with the child. As children get older, they can provide much information and feedback themselves.
- Allow students to remain with the same teacher(s) for several years, so that they can get to know one another very well.
- Assign teachers and students flexibly, so that more compatible matches can be made.
- Have an effective information-transmission system in the schools, so that the next year's teachers know as much as possible about their new students. Also, make sure that the teachers have ready access to this information and can update it as needed.
- Have older students work with younger students, or have students with compatible or complementary learning approaches work together.

One fact will make individually configured education a reality in my lifetime: the ready availability of new and flexible technologies. Already, it is possible to use technology to vary the presentation of important materials—from physics lessons to musical composition.

Such technology can also be "smart": It can adjust on the bases of earlier learning experiences, ensuring that a student receives lessons that are optimally and individually crafted.

Once parents learn that there are indeed several ways to teach most topics and most subjects, affluent families will acquire the materials for home use. And pressures will mount for schools and teachers to have available, say, the "Eight Roads to Pythagoras" or the "Eight Paths to Plato." No more will teachers say, "I taught it well, and she could not learn it." Rather, all involved in education will be motivated to find the ways that will work for *this* student learning *this* topic, and the results will be widely available in planning for future work.

One critique of this approach should not be ignored: the apparent success of uniform schooling in some societies. Some of the most effective societies, such as those in East Asia, embrace uniform-schooling methods, and they sometimes get results far more impressive than those achieved in seemingly more progressive Western societies. I do not want to belittle the East Asian achievements, which I respect. Nor do I want to offer the usual defenses: Those societies are more authoritarian, less interested in creativity and flexibility, have a more homogeneous population, and may even have genetic or neural structures that differ from those of other cultures. Instead, I want to suggest that such educational approaches may actually be more individualized than we believe they are. Consider the fact that the first years of education in countries like Japan are spent developing social understanding and students' capacity to work well together. Much of the work is done in groups, in which students are encouraged to help one another and to take seriously the other children's ways of learning. Most important, however, are the institutions auxiliary to school. Precisely because the socializing aspects of school are so important in East Asia, the society makes sure that cognitive aspects are not neglected. And so, in Japan, many students go to after-school tutoring, where the lessons are as individualized as needed. And nearly every student has at least one tutor—the parent, most often the mother. Since this tutor has but one goal—the preparation of her child for the decisive examinations—the education can become as individually configured as necessary.

I have sought to indicate how MI ideas can be introduced into a school community and how they can be put to work for the general purpose of providing a good education. I have also tipped my hand as to the centrality of individually configured education. And yet, in the absence of clearly stated goals, the foregoing discussion retains a generic quality. Indeed, so many of the recommendations about how to teach to the multiple intelligences, while well intended, are essentially vacuous, because they are provided without context. Therefore, in the next chapter, I put my cards on the table about a very specific goal: an education for understanding. Then I seek to show how an education informed by MI thinking can achieve that goal.

MULTIPLE APPROACHES
TO UNDERSTANDING

Some topics suffuse the discourse of an era. Hardly a week goes by without references in the media to key scientific ideas, like the theory of evolution, or to pivotal historical events, like the Holocaust. Even the "culturally challenged" have heard of these topics; all who consider themselves culturally literate should be able to recall central facts about evolution or the Holocaust from their formal education, their casual reading and movie or television viewing, and their residence in a news-saturated culture. Educated people should also be able to assimilate new information. They should be able to comment on news stories about the disappearance of dinosaurs, the rise of creationism, the development of computer software that simulates evolution or itself evolves, and the periodic bursts of new species in the evolutionary record. They should have views about the Swiss hoarding of Nazi gold, the collective guilt of the German people, or a fictional work about an individual who survived a year in a death camp. Too often, however, discussions of education skirt these hallmarks of the educated person. We find ourselves impaled on questions of methods: Should we encourage tracking, cooperative learning, the use of projects in the classroom? Or we debate political topics: Should we embrace vouchers, choice, national standards? While worth discussion, these issues seem suspended in surreality when they are considered in the absence of consensus—or even debate—about *what* should be taught and *why*.

Issues of curriculum inevitably arouse the community. While texts on evolution or the Holocaust would seem straightforward in most educational contexts, we have recently seen fundamentalist efforts to denigrate Darwin's work as "just another theory," or to exclude evolution from textbooks. And while few U.S. educators directly question the occurrence of the Holocaust, cultural commentators have attacked Holocaust curricula either as not adequately representing the German point of view or as inaccurately claiming that the treatment of six million European Jews was qualitatively different or qualitatively more brutal than that of other victims at other times. The attitude seems to be that it is safer simply to have students memorize a few facts or definitions and then move on swiftly to other theories, and historical events and claims.

MULTIPLE INTELLIGENCES AND
THE GOALS OF EDUCATION

It is not possible to talk coherently about MI ideas in the classroom unless one has taken a stand on what should be taught and why. And even if one's position on these questions may seem straightforward (particularly in the company of friends), it is helpful to lay one's curricular cards on the table. Here are my cards. Education in our time should provide the basis for enhanced understanding of our several worlds—the physical world, the biological world, the world of human beings, the world of human artifacts, and the world of the self. People have always been interested in these topics; contemporary disciplines have reworked insights from mythology, art, and folk knowledge. Evolution and the Holocaust are hardly the only topics worth understanding. Yet it is hard to see how a person could understand the world of biology without some mastery of evolutionary theory or comprehend the world of human beings without a study of the Holocaust (or another episode of mass wanton killing). Note that this goal does not mention the acquisition of literacy, the learning of basic facts, the cultivation of basic skills, or the mastery of the ways of thinking of the disciplines— achievements that should be seen as means, not ends in themselves. We learn to read, write, and compute not so that we can report these milestones (as we might post an attendance record), nor even so that we can achieve a certain score on an admissions test. Rather, literacies, skills, and disciplines ought to be pursued as tools that allow us to enhance our understanding of important questions, topics, and themes.

These goals may sound quaint or idealistic. After all, aren't the *real* purposes of education to learn to get along with others, to acquire personal discipline, to become well rounded, and to prepare for the workplace and for the ultimate rewards of success and happiness? Certainly, arguments can be mounted in favor of these and other instrumental ends. But all of these goals are the responsibility of the broader society, from parents and families on one end, to religion, the media, and community institutions on the other. Resources invested in formal education can best be justified if, at the end of the day, all students show enhanced understanding of the important questions and topics of their time. And once such a commitment has been made, the powerful ideas of multiple intelligences can be mobilized to achieve that goal.

A PERFORMANCE VIEW OF UNDERSTANDING

Both folk wisdom and contemporary psychology convince us that understanding is an event or process that occurs between the ears—in the mind or brain. As a psychologist who honors common sense, I underscore the importance of the processes of mental representation that occur in the assimilation and transformation of knowledge. But from the perspective of the teacher and the learner, the physical events that occur in the mind or brain are far from transparent and, strictly speaking, are irrelevant to their educational missions. Instead, when it comes to understanding, the emphasis falls properly on performances that can be observed, critiqued, and improved. We do not care about the elegance of a mental representation if it cannot be activated when needed. And while it is unlikely that performances of quality will emerge in the absence of intricate, appropriate mental representations, such performances may in fact emanate from a variety of cognitive schemas across situations and individuals.

Accordingly, when it comes to probing a student's understanding of evolution, the shrewd pedagogue looks beyond the mastery of dictionary definitions or the recitation of textbook examples. A student demonstrates or "performs" his understanding when he can examine a range of species found in different ecological niches and speculate about the reasons for their particular ensemble of traits, or when he can describe the similarities and differences among the Malthusian, Darwinian, and social Darwinist versions of "survival of the fittest." By the same token, a student performs her understanding of the Holocaust when she can interpret the contents of an SS officer's diary in light of claims about the "good German," or when she can compare events in a Nazi concentration camp to such contemporary genocidal events as those in Bosnia, Kosovo, or Rwanda in the 1990s.

"Measures of understanding" may seem demanding, particularly in contrast to current, often superficial, efforts to measure what students know and are able to do. And, indeed, recourse to "performing" one's understanding is likely to stress students, teachers, and parents, who have grown accustomed to traditional ways of doing (or *not* doing) things. Nonetheless, a performance approach to understanding is justified. For one thing, the fact that something is new is hardly a justification for avoiding it, even though ready implementation may be difficult. More important, focusing on performances immediately marks an important shift: Instead of "mastering content," one thinks about the reasons *why* a particular content is being taught and how best to display one's comprehension of that content in a publicly accessible way. When students realize they will have to apply knowledge and demonstrate insights in a public form, they assume a more active stance vis-à-vis material, seeking to exercise their "performance muscles" whenever possible.

Let me offer a personal example. Some years ago, I revised my standard graduate student course on theories of cognitive development, with the goal of teaching students to go beyond "knowing the theories" to being able to use them productively. With this new approach, each week I assigned a particular theory of development such as the one associated with Jean Piaget or his influential Russian contemporary, Lev Vygotsky. Then I gave the students prompts—sets of data or a story about an educational practice—and asked them to illuminate that prompt by invoking the theory of the week. One day a student asked, "Dr. Gardner, how can I apply the theory if I don't understand it?" I thought for a moment and responded, "You'll never understand the theory unless you apply it . . . and then apply it again." Emphasizing performance not only stimulates active consumption of classroom material but also enhances understanding of the material.

OBSTACLES TO UNDERSTANDING

I have yet to mention an important and troubling consideration. There has been a virtual conspiracy to avoid assessment of understanding, though this avoidance may have been innocent. If one assumes that understanding is equivalent to mastery of factual materials, or if one assumes that understanding follows naturally from exposure to materials, then there is no reason to require explicit performances of understanding. But it is more likely that we have avoided assessing understanding because doing so takes time and because we have lacked confidence that we will actually find clear evidence of understanding. Thanks to hundreds of studies during the past few decades by cognitively oriented psychologists and educators, we now know one truth about understanding: Most students in most schools—indeed, many of the best students in the best schools—cannot exhibit appreciable understandings of important ideas.

The most dramatic findings are manifest in physics. Students with top grades in high school and college courses not only are unable to apply their presumably mastered knowledge, but, even more damning, they tend to respond much the way young children do—in a manner that merits the label "unschooled." In the typical study, students are asked outside of a classroom context to explain the forces that operate on a coin that is being flipped, the reasons for different temperatures in summer and winter, or the trajectory of a pellet that has been shot through a tube. Surprisingly, most physics students revert to the same answers that are produced by children who have never heard of physics.

Would that such problems surfaced only in physics! In all sciences, students' misconceptions abound. In evolution, for example, students gravitate almost ineluctably to a teleological and perfectibility view. That is, even though evolution consists of random mutations that do not follow a predetermined script, students typically describe evolution as if it were guided by an unseen hand with each species being in some sense more perfect than the previous ones, and the height of evolution magically coinciding with our own species in our own time. Similar misconceptions crop up in physics, biology, geology, astronomy, and other sciences. In other areas of the curriculum, analogous "unschooled" difficulties abound. In mathematics, students are at the mercy of rigidly applied algorithms. They learn to use certain formalisms in certain ways, often effectively, if provided with a pre-arranged signal that a particular formalism is wanted. And so, for example, they memorize the theorem for the binomial equation or the quadratic equation and learn to produce it when certain "cues" are provided. If, however, no cue is provided to activate the formalism in question, or if the students have to derive the formalism afresh, they are stymied; after all, they never really understood the formalism and recognized only the tip-off signals from previous situations.

In social studies and the humanities, the enemies of understanding are scripts and stereotypes. Students readily believe that events occur in typical ways, and they evoke these scripts even inappropriately. For example, they regard struggles between two parties in a dispute as a "good guy versus bad guy" movie script—often dubbed the "Star Wars" script. Far too many students have a superficial understanding of the Holocaust; they may deny its existence, blame it entirely on the evil Germans, treat the Jewish people as unique, or say such an event could never happen again. A deeper understanding—that human beings everywhere have the potential to engage in genocide or to become victims of such cruelty, that in fact the Holocaust starkly reveals what some people did to others—requires more intensive and extensive grappling with historical, social, and personal worlds.

ENCOURAGING PERFORMANCES
OF UNDERSTANDING

Obstacles to understanding are ubiquitous and cannot be averted readily. Moreover, misunderstandings are inevitable as long as people succumb to the temptation to "cover everything"—for instance, in a course on Western history to go from Plato to NATO in thirty-six weeks. Nonetheless, in recent years, four promising approaches to understanding have evolved, and each recognizes the obstacles and seeks to inculcate more productive performances of understanding. I will mention three briefly and then turn to the fourth and featured approach: the use of MI theory to enhance student understanding.

Observational Approaches

The first approach involves observing and applying the practices of institutions that have successfully inculcated understanding. The traditional institution of the apprenticeship is one example. Young apprentices spend much time with a master practitioner, observe him up close, and gradually engage in the daily practices of problem solving and product making. The contemporary institution of the children's museum or the science museum is another exemplary way to mold understanding (see chapter 11). Students have the opportunity to approach intriguing phenomena in ways that make sense to them, they can take their time, and they face no test pressures. More important, they may bring issues with them from home to school, to the museum, and back again—gradually constructing sturdier understandings by using multiple inputs (and multiple ways of reacting to those inputs) in diverse settings. In learning how these institutions have generated deeper understandings, we receive clues about how best to teach for understanding.

Confrontational Approaches

A second approach features frontal tackling of the obstacles to understanding. One comes to grips directly with one's own misconceptions. For example, if a person believes in the inheritance of acquired characteristics, he can cut off the tails of generations of salamanders and see whether a shorter-tailed salamander gradually (or abruptly) emerges. If another person regularly invokes memorized algorithms to solve problems, she can be given the opportunity to construct her own mathematical formula through experimentation with relevant (and irrelevant) variables. And if someone else habitually engages in stereotypical thinking, he can be encouraged to consider each historical event or work of art from multiple perspectives. Note, however, that none of these is foolproof; moreover, occasionally adopting "multiple perspectives" or challenging misconceptions will not suffice. Teachers need to encourage understandings by pointing out inadequate conceptualizations and asking students to reflect on the consequences. Students gradually learn to monitor their own intuitive theories and thus cultivate habits of understanding.

A Systematic Approach: Teaching for Understanding

In collaboration with the educational researchers David Perkins, Vito Perrone, Stone Wiske, and others, I have developed a third, more systematic approach to the problem, Teaching for Understanding, which features an explicitly performing stance. Teachers are asked to state explicit understanding goals, stipulate the correlated performances of understanding, and share these perspectives with the students. Other key features of this "understanding framework" include a stressing of generative topics that are both central to the discipline and attractive to students (for example, Why are there fourteen varieties of finches on the Galapagos Islands? When and how was the "Final Solution" arrived at?); identifying "through-lines" that permeate a unit or course (for example, how to go from an observation to a hypothesis and back again to fresh observations that will ultimately yield further hypotheses); and assessing students' understandings not simply at the end of the course, but through regular, interim "practice" performances.

I have suggested that understanding is a generic problem with generic solutions. It is important for students to understand, the achievement of understanding is challenging, and there are a variety of means that might aid students. A generic approach would seem justifiable, since it is reasonable to approach a problem in terms of its fundamental constituents. Certain tacks might in fact prove successful with all students, or at least the vast majority. But as I've now established, human minds do not all work in the same way, and human beings do not have the same cognitive strengths and weaknesses. Knowing this should strongly influence how we teach students and how we assess what they learn. We all possess the same ensemble of intelligences—in one sense, they represent our species' intellectual heritage—but we do not exhibit equal strengths or similar profiles. Some people are strong in one intelligence and weak in others, and strength in a particular intelligence does not necessarily predict strength (or weakness) in others.

As I've pointed out, many educators see MI theory as an end in itself. That is, a school or program is meritorious to the extent that it extols MI ideas or measures students' intelligences or features the intelligences in curriculum or pedagogy. But enhancing "multiple intelligences" is not in itself a suitable goal of education. Rather, it is better thought of as a handmaiden to good education, once educational goals have been established on independent grounds. Indeed, I would argue that MI is most usefully invoked in the service of two educational goals. The first is to help students achieve certain valued adult roles or end-states. If one wants everyone to be able to engage in artistic activities, it makes sense to develop linguistic intelligence (for the poet), spatial intelligence (for the graphic artist or sculptor), bodily-kinesthetic intelligence (for the dancer), and musical intelligence (for the composer or performer). If one wants everyone to be civil, then it is important to develop the personal intelligences.

The second goal—and the one most relevant to this chapter—is to help students master certain curricular or disciplinary materials. Given that, students might be encouraged to take a course in biology, so as to better understand the origins and development of the living world, and to study history, so as to better understand people's plans, actions, and consequences in the past. One could take the position that everyone should study the same thing in the same way and be assessed in the same way. The standard view of intelligence leads readily, perhaps ineluctably, to that educational course. Yet, if there is validity to the idea of multiple intelligences—if individuals indeed have different kinds of minds, with varied strengths, interests, and strategies—then it is worth considering whether pivotal curricular materials could be taught and assessed in a variety of ways.

FOCUSED APPROACHES
THROUGH MULTIPLE INTELLIGENCES

Here, at last, I can introduce the core ideas of the educational approach I embrace. I believe that every person ought to master a central body of curricular materials and approaches, though I am not thereby wedded to a specific canon. For this chapter I have selected the examples of evolution and the Holocaust—though they are not without controversy—because I think they lie comfortably within the ensemble of ideas that every educated person of our time should have encountered, grappled with, and mastered. [In *The Disciplined Mind*, I have added to the true (evolution), and the evil [the Holocaust] an example of the beautiful (the music of Mozart).] I depart from the assumption of traditional educators—and of their allies in psychology—that such topics need to be taught or assessed in a single way. Because of their biological and cultural backgrounds, personal histories, and idiosyncratic experiences, students do not arrive in school as blank slates, nor can they be aligned unidimensionally along a single axis of intellectual accomplishment. While this variation (a product of evolution!) complicates the teacher's job, it can actually become an ally in effective teaching. When teachers are able to use different pedagogical approaches, they can reach more students in more effective ways.

Assume, then, that our educational goals include an enhanced understanding of the theory of evolution and the events called the Holocaust—topics drawn, respectively, from biology and history. We want students to appreciate that evolution, a process of random mutation in the genes of earlier organisms, is the driving force behind the variety of species that have existed historically and contemporaneously. The diverse members of a species yielded by genetic variation at a historical moment result in organisms that are differentially able to survive in specific ecological contexts. Those who survive to reproduce in abundance have a competitive advantage over those who, for whatever reason, do not adjust adequately to a given ecological niche. If these trends continue over the long run, the survivors prevail, while those who cannot compete successfully are doomed to extinction. The fossil record documents the course and fate of different species historically; one sees the gradual increase in diversity of species as well as the increase in complexity of certain lines of descent. It is possible to study the same processes contemporaneously, with relevant research ranging from the breeding of various strains of fruit fly to experimental investigations of the ways in which genes may have originated in the distant past.

Turning to the Holocaust, we want students to appreciate what happened to the Jewish people, and to certain other condemned minorities and political dissidents, during the Nazi Third Reich's reign, from 1933 to 1945. Efforts to castigate and isolate the Jewish people began with simple verbal attacks and laws of exclusion, gradually evolved to more violent forms of abuse, and culminated in the creation of camps whose explicit goal was the extinction of European Jewry. The contours of anti-Semitism were laid out in Hitler's early speeches and writings, but the historical course from plans to actualities took several years and involved tens of thousands of people in various capacities. Genocide—the effort to eliminate a people in its entirety—is hardly a new idea or a new phenomenon; it dates back to biblical times, if not before. Yet, the systematic manner in which an allegedly civilized, modern nation proceeded to eradicate six million Jews is unprecedented.

These understandings constitute a reasonable goal for a course or a unit, but memorizing or paraphrasing these paragraphs does not count for understanding. Rather, students exhibit understanding when they can invoke these ideas flexibly and appropriately to carry out specific analyses, interpretations, comparisons, or critiques—and, especially, to perform their understandings with respect to new material, perhaps as new as today's newspaper or tomorrow's technological or biological breakthrough.

How can we help students understand these formidable topics? From the vantage point of multiple intelligences, I propose three increasingly focused approaches.

Entry points

One begins by finding a way to engage the student and to place her centrally within the topic. I have identified at least seven discrete entry points, which can be roughly aligned with specific intelligences:

1. *Narrational*—The narrational entry point addresses students who enjoy learning about topics through stories. Such vehicles—linguistic or filmic—feature protagonists, conflict, problems to be solved, goals to be achieved, and tensions aroused and, often, allayed. Thus, evolution may involve the story of Darwin's voyages (as it contrasts with the

story of origins told in the Bible) or of the life course of a particular species. The Holocaust can be introduced through a narrative account of a particular person (like Adolf Hitler or Anne Frank) or through a year-by-year chronicle of events in the Third Reich.

2. *Quantitative/Numerical*—The quantitative entry point speaks to students who are intrigued by numbers and the patterns they make, the various operations that can be performed, and insights into size, ratio, and change. One can examine evolution by looking at the incidence of different individuals or species in varied ecological niches and at how those aggregates change over time. With respect to the Holocaust, one can look at the movements of people to various camps, the survival rates at each, and comparisons of the fates of Jews and other groups of victims in different cities, nations, and regions.

3. *Logical*—The logical entry point galvanizes the human capacity to think deductively. Many events and processes can be conceptualized in terms of syllogisms. Here are ones linked to our two topics:

If there are more individuals/species in a territory than can be supported, and
If there are variations among individuals/species,
Then those variants that survive best in a particular ecology will be able to reproduce and flourish there.

*   *   *

If one wants to remove all Jews from Europe, and
If the Jews can neither be moved elsewhere nor allowed to die natural deaths,
Then one must devise ways to eliminate them.

4. *Foundational/Existential*—This entry point appeals to students who are attracted to fundamental kinds of questions. Nearly all children

raise such questions, usually through myths or art; the more philosophically oriented pose issues and argue about them verbally. Evolution addresses the question of who we are and where we—and all other living things—come from. The Holocaust challenges us to ask what kinds of beings humans are, what their virtues and vices are, and how people can find meaning in life after surviving a concentration camp.

5. *Aesthetic*—Some people are inspired by works of art or by materials arranged in ways that feature balance, harmony, and composition. The tree of evolution, with its many branches and interstices, may attract these students. Darwin himself was intrigued by the metaphor of the "tangled bank" of nature. The Holocaust has been portrayed in works of art, literature, and music, both by victims and by observers who have sought to capture its horror.

6. *Hands On*—Many people, particularly children, most easily approach a topic through an activity in which they become fully engaged—where they can build something, manipulate materials, or carry out experiments. Breeding generations of fruit flies lets a student observe the incidence and fate of genetic mutations. A Holocaust museum can provide a harrowing introduction to that historical event: giving students alternative "identities" when they enter such a museum, so they can learn what happened to particular people in the Holocaust, can be a powerful educational experience. Students can also participate in variations of the classic Milgram experiments on obedience to authority. In those chilling experiments, conducted during the 1960s, subjects were asked to deliver electric shocks to individuals who (unknown to the subjects) were actually confederates of the experimenter. Defying both common sense and the predictions of psychiatrists, most subjects shocked the confederates to a "danger level," presumably because the experimenter, dressed authoritatively in a white coat, insisted that "The experiment must go on."

7. *Social*—The entry points I've been describing address the individual. Many people learn more effectively, however, in a group setting, where they can assume different roles, observe others' perspectives, interact regularly, and complement one another. A group of students can be given a problem to solve: What happens to various species in a given environment following a dramatic change in climate? How would the Germans have reacted if the Allies had blown up the train tracks that led to major concentration camps? Or students can be asked to role-play—different species in a shifting ecology or different participants in a rebellion in a ghetto under siege.

Telling Analogies

An entry point perspective places students directly at the center of a disciplinary topic, arousing their interests and securing cognitive commitment for further exploration. But the entry point does not necessarily inculcate specific forms or modes of understanding. Here, the teacher (or the student) is challenged to come up with instructive analogies, drawn from material they already understand, that can convey important aspects of the less familiar topic. In the case of evolution, analogies can be found in history or the arts. Societies change over time, sometimes gradually, sometimes apocalyptically. The processes of human social change can be compared with those of biological change within and between species. Evolution can also be observed in works of art. Characters change within the course of a book, and sometimes over a series of books; and themes in a fugue evolve and develop in certain ways, and not (ordinarily) in others. There are even intriguing evolutionary trends in the realm of fashion. Similarly, one may search for analogies to the Holocaust. The effort to annihilate a people can be analogized to the eradication of traces of an event or even of an entire civilization. Sometimes these efforts at eradication are deliberate, as when the criminal seeks to hide all evidence of a crime. Sometimes they occur as a result of time, as when the traces of an ancient city are virtually destroyed (absent relevant historical records, we do not know, of course, about those cities whose vestiges have vanished as the result of natural disaster or a vengeful enemy).

Analogies are an excellent way to convey important facets of a topic to people largely unfamiliar with it. Analogies can be powerful, but they can also be misleading. Each analogy can suggest parallels that do *not* hold: for example, the informing human intelligence that constructs the theme of a fugue differs from the random nature of biological evolution, and a murderer working in isolation differs from a sector of society, committing genocide secretly but in concert. A teacher must qualify each analogy as appropriate and ensure that the misleading parts of the analogy will not distort or cripple the students' ultimate understanding. Metaphors can also be invoked to illuminate new topics. Darwin thought of evolution as a branching tree; concentration camps have been described as factories of death. Again, the power and the dangers of such metaphors must be noted. Thus, while evolution is often thought of as a ladder, it is misleading to think of the latest-emerging species as in any sense the "highest" one.

Approaching the Core

Entry points open up the conversation, and apt analogies convey revealing parts of the concept in question. But the challenge of conveying the central understandings remains—and this challenge leads me to the most vexing part of my analysis. Educators have traditionally relied on two seemingly opposite approaches. Either they have provided explicit instructions—usually didactic—and assessed understanding in terms of linguistic mastery of materials *(Evolution is . . . The five central points about the Holocaust are . . .)*, or they have supplied copious information and hoped that somehow the students would forge their own syntheses (*On the basis of your reading, our trip to the museum, and various classroom exercises, what would you do if . . .*). Some teachers have pursued both approaches, either simultaneously or successively.

Let me pose the crucial educational question: Can one use psychological insights about individual differences in strengths and modes of representations to create educational approaches that can reliably and thoroughly convey the most important, or core, notions of a topic? To answer this question, one must first acknowledge that there cannot be a formulaic approach. Every topic is different—just as every classroom context is different—and so each topic must be considered in terms of its own specific core ideas, network of concepts, issues, problems, and susceptibilities to misconception.

Next, one must acknowledge that topics do not exist in isolation; they come from and are partially defined by the ensemble of existing and emerging disciplines. Thus, a study of evolution occurs within the domain of biology and, more generally, within the realm of scientific explanation; as such, it involves the search for general principles and for models that will apply to all organisms under all kinds of circumstances (though some branches of science seek to explicate one-time events like the disappearance of dinosaurs). In contrast, a study of the Holocaust occurs within the field of history—and sometimes within literary or artistic efforts to render this event or within philosophical courses on ethics or morality. Parts of the Holocaust may resemble other historical events, but a foundational notion is that history offers an account of specific events occurring in specific contexts. One can neither expect general principles to emerge nor build models that can be experimentally tested (though some scientifically oriented historians have attempted to construct such models and to test them after the fact).

As a third consideration, one must acknowledge the commonly used ways of describing and explaining a concept. Evolution is typically described using certain examples (such as the disappearance of Neanderthal man and the branching tree of evolution). The Holocaust is typically presented in terms of key events and documents: Hitler's early tract *Mein Kampf*, the formulation of the Final Solution at the January 1942 Wannsee Conference, the records kept at Auschwitz, the reports by the first Allied soldiers to liberate the camps, and the chilling photographs of the survivors. These familiar examples are not randomly chosen; rather, they have helped scholars define these topics in the past, and they have proved effective pedagogically with many students.

Although these examples have clearly proved valuable, one must not infer that they are uniquely or permanently privileged. Considering these examples does not guarantee understanding, and, by the same token, it is surely possible to enhance understanding of evolution or of the Holocaust by using other examples, other materials, and differently formulated causal accounts. We know that this ensemble of pivotal examples changes, because there are new historical or scientific discoveries as well as novel pedagogical approaches. Thus, for example, the opportunity to use a computer to simulate evolutionary processes or to create virtual realities spawns educational opportunities unanticipated a generation or two ago. And new scholarship clarifies the roles of Hitler and his "willing executioners," the German people.

The key step is recognizing that a concept can be well understood— and can give rise to convincing performances of understanding—only if a person represents the core features of that concept in several ways. Moreover, it is desirable if the multiple modes of representing draw on a number of symbol systems, schemas, frames, and intelligences. By going beyond analogies—indeed, proceeding in the opposite direction—teachers and students can seek to make representations as accurate and comprehensive as possible. And inasmuch as each representation necessarily highlights certain features of the topic while minimizing others, the ultimate goal is to synthesize the various representations as comprehensively as possible.

Several implications follow from this assertion. First, it is necessary to spend significant time on a topic. Second, it is essential to portray the topic in a number of ways, both to illustrate its intricacies and to reach the various students. Third, it is highly desirable if the multiple approaches explicitly call on a range of intelligences, skills, and interests.

This tack is much more than a "smorgasbord" approach to education—throw enough of the proverbial matter at students, and some of it will hit the mind or brain and stick. The theory of multiple intelligences provides an opportunity to transcend mere variation and selection. It is possible to examine a topic in detail, to determine *which* intelligences, *which* analogies, and *which* examples are most likely both to capture important aspects of the topic and to reach a significant number of students. We must acknowledge here the cottage-industry aspect of pedagogy, a craft that is not susceptible to an algorithmic approach. This craft aspect lies at the heart of the pleasure of teaching—the chance to revisit a topic and to consider fresh ways of conveying its crucial components to different minds as powerfully and accurately as possible.

The history of disciplinary progress makes it inevitable that experts will think about a topic in terms of privileged considerations—perhaps genetic mutations and ecological niches in biology, perhaps human intentions and impersonal forces in history. But one should never lose sight of the fact that evolution and the Holocaust did not occur within academic fields: They are events and processes that somehow happened and became available for observers and scholars to interpret and explicate. Fresh discoveries, as well as new disciplinary trends, will gradually undermine today's orthodoxy; tomorrow's scholars might remake our understandings. Just as Darwin rewrote the view of evolution expounded by the French naturalist Chevalier de Lamarck, believers in punctuated equilibrium—the view that evolution occurred in fits and starts—aim to overthrow Darwinian gradualism. By the same token, Daniel Goldhagen's recent *Hitler's Willing Executioners* gives a far more "ordinary Germanic" cast to the Holocaust than had earlier historical analysis.

I must stress that I have not touched the vast majority of the curriculum. I have had in mind high school, or perhaps college, and topics from the natural sciences and history. And I must stress as well that there is nothing privileged about the two topics. It is important that educators focus in depth on topics of consequence to their community; innumerable topics fit that bill. I would be remiss if I implied that the trio of stances sketched here could be applied equivalently to every topic on a syllabus. Indeed, I deliberately selected two topics that are relatively rich and multifaceted and that readily allow consideration from several perspectives. No pedagogical approach is going to prove equally effective for the full range of topics and skills that need to be conveyed across the disciplines.

Still, an MI-based approach can have wide utility. First, it raises key questions: Why teach certain topics? What will students retain? Much of what we teach takes hold through habit; it makes sense to teach fewer topics and to treat them in greater depth. The approach also makes it possible to relate materials to a few central themes—like evolution in biology, the Holocaust in history, energy in physics, or character in literature—and to eliminate topics that cannot be reasonably connected to powerful themes. Having determined which topics require sustained attention, one can then exploit an ensemble of pedagogical approaches, choosing not only entry points that attract the interest and attention of diverse students but also examples, analogies, and metaphors that convey important parts of the topic in powerful, clear ways. Finally, one seeks an ensemble of literally appropriate descriptions that, taken together, provide a rich and differentiated set of representations of the topic under consideration. Such an ensemble conveys to students what it is like to be an expert. And to the extent that the representations involve a range of symbolic systems, they will prove more robust and more useful to students.

Fostering multiple representations is one component of effective teaching; providing many opportunities for performance, which can reveal to the student and to others the extent to which the material has been mastered, is a complementary component. Teachers need to be imaginative and pluralistic if they hope to stimulate revealing performances of understanding. While it is easy to fall back on the tried-and-true, such as the short-answer test or the essay question, there is no imperative to do so. Performances can be as varied as the different facets of the topic and the diverse skills of students. A variety of sanctioned performances not only provides more students with an opportunity to show what they have understood; it also ensures that no single "take" on a topic inappropriately dominates students' (or test makers') understandings of that topic.

I encourage teachers to have students deal with challenges: debate with one another about the causes of the Holocaust or the merits of Darwinism, conduct experiments that probe different aspects of the evolutionary process, interview Holocaust survivors, create works of art that commemorate heroes of the Resistance, or design a species that can survive in an environment that has become highly toxic. Most challengingly, students can be asked to discuss the factors that permitted the Holocaust in terms of what we know about the evolution of human behavior. Hence, at last, our two topics would be meaningfully joined.

Is this just another call for projects—the sins of the Progressive movement—recently castigated by such conservative educational critics as E. D. Hirsch? Quite the contrary. Student projects need to be considered critically in two respects: (1) adequacy as an example of a genre (*Is it a coherent essay? Is it an effective monument? Does it qualify as a causal explanation?*); and (2) adequacy as an occasion for performing one's understandings (*Does the debater stick to the consensual facts, or does she distort what is known? Does the newly designed species have a life span that allows for reproduction and rearing of offspring?*). Far from being a superficial measure of understanding, such projects and performances hold students to high standards; the key features of the concept should be performed in vehicles that meet the criteria of the relevant genre.

CODA: TECHNOLOGICAL MEANS, HUMAN ENDS

I have restricted myself until now almost entirely to the simplest forms of technology—books, pencils, papers, a few art supplies, a simple biological laboratory. This is appropriate; fundamental discussions of educational goals and means should not depend on the latest technological advances. But the approach promises to be enhanced significantly by technology. It is not easy for teachers to provide individualized curricula and pedagogy for a class of thirty elementary school students, let alone several high school classes totaling more than a hundred students. And it is challenging to ask students to provide a variety of performances and then give them meaningful feedback.

Happily, we have in our grasp today technology that should allow a quantum leap in the delivery of individualized services for both students and teachers. It is already possible to create software that addresses the different intelligences, provides a range of entry points, allows students to exhibit their own understandings in diverse symbol systems (linguistic, numerical, musical, graphic, and more), and begins to allow teachers to examine student work flexibly and rapidly. Student work can even be examined from a distance, thanks to electronic mail, Web sites, video conferencing, and the like. The development of "intelligent systems" that will be able to evaluate student work and provide relevant feedback is no longer simply a chapter from science fiction. Indeed, such systems should be able to vary both exercises and pedagogical feedback based on the success or failure of earlier interventions. The earlier arguments against the feasibility of individualized instruction are no longer tenable. Future reluctance will have to be justified on other grounds. My strong hunch is that such resistance is not likely to persuade students and parents who are not experiencing success "in the usual way" and who might benefit from alternative forms of delivery, or scholars who have arrived at new ways of conceptualizing materials, or teachers dedicated to a variety of pedagogies and assessments.

Educators have always tinkered with promising technologies. Much of the history of education chronicles the varying fates of paper, books, lecture halls, filmstrips, television, computers, and other human artifacts. Current technologies seem tailor-made to help bring into reality the kind of MI approach I have endorsed here. Still, there are no guarantees. Many technologies have faded, and many others have been used superficially and unproductively. And we cannot forget that some of the horrible events of human history—such as the Holocaust—featured a perversion of the existing technologies. That is why any consideration of education cannot remain merely instrumental: If we get more computers, what do we want them for? More broadly, what do we want education for? I have taken here a strong position: Education must ultimately justify itself in terms of enhancing human understanding. But that understanding itself is up for grabs. After all, one can use knowledge of physics to build bridges or bombs; one can use knowledge of human beings to free or to enslave them.

I want my children to understand the world, but not just because the world is fascinating and the human mind is curious. I want them to understand it so that they will be positioned to make it a better place. Knowledge is not the same as morality, but we need to understand if we are to avoid past mistakes and move in productive directions. An important part of that understanding is knowing who we are and what we can do. Part of that answer lies in biology—the roots and constraints of our species—and part of it lies in our history—what people have done and are capable of doing. Many topics are important, but I personally believe that evolution and the Holocaust are especially important. They bear on the possibilities of our species, for both good and evil. A student needs to know about these topics not primarily because they may appear on an examination but rather because they help us to chart human possibilities. Ultimately, we must synthesize our understandings for ourselves. The performances of understanding that truly matter are the ones we carry out as human beings in an imperfect world which we can affect for good or for ill.

11

THE SCIENTIFIC CONCEPT of intelligence has scholastic roots. At the turn of the nineteenth century, Alfred Binet and his colleagues were interested in helping students who were likely to have difficulties in school. I have often wondered how different things would have been if the first tests of intelligence had been devised by performers, business-people, or members of a hunter-gatherer society.

It was perhaps inevitable that schools emerged as the first host for multiple intelligences theory. I developed my theory as a critique of standard psychometric theory, and so those with the greatest stake in that theory took notice of what was being said. But, like any of its scientific counterparts, MI theory can lead to a range of practices and speak to a variety of institutions. As MI theory has begun to penetrate the wider society, it has appealed to institutions that bear some resemblance to schools—particularly museums. More recently, it has also begun to influence an institution as vast as, and more powerful than, schools—the world of business.

THE CHILDREN'S MUSEUM AND ITS COUSINS

The children's museum is a relatively new phenomenon. Traditionally, museums have been depositories for highly valued cultural artifacts and have been off limits to children, who like to touch and play with things and who might harm irreplaceable objects. The children's museum is a relatively new phenomenon. This type of institution began in the United States and has spread rapidly to other countries. (Often, if ironically, it becomes the perfect project for the wife of the leader of a nation.) Most children's museums are geared toward very young children and offer a variety of materials and experiences. In a typical children's museum, there are areas for free play, climbing structures, water areas for making bubbles and spraying patterns, an assembly line where a child can (alone or with others) put together simple and attractive products, common household objects magnified in size, materials for creating unusual works of art (like moving cartoons or zootropes), devices (including computers) for creating sound patterns and music, interactive demonstrations that illustrate scientific principles, small fish and animals that children can observe and even play with.

The children's museum also has its close relatives. Some specialize in particular age groups, such as toddlers or adolescents. Some specialize in topics, such as the arts or computers. Especially appealing to older children and adolescents are science museums or exploratoriums. And some museums blend into the broader theme parks that have become popular (and profitable) in different regions of the world.

Children's museums skate the line between entertainment and education. The displays must be appealing to attract families, who typically pay to enter the museum and then spend money in the restaurant and gift shop. At least in the United States, if these institutions were not inviting and did not promise fun, they would not survive. At the same time, however, many of the exhibitions and parts of a children's museum have educational aspirations, especially if the museum specializes in the sciences. Sometimes the founders or directors of the museum have a generic commitment to education; sometimes funding sources expect an educational interface. Some museums see themselves as supplements to the school, and some staff believe that there should be no tension between education and entertainment.

Whatever the reasons, there has been a natural affinity between museums for children and the theory of multiple intelligences. Here, the contrast with schools works to the advantage of MI theory. Children have to attend school, there is generally a required curriculum, teachers feel bound to reach all students efficiently, and there is an age-old tradition of exploiting linguistic and logical intelligences, often to the exclusion of others. But these requirements do not burden museums for children. Here, children can proceed at their own pace and direct their energies wherever they like. There is no need to focus on language or logic and there is no explicit teacher or curriculum. As Frank Oppenheimer, the founder of San Francisco's Exploratorium, once quipped, "Nobody flunks museum."

But there is a downside to this freedom, flexibility, and fun. Because most people visit a museum for children only once or twice a year, the educational possibilities are limited. The time at the museum may be enjoyable, but from an educational perspective, it may not be spent productively. And if other institutions—the home, the school, the mass media—cannot exploit the cognitive sparks set off by the museum experience, the sparks are likely to dim.

As I have argued with respect to schools, MI theory cannot provide a goal for an institution. But once a children's museum adopts educational goals, MI theory can become pertinent and useful. Because they can devote considerable resources to the exhibitions, these museums can create materials that deliberately arouse and use a range of intelligences in a provocative mix. And because the exhibitions often travel to (or can be borrowed or bought by) other museums, they can have a long shelf life.

I've seen multiple intelligences at work in children's museums in three ways. First, they provide rich exhibitions with a variety of entry and exit points. In an exhibit on computers, for example, students behold the history of computing and experiment with the variety of computers that were popular over the last fifty years, they climb into and explore a large replica of a computer, they carry out experiments that demonstrate the potentials and limitations of different kinds of computational devices and languages, they compare computers with other modes of communication and problem solving, they create works of art and music with computers, and they program a robot and observe how it carries out "human" functions. They may also explore virtual realities and get acquainted with people at a distance through electronic mail, video broadcasting, and other ways of spanning the globe.

As a second practice, museums have mounted exhibitions on the topic of multiple intelligences. Typical MI exhibitions show how the brain handles different kinds of information in different regions of the cortex. They demonstrate the relation between sensory and motor systems and the several intelligences. They re-create the lives and works of people who have excelled in various intelligences. And most important, they allow children to practice their own intelligences, to see what can be accomplished by each intelligence and learn what its strengths and limitations are. These exhibitions can make children more aware of the specific accents of their own minds; they provide a vocabulary that helps young people talk about how they approach and encode experience.

Finally, a few museums, such as the Junibacken Museum in Stockholm, are actually organized around the multiple intelligences, with an explicit focus on the nature of each intelligence and what it can accomplish. Youngsters are invited to think of themselves and of the world in terms of the various intelligences that humans (and other entities) possess and use.

Each museum and museum community makes its own decisions

about how far to push the MI concept. In the most ambitious cases, museums provide curricula for use at home or at school. These may resemble school curricula but they have the advantage of making use of materials and experiences available only through the museum. (Nearly every school can have a computer or a life-sized plastic heart, but few schools can afford giant replicas, which a student can literally walk through and visit again and again. If students learn about a topic before visiting the museum, if they can take materials (and memories) and bring them into their daily life, then these experiences are likely to become part of the children's understanding, new entries in their library of mental representations.

ART MUSEUMS

Art museums have historical, curatorial, and aesthetic purposes that are marginal to most children's museums. Because they contain unique objects that may not survive touching or holding, they are less inviting for most children. Indeed, while nearly every youngster can enjoy a children's museum without adult explanation or encouragement, art museums rarely "speak" to children without adult guidance.

One way to make art museums more inviting to children is to create, within the museum, objects and experiences that more closely resemble those of children's museums. It is possible to mount a gallery where youngsters can explore less fragile or less costly works of art, to install CD-ROM or other video and computational devices that are more inviting to children, and to create ateliers where children can fashion their own art objects and compare them to those mounted in the museum. It is also possible to increase the range of approaches to the permanent installation for children and for adults who have not had much exposure to the fine arts. The key idea is the "entry point."

As I've argued with respect to school curricula, most topics can be approached in a variety of ways. Once a topic—evolution, the Holo-caust, or the music of Mozart—has been introduced, it can be illuminated further by using metaphors and analogies. And the central themes can be captured by several symbol systems, each of which highlights an aspect of the topic. Taken together, these complementary representations capture the fullest understanding of the topic at hand.

Building on the concept of the entry point, the art educator Jessica Davis and her colleagues devised Project MUSE (Museums Uniting with Schools in Education). The basic idea of MUSE is disarmingly simple: When viewers examine works of art, they encounter questions that span a range of entry points:

1. *Narrative* (e.g., Tell the story of what you see and hear.)
2. *Quantitative* (e.g., Figure out the cost of the materials and how that relates to the selling price.)
3. *Logical* (e.g., Share your theory about why this object is important.)
4. *Aesthetic* (Describe the colors and shapes and how they fit together.)
5. *Hands On* (e.g., Design a dance about what you see.)

Teachers, docents, or curators can use MUSE materials in various ways. They can pose questions directly to viewers, or viewers can pose the questions to themselves. A MUSE game lets people choose questions at random from a query-filled box. Or participants can pose previously formulated or original questions to one another and compare answers.

It might seem that the MUSE approach emphasizes language too much. But one must distinguish between language as a means of communication and language as the essence of learning. As long as viewers understand the questions and are comfortable speaking, language becomes a mere convenience, and the questions themselves soon become invisible. The viewers' activities and mental representations span a range and combination of intelligences.

Of interest is MUSE's relation to another psychologically oriented approach to the arts: the Visual Thinking Curriculum (VTC). Developed at New York's Museum of Modern Art, VTC is based on the assumption that there are stages of sophistication in a person's grasp of art objects and that educational interventions work best when they honor this sequence. So, for example, novices focus on color and subject matter; journeymen, on style and expression; and experts, on a more individualistic, interpretive approach to each work of art.

Considerable evidence supports the VTC stage sequence. Yet, it may be too comfortable a reaction simply to accept the stage sequence and conform to it (for example, pointing out only color and subject matter to a novice viewer). By posing challenging questions to individuals of different degrees of sophistication, one may actually give such individuals a sense of the range of possible approaches to works of art. When someone hears or observes the responses of others, particularly those at a higher stage, their own thinking may become more complex and rich. A stage sequence—like psychological theories—should not dictate practice.

Just as schools appear to favor a linguistic or logical approach, art museums appear to speak most directly to those who have strengths in the visual-spatial and the aesthetic areas. But even if this is true, it bypasses the issue of *why* certain people have readier access to visual arts. They may have been born with heightened mental representations or intelligences in these areas, but it is more likely that experience and training sharpened their eyes and provided the contexts whereby they could learn to appreciate and interpret works of art.

MI theory assumes many routes to expertise, in school and out. The interventions favored for children's museums, art museums, and other cultural institutions open up a variety of entry points and then, in turn, allow free use of one's own strengths. Under favorable circumstances, museum visitors master these various points of entry and apply them broadly, even when exhibitions have not been crafted with such pluralism in mind. These entry points and modes of representation can also be used for communication about works of science or art. And perhaps someday, when the young viewers become parents or teachers, they can return the favor by offering broader access to a new generation of museum visitors.

THE WORLDS OF BUSINESS AND EDUCATION

In most parts of the world, the realms of business and education peer nervously at one another. Business is seen as powerful and headstrong, education as caring and vulnerable. When conditions are favorable in the land, the tensions between business and education are muted. In times of conflict or scarcity, mistrust flares up. In good times and bad, businesses complain about students' lack of preparation; schools deplore the lack of financial support for education. In the United States and some other countries, businesses have come to believe that they have the expertise to run schools. Either they seek to introduce that expertise into the schools, for example, through site-based management or total quality management, or they offer to operate schools, either as nonprofit or for-profit entities. The mutual conviction that they are operating in different spheres has made it difficult for schools and businesses to enter into comfortable contact and meaningful collaboration with one another. As a result, neither institution has sufficiently appreciated that they share many common challenges and opportunities. Both are fundamentally concerned with learning: to remain viable within a business, one must continue to learn on the job. Both institutions suffer if they do not create a community in which people can be comfortable. Both institutions require leadership that is fixed determinedly on its goals and yet sensitive to the often conflicting motivations and desires of its "workers."

Looking closely at three major differences between schools and businesses, we can see that the distinctions are not as sharp as many people believe.

1. *Businesses make products.* Business entails the fashioning of products, whether pens, processed foods, or planes. However, particularly in the developed world, an increasing proportion of businesses are now involved with human services or the creation and transmission of information. Schools do not usually think of themselves as creating products, but they also have an obligation to fashion "human" products of quality and should be concerned when they fail to do so. In these respects, the missions of schools and businesses are converging.

2. *Businesses must make profits, and, nowadays, increasingly high ones.* Once a market model is in place, businesses have at least to break even, and those that surpass the minimum are the ones likely to thrive. But businesses differ from one another in how they conceive of profits. Many take a short-term view—how much profit can be made next season for shareholders?—but others (particularly abroad) adopt a more extended time frame and willingly forego current profits for long-term viability. Businesses also differ from one another in how they regard achievements other than sheer profitability. Some, particularly those associated in the public mind with a specific family or community, are deeply concerned about the quality of their products. Some businesses embrace prosocial goals; they do not use certain materials or make certain products, even if these self-restraints make them less competitive. And, recently, the notion of "stakeholders" in business has developed,

particularly in Great Britain. In contrast to "shareholders," whose interest in corporations is financial, stakeholders include the panoply of involved people—from manufacturers to purchasers to those who live in communities that will be affected by a business's operations.

Schools usually do not have to make a profit, though independent schools cannot survive indefinitely if they remain in debt. Indeed, nowadays many schools—public as well as independent—spend much of their energy in fund-raising so as to survive and attract new parental customers or voucher bearers. Metaphorically, however, schools do need to remain in the black. They must demonstrate that their students are receiving value from their schooling. Without signs of profit or productivity, schools become vulnerable to the charge that they are achieving little and expending their resources unwisely. While few schools have yet been dissolved because of a string of losses, a "performance" set and rhetoric is becoming increasingly common in the academic marketplace.

Is it fair to hold schools to such standards? The staunchest defenders point out that schools often operate under deplorable conditions. And the most vociferous critics typically purchase expensive private education (or well-supported suburban public education) for their own children. No one can educate students effectively if most of the students come from homes that are seriously troubled or if the population is overwhelmingly transient or is unwilling or unable to learn in the language and mores of the dominant culture. Still, all too often, objectively poor conditions are used as an excuse to argue that the schools should not be accountable. Whatever its emotional or sentimental appeal, this line of argument cannot be sustained indefinitely.

3. *Schools serve a vital civic function.* Because schools focus determinedly on the acquisition of basic skills and the transmission of disciplines, we sometimes forget that, at least in a democracy, they also

serve important civic functions. Students learn about the history and the governance of their country; they come to know peers of different backgrounds and points of view; they review current events; they are exposed to argument and debate about controversial issues, and in some circumstances are encouraged to become participants; they observe how decisions are made, carried out, and reviewed in a community like theirs; and they note how adults relate to one another in formal and informal settings.

Admittedly, this description is ideal. In many schools, civic functions have been compromised or have disappeared. Often, the staff members would like to fulfill these functions but find themselves diverted by seemingly more pressing matters. In some schools, the notions of civility and civic-mindedness vary so much within the community that the school becomes paralyzed when it attempts to address these responsibilities. But despite these obstacles, schools remain society's most appropriate setting for inculcating civic-mindedness. In the United States, as in many other countries, the schools have also served as a "hot-button" institution where sensitive issues come to the fore: patriotism, morality, cultural values, the relationship among groups, the need to integrate newcomers, and access to higher education have been tackled head-on. Societies need to maintain this function—in schools and elsewhere—if they are to achieve any success in building a more integrated polity.

Here, too, we must not exaggerate the difference between schools and businesses. Businesses are communities, if also increasingly transient ones, where people must learn to get along with one another. Perhaps paradoxically, issues of trust loom even larger in the new economic order, which features takeovers by new owners, rapid changes of roles, and tasks increasingly being performed by consultants or out-sourced or carried out without face-to-face contacts. Unless agreed-upon norms are developed about expectations, consequences, and civility, the business terrain is likely to become a permanent battlefield.

But businesses also see themselves as part of the social fabric of their communities, and they realize that they cannot thrive where rancor and tensions abound. As institutions of power and influence, they are increasingly asked to lend support to schools, museums, and other civic and community institutions. Wise businesses do not resist these overtures, and it is reasonable for them to ask for certain services and standards in return.

MI THEORY AND THE WORKPLACE

Up to this point, I have committed the sin of lumping a myriad of enterprises together under the single label of "business." Of course, there are hundreds, if not thousands, of kinds of businesses, each with its peculiar mission and problems. Just like no two people are exactly alike, no two businesses are identical. MI theory was devised as a description of individuals, based on their evolutionary past and their survival in ecological and cultural niches. It is not self-evident that organizations exhibit the same intelligences as individuals, nor that they create and lead in the same ways. But the corporation itself was set up in direct analogy to the person, and it is at least worth considering whether one might profitably think of businesses—individually and collectively—as having multiple intelligences that can be nurtured and deployed more or less productively.

Sectors and Roles

As a start in disaggregating the terrain of business, I suggest two primary distinctions. The first has to do with the sphere or sector, the second with the roles performed within each sector. Obviously, businesses are involved with diverse products and services. Some make products that go directly to the consumer, some make products that are used in making other products, and some deal in direct services (like those handled by a bank teller, an airplane steward, or a nurse) or in indirect services (like doing accounting or scheduling airlines). An increasing number of businesses deal with information per se (for example, compiling statistics about the weather or the preferences of customers in different zip-code areas); are involved chiefly in finance (buying and selling money); or manage aspects of other businesses (consulting, acquisitions and mergers, creation of computer networks and Web pages, and feedback on consumer preferences).

Focusing on sectors suggests one business application for MI ways of thinking. Sectors that deal primarily with communication use language and other symbol systems. Those that deal primarily with finance, accounting, or science draw on logical-mathematical intelligence. Sectors that interact with the public highlight the personal intelligences. There are businesses that explore the other intelligences: The entertainment business highlights musical and other artistic intelligences; athletics, arts, and crafts focus on bodily-kinesthetic intelligence; businesses involved in navigation, transportation, advertising, or graphics feature spatial intelligence; businesses that have contact with the environment, plants, animals, textiles, and ecology exploit the naturalistic intelligence; businesses that deal with career guidance, self-knowledge, and self-transformation address intrapersonal intelligence; and businesses that focus on spiritual matters, matters of personal or communal identity address existential intelligence.

Of course, just as intelligences differ from scholarly domains, there is no one-to-one correspondence between sectors and intelligences. Any sector can make use of the range of intelligences. Moreover, people with varying strengths in the intelligences are free to gravitate to whichever sector they like, depending on interest, passion, or training. Still, one should not lump all businesses together but instead consider the specific content of the major traditional sectors as well as emerging ones.

The second major distinction pertains to the different roles present in businesses. Most businesses have leadership and management positions, plus a variety of departments: human resources, production, accounting, finance, marketing, sales, customer relations, philanthropy, and community outreach. As noted in chapter 8, leaders generally rely especially on linguistic, personal, and existential intelligences, whereas managers avoid the existential issues—unless they want to become leaders—but need to be strong in other intelligences, the specific intelligence reflecting the work of their department.

Going beyond these structural roles, it is easy to match niches to intelligences. For those involved in human resources, sales, customer relations, and marketing, knowledge of other people is key. Human resource workers may have to exploit existential intelligence when dealing with health and other crises or with hiring and firing, issues that involve fundamental tensions and dilemmas of existence. Logical-mathematical intelligence is essential for workers in accounting and finance. Marketing, advertising, and product design people rely on aspects of their aesthetic intelligences, particularly poetic language, musical forms, and the growing panoply of graphic, video, and pictorial devices. Bodily-kinesthetic intelligence is necessary for those involved directly with production or the handling of products, and graceful bodily movements prove valuable for those who wish to put others at ease in meetings and other personal contacts.

At first, it may seem that including naturalist intelligence is a stretch, except in industries that deal with plants and animals. But I believe that naturalist intelligence is extremely important in the business world. Commercial businesses exploit the smallest perceptible differences in products to convince consumers that they should go to MacDonald's rather than Burger King, drive a Ford rather than a Plymouth, or jog in Nikes instead of Adidas shoes. We are capable of making the necessary perceptible distinctions among products because of our naturalist intelligence. Although we did not evolve to be able to discriminate between two similar man-made objects, the ability to discriminate depends on precisely those evolved mechanisms that allow us to know which plants to eat and which to spurn, which animals to pursue and which to run away from. These capacities have, as it were, been "hijacked" by the world of commerce. Without naturalist intelligence we can neither participate in the creation of these products nor, perhaps happily, fall prey to advertisers' and marketers' blandishments.

Across business sectors and functions, the full range of intelligences should be employed. This assertion challenges the prevailing idea that there is a single "business intelligence"—an assumption rarely made explicitly, but entrenched in a "business school way of thinking." (Indeed, if there were a business IQ, it would no doubt sample a wide set of skills and abilities.) Business schools highlight linguistic and logical intelligences, and students who excel in these areas are recruited by major corporations. This classical views of intelligence has always its place in business. And if the "symbol analyst" remains important in the businesses of tomorrow, then the role of linguistic and logical intelligences cannot be minimized. But as I have argued with respect to schooling, we need to be more flexible in considering the roles and functions valued in the business world. Each of the intelligences can be marshaled in an entrepreneurial environment, and the roles most crucial in business should be assumed by people who have varying blends of intelligences.

For those involved in hiring, promoting, and firing, clear implications follow. It does not make sense to judge people in terms of a single set of dimensions. Rather, one should attempt to learn as much as possible about candidates' and employees' favored ways of thinking and problem solving, and use this knowledge to hire and train people, to set up teams, and to make critical decisions about reployment, advancement, and termination. In some cases, information about intelligences can be secured through self-report or recommendations. In other cases, simple tasks or assignments can reveal candidates' favored intelligences.

When it comes to actual methods of selecting employees in the future, all bets are off. For some time, it has been true that people with the most formal credentials or the longest resumé have the easiest time gaining and maintaining employment. But credentials are expensive, and they may not be necessary for accomplishing a job.

Traditionally, credentials have signaled that a person has carried out the requisite studies or has performed the required tasks in other comparable business settings. In the future, however, it should be possible to devise computer-based simulations that will show, with a high degree of accuracy, whether an individual will be able to carry out the job for which he or she is applying. This process could be carried out not only with respect to professions—arguing a legal case, performing surgery—but also with respect to various business roles—designing a product, creating a marketing strategy, or even conducting a delicate meeting. Should it turn out that only those who have credentials or documented experience can handle these situations, then hiring will proceed as it has in the past. But if it turns out that people without such expensive backgrounds can perform as well, or nearly as well, on simulations, costly credentials may not be so important. A cost-conscious business community may turn instead to self-trained experts.

From the perspective of MI theory, what is important is whether people can do their jobs, not what particular intelligences they happen to be applying. To the extent that professional schools require admissions or exit tests that measure intelligences only marginally important for core functions, schools will either have to change or close, yielding to institutions that can develop the desired skills more directly.

While acknowledging the differences between business and educational settings, it should be possible to draw inspiration from some of the educational interventions discussed in earlier chapters. For example, recruiters can make use of informal assessments of intelligence, or can even create Spectrum-style settings where relevant intellectual strengths can be assessed in a naturalistic setting. On-the-job training and retraining can certainly make use of our knowledge of various entry points, analogies, and ways of representing the key concepts in a role or task. Finally, those involved in promoting or transferring personnel will benefit from records, self-reports, or on-line experiments that reveal the particular intellectual configurations of employees.

Business and the Personal Intelligences

An awareness of the intelligences involved in different business sectors and roles is significant. But other aspects of multiple intelligences may be even more important—those involving the personal intelligences.

While I am primarily a teacher and a scholar, during the nearly thirty years that I have codirected Harvard's Project Zero, I have supervised dozens of research projects and hundreds of gifted young researchers, and can reasonably say that I have been raising funds for and managing a small, nonprofit organization. Two decades ago, when I chose personnel, I looked for people like me. But studying the personal intelligences has taken me in new directions. I now rarely look for individuals with skills like mine. Instead, I ask these questions:

What skills or intelligences are needed for particular roles, and particularly for new ones?

Who on my staff already has these skills or intelligences? Who could readily acquire them?

Who can work well with a person who has a particular profile of intelligences and fulfills a certain role?

Which persons, or kinds of persons, can train others in new skills?

How will a project benefit from different mixes of individuals?

Not only do these questions bring to the fore people who work well with others, who are strong in the personal intelligences—the entire way of thinking also becomes more person-centered. They ask about individual strengths and probe how these strengths can be mobilized to create effective work groups and bring out the best in each person. And they also ask individuals, including me, to think about our own profile of intelligences, how we interact with others, and—to use Peter Drucker's apt phrase—how we manage ourselves.

Businesses used to be set up so that employees would remain with them indefinitely; indeed, it was assumed that people who did their jobs well had lifetime employment. But for at least fifteen years, these assumptions have not held true in the United States; and with every new economic twist in Europe, Asia, or Latin America, they are undermined further. In this rapidly changing environment, the role of intrapersonal intelligence becomes increasingly important—indeed, essential. When people did the same work as their predecessors, self-knowledge was a luxury, if not a burden. Given today's extreme fluidity of jobs, roles, and preferences, it is essential that people have an accurate, up-to-date, and flexible understanding of their own desires, needs, anxieties, and optimal ways of learning. People with particularly strong intrapersonal intelligence are prized in the business world because they can make optimal use of their talents, especially under rapidly changing conditions, and they know best how to mesh their talents with those of their coworkers. In contrast, those with inaccurate self-perceptions behave in nonproductive ways, personally or professionally, and are a burden to a company. It is easier to fire such people than to try to instruct them in knowledge of self.

Unfortunately, we don't know a lot about the personal intelligences. We do not understand their operations well, we do not know how to measure these intelligences, and we are not skilled at training them. This fact helps to explain why businesses have little patience for people deficient in personal intelligences. One might argue that personal intelligences are important in companies that require face-to-face interaction and less so when people work at home or communicate via the Internet. It may well be true that the particular mix of personal intelligences may change, but I am convinced that these intelligences will remain equally important, if not more so. To work effectively at a distance, one must be able to transmit and interpret subtle linguistic cues and, if face-to-face contacts occur, behave appropriately in light of the earlier, more "distant" contacts.

Furthermore, in the future, more work may be temporary. When a job needs to be done, the producers will assemble a staff, with varying skills and intelligences, and ask them to accomplish the work as expeditiously and expertly as possible. (About 90 percent of the employees of the influential management company McKinsey and Co. are considered consultants rather than employees or partners.) If these staff are to be well assembled and work effectively with one another, individuals will need better personal intelligences than ever before.

Work Beyond the Individual

There is, finally, the question of education and learning beyond the boundaries of the individual. Even as people move rapidly from one business or niche to another, the organizations will remain. In addition to teams of workers and professional partnerships, there will be businesses of varying sizes and shapes, ranging from start-ups to nongovernmental organizations to multinational corporations, either loosely or tightly coupled. And to remain viable, all organizations will have to continue to learn and to change. They must not only be "intelligent" and "creative," but also be "effective leaders" or "attentive followers" or "wise counselors" as appropriate. They will need to be aware of their own explicit and tacit strengths and weaknesses, their positions vis-à-vis competitors, their long-term goals, and the optimal strategies for achieving them.

Starting as a contribution to the psychology of intelligence, MI theory has moved a long way. In education, the original interest among elementary educators has expanded through high school and to the college level. In the world of museums, MI ideas have helped navigate the line between education and entertainment. In recent years, a growing number of businesses have been attracted as well to the themes of MI: as input to the human resources department, as a means for creating or marketing products, or as training for a more effective working environment. These trends are gratifying. I have learned much by observing experiments in various settings, and I expect to learn more in the years to come. And, naturally, this has led me to consider the final topic of this book: work on intelligence in the future.

WHO OWNS

INTELLIGENCE?

THE THEORY OF multiple intelligences has helped break the psychometricians' century-long stranglehold on the subject of intelligence. While we may continue to use the words *smart* and *stupid*, and while IQ tests may persist for certain purposes, the monopoly of those who believe in a single general intelligence has come to an end. Brain scientists and geneticists are documenting the incredible differentiation of human capacities, computer programmers are creating systems that are intelligent in different ways, and educators are freshly acknowledging that their students have distinctive strengths and weaknesses.

In this book, I have laid out a position that challenges the psychometric consensus. I have proposed a set of several intelligences, each resting on its own neurological substrate, each of which can be nurtured and channeled in specific ways, depending on a particular society's values. I have listed the criteria for an intelligence and shown how these can be evoked in evaluating potential new intelligences. But where does one draw the line? Are my criteria the right ones? In the future, the new dimensions and boundaries of intelligence will likely be thrashed out on a pivotal battlefield. Now that the Scylla of the psychometricians has been overcome, we risk succumbing to the Charybdis of "anything goes"—emotions, morality, and creativity all being absorbed into the "new intelligence." The challenge is to chart a concept of intelligence that reflects new discoveries and understandings and yet can withstand scrutiny.

THE STRETCH AND LIMITS
OF MULTIPLE INTELLIGENCES

One can think of intelligence as an elastic band. For many years no one effectively challenged its definition, and the band seemed to have lost its elasticity. Some of the new definitions of intelligence have expanded the band and renewed its resilience, even while incorporating the earlier work on intelligence that is still germane. Other definitions have expanded the band to the snapping point, rendering unusable the earlier foundational study of intelligence.

Until now, the term *intelligence* has been largely limited to linguistic and logical capacities, although (as I've argued) humans can process other elements as diverse as the contents of space, music, or their own and others' psyches. Like the elastic band, conceptions of intelligence need to encompass these diverse contents—and stretch even more. We must move beyond solving existing problems and look more at the capacities of human beings to *fashion products* (like works of art, scientific experiments, classroom lessons, organization plans) that draw on one or more intelligences.

As long as intelligences are restricted to the processing of "contents in the world," we avoid epistemological problems. So it should be. The concept of "intelligence" should not be expanded to include personality, motivation, will, attention, character, creativity, and other valued human capacities. If we conflate intelligence with creativity, as we have seen in chapter 8, we can no longer distinguish between the expert (the person highly skilled in a domain) and the creator (one who expands a domain in new and unexpected ways). We would also fail to recognize that creative individuals stand out particularly in terms of their restless temperament and personality, whereas experts efficiently process informational content and accept the status quo.

Consider also what would happen if we stretched intelligence to include good or evil attitudes and behaviors. By making that incursion into morality, we would confront human values within a culture. Granted, a few values probably can be expressed generically enough so that they command universal respect: One promising candidate is the Golden Rule (in its biblical version, in other religions' versions, or in the contemporary version introduced by the sociologist Amitai Etzioni: Respect the mores of your society). However, most other values—even such seemingly unproblematic ones as the rejection of theft, killing, or lying—turn out to be specific to cultures or subcultures.

If we conflated morality and intelligence, we would need to deal with widely discrepant views of what is good and bad, and why—vexing questions about abortion, capital punishment, holy wars, marriage between relatives, patriotism, treatment of strangers, and more. Consider too that people who score high on tests of moral reasoning often act immorally outside the test situations, even as courageous and self-sacrificing people turn out to be unremarkable on tests of moral reasoning. Many of those who hid Jews or other persecuted people during World War II lacked education or sophistication. In contrast, eight of the fourteen men who laid plans to implement the Final Solution held doctoral degrees from major European universities.

Furthermore, Adolf Hitler and Joseph Stalin probably knew full well which situations were considered moral in their culture, but they either did not care (Stalin commented, "How many divisions does the Pope have?" and Hitler extolled the Big Lie) or embraced their own peculiar codes ("Wiping out a generation is a necessary, indeed inevitable, move if you are committed to the establishment of a Communist state." Or "Eliminating Jews is the moral imperative in quest of an Aryan society.")

The notion of an "emotional intelligence" proves problematic in certain respects (as discussed in chapters 1 and 5). Unlike language or space, emotions are not "contents" to be processed. Rather, cognition has evolved so that we can make sense of human beings (self and others) who have and experience emotions. Emotions do accompany cognition, and they may well prove more salient under certain circumstances; they accompany our interactions with others, our listening to music, and our efforts to solve mathematical puzzles. Calling *some* intelligences emotional implies that other intelligences are not, and that implication flies in the face of experience and empirical data. Further problems arise when we conflate emotional intelligence with a certain recommended pattern of behavior—a temptation to which Daniel Goleman sometimes succumbs in his otherwise admirable *Emotional Intelligence*. Goleman singles out as "emotionally intelligent" people who use their understanding of emotions to make others feel better, solve conflicts, or cooperate in home or work situations. I certainly cherish such people, but we cannot assume that being emotionally intelligent means those skills will be used for socially desirable ends.

For these reasons, I prefer the term *emotional sensitivity*, which applies to those who are sensitive to emotions in themselves and others—that is, individuals who exhibit the personal intelligences (in my own terminology). Presumably, clinicians and salespeople excel in sensitivity to others; poets and mystics, in sensitivity to the melodies of their own psyches. And there are others—autistic or psychopathic persons, for example—who seem completely deaf to the emotional realm. I insist, however, on a strict distinction between being emotionally sensitive and being a "good" or "moral" person, since someone who is sensitive to others' emotions may still manipulate, deceive, or create hatred. I call, then, for a delineation of intelligence that includes the full range of contents to which human beings are sensitive, but excludes such valued but separate human traits as creativity, morality, and emotional appropriateness. This delineation makes scientific and epistemological sense; it reinvigorates but does not break the elastic band; and it helps resolve two remaining struggles: how to assess intelligences and how to connect intelligences to other virtues.

THE ASSESSMENT OF INTELLIGENCES

All societies want to place the most appropriate people in positions of importance, but the most desirable niches often have far more candidates than can be accommodated. Hence, some forms of assessment are almost inevitable. Once we restrict the definition of *intelligence* to human information-processing and product-making capacities, we can use and supplement the established technology of assessment. We can continue to use paper-and-pencil or computer-adapted techniques, while simultaneously looking at a broader range of capacities, such as sensitivity to musical patterns or the understanding of people's motivations. And we can avoid ticklish, and possibly unanswerable, questions about the assessment of values and morality. But even with a limited definition of intelligence, important questions remain about which assessment path to follow. Here I hold strong views. I consider it a fool's errand to embrace the search for a "pure" intelligence—whether general intelligence, musical intelligence, or interpersonal intelligence. I do not believe that such alchemical cognitive essences actually exist; they are an outcome of our penchant for creating (and then attributing reality to) terminology rather than searching for determinable, measurable entities. Morever, the correlations that have been found between allegedly "pure measures" (like certain brain-wave patterns that purport to measure intelligence directly) and the skills we actually value in the world (like mathematical problem solving and good writing) are too modest to be useful.

What matters is the use of intelligences, individually and in concert, to carry out tasks valued by a society. Accordingly, we should be assessing people's success in carrying out valued tasks that presumably involve certain intelligences. For example, instead of testing musical intelligence by looking at evoked cortical responses when someone is listening to pure tones, we should teach people to sing songs, play instruments, or compose or transform melodies, and then determine how well they have mastered these tasks. By the same token, we should not search for immaculate emotional sensitivity—for example, with tests of galvanic skin response to a word or photograph. Rather, we should observe people in real-life situations where they have to be sensitive to the aspirations and motives of others. For example, we can see how someone handles a fight between two teenagers or convinces a supervisor to change an undesirable policy. These are realistic contexts for assessing mastery of the emotional realm.

Increasingly, we have another assessment option: simulations. We are now in a position to use technologies that not only can present realistic situations or problems but also can also measure performance through virtual realities, and even "intelligently" select subsequent steps in light of responses on earlier phases of the simulations. Thus, presenting a student with an unfamiliar tune on a computer and having him learn the tune, transpose it, and orchestrate it, can reveal much about his intelligence in musical matters. Similarly, we can learn about interpersonal or emotional sensitivity by simulating human interactions and asking people to judge the shifting motivations of each actor. For example, subjects can give their running reactions to members of a jury who are attempting to reach a verdict on a sensitive case. Or one can create an interactive hypermedia program—for example, a progam that features members of an organization as they are grappling with a major change in corporate strategy—and ask respondents to react to the virtual (or "real") people's moves even as those moves are being altered by the program.

An increase in the breadth, or elasticity, of our concept of intelligence, then, should open the possibility for innovative forms of assessment that are far more authentic than the classical short-answer examinations. Why settle for an IQ test or an SAT, on which the items are at best remote "proxies" for the ability to design experiments, write essays, critique musical performances, or resolve a dispute? Why not instead ask people to *do* the things—either in person or on-line? As long as we do not open the Pandora's box of values and subjectivity, we can continue to use established insights and technologies judiciously. Of course, if we used the psychometricians' traditional armamentaria, we could create an instrument to test any conceivable virtue (or vice), including morality, creativity, and emotional intelligence. Indeed, since Goleman's landmark book, there have been dozens of efforts to create tests for emotional intelligence. But such instruments are far more likely to satisfy the test makers' desires for reliability (that is, each testee would get roughly the same score on two separate administrations of an instrument) than the need for validity (that is, the test measures the trait it purports to measure, such as emotional sensitivity within one's family or at the workplace).

These kinds of instruments are questionable for two reasons: First, it is too difficult to agree on what it means to be emotionally intelligent—consider the different interpretations that might be given by Jesse Helms and Jesse Jackson, or Margaret Thatcher and Margaret Mead. Second, "scores" on such tests are more likely to reveal test-taking savvy (people's skills in language and logical inference) than fundamental emotional acuity.

We are at a turning point. A tight view of assessment is likely to produce reliable instruments that correlate well with one another but do not broaden the sample of talents to be surveyed nor the range of individuals who will stand out. A subtler view opens up many new and exciting possibilities. We will be able to look directly at the skills and capacities we value, and we will give people a variety of ways to demonstrate what they know and what they can do. Rather than just selecting one kind of a person, we may help to place many kinds of people in positions well matched to their skills and aspirations. If assessment is to be reinvented, such innovations point the way.

CONNECTING INTELLIGENCES TO OTHER VIRTUES

While broadening the definition of intelligence, I have steadfastly argued that the expansion of the band must be regulated. We cannot hijack the word *intelligence* so that it becomes all things to all people—the psychometric equivalent of the Holy Grail. Yet the problem remains: How, in a post-Aristotelian, post-Confucian era, one in which psychometrics still looms large, should we think about the virtuous human being—the human being who is justly admired because of his or her personal qualities? One promising approach is to recognize that intelligences, creativity, and morality—to mention just three commonly recognized virtues—are separate. Each may require its own measurement or assessment, and certain species or subspecies of these virtues will prove far easier to assess objectively than others. Indeed, with respect to creativity and morality, we are more likely to rely on overall judgments by disinterested experts than on any putative test battery. At the same time, we might well look for people who combine attributes: people who have musical *and* interpersonal intelligence, who are psychometrically intelligent *and* creative in the arts, who combine emotional sensitivity *and* a high standard of moral conduct.

Consider that selective colleges pay much attention to scholastic performance, as measured by the College Entrance Examination Board and secondary school grades; but they also weigh other features, and sometimes a student with lower test scores but high value in citizenship or motivation is chosen over one who has "aced" the tests. Admissions officers do not confound these virtues (indeed, they may use different "scales" and issue different "grades"), but they recognize the attractiveness of candidates who exemplify two or more of these desirable traits.

We probably will never re-create an Eden where intellectual and ethical values commingle, and we should recognize that these virtues can be separate. Indeed, despite the appeal of the Confucian or Grecian hero, these virtues are often all too remote from one another. Thus, when we attempt to aggregate the virtues, through phrases like "emotional intelligence," "creative intelligence," or "moral intelligence," we should realize that we are expressing a wish rather than describing a probable reality. Despite this caution, it is important to recognize that there are powerful models—people who successfully exemplify two or more cardinal human virtues. In the recent past, one can without reservation name the scientist Niels Bohr, the writer Rachel Carson, the athletes Arthur Ashe, the statesman George Marshall, and the musicians Louis Armstrong, Pablo Casals, and Ella Fitzgerald. In our own time, few would challenge the singling out of Nelson Mandela.

Examining lives like these reveals human possibilities. Young people learn primarily from the examples of powerful adults around them, ones who are admirable as well as ones who are simply glamorous. Sustained attention to admirable examples may well increase the incidence of people who will eventually link capacities now considered scientifically and epistemologically separate.

First-hand acquaintance with exemplary models probably constitutes the first step in becoming a person of multiple virtues, but exposure is not enough. Capacities must be trained. Threats to morality and decency must be identified and confronted. We need practice, with feedback, in handling morally charged situations, dilemmas that pull us in competing directions. We must learn from others but also recognize that we must sometimes go our own way. And ultimately, we must be ready to serve as role models for younger people.

The British novelist E. M. Forster counseled: "Only connect." Some expansionists in the territory of intelligence have prematurely claimed connections that do not exist. But it is within our power to help forge connections that are important for our physical and psychic survival. Just how the precise borders of intelligence are drawn is a question we can leave to scholars. But the imperative to broaden the definition of intelligence responsibly goes well beyond the academy. Who "owns" intelligence promises to be an even more critical issue in the twenty-first century than it has been in this era of the IQ test.

REMAINING PUZZLES: THE RESEARCH AGENDA

The first half of the twentieth century was the period of physics; the second, the period of molecular biology and genetics. Few doubt that the next century will highlight the study of the brain and mind. And, of course, exploring the nature of intelligence will be an important part of the research agenda. The research of the coming years will explore three major areas—each with two main thrusts.

The Basic Sciences of Intelligence

While intelligence has belonged largely to psychology, I see it increasingly being explored by other disciplines. On the one hand, those who work at the cellular and genetic levels are asking which genes control which aspects of intellectual functioning and how the genes work together to produce intelligent behavior. On the other hand, there is a growing interest in, and knowledge of, the ways human intelligence is applied in different social and cultural contexts.

We already know of genes or gene clusters that code for specific cognitive abilities like reading and spatial capacities, and there may be others that are critical in the attainment of high IQ-test scores. The interest in the structure of specific human abilities is magnified by new imaging techniques; we now can examine the neural structures involved in particular aspects of language (like reading, naming, and learning foreign languages), music (like rhythm and tonal perception), and even the understanding of people's minds, which proves crucial in interpersonal intelligence. At the other end of the scientific spectrum, within our own society, ethnographic investigators are studying different work settings and trying to determine which intelligences people use alone and in concert to accomplish important tasks. Studies of the building of a computer and of the navigation of a huge carrier reveal, for example, that no single individual understands the entire process; rather, this type of intelligent behavior depends upon capacities distributed across numerous individuals.

Cross-cultural studies continue to challenge our notions of human intellect. We look at contemporary societies and note the different emphases placed, for example, on sensitivity to others, on the capacity to cooperate with strangers, or on various putative psychic capacities like meditation or healing. And retrospectively we can also study intelligences of an earlier era. The archaeologist Stephen Mithen, for example, has described the naturalist and technological intelligences that may have been important for the forerunners of *Homo sapiens* 250,000 to 500,000 years ago.

These lines of study help us appreciate the limitations of singular views of intelligence, formulated largely in terms of the capacities

needed to exist in a certain kind of European or American school one
century ago.

The Operations of Intelligences

Information-processing techniques and computer simulations offer
powerful ways of learning how people perform specific tasks, from
understanding a foreign language to creating a piece of music. Such
studies not only will facilitate the development of software that excels
at these tasks but also will suggest the kind of training that can
improve the performance of ordinary (and extraordinarily talented or
impaired) people. It is equally important to understand those capacities that extend beyond the operations of single intelligences or subintelligences. Cognitively oriented researchers will probe in two
directions. They will investigate the ways in which particular intelligences work together, in general or on specific tasks. And they will
explore those capacities that seem to cut across different intelligences—the making of metaphors and analogies, the capacity to synthesize information, the emergence of wisdom. Unfortunately, MI
theory has not made much progress in explicating the nature of these
transintellectual capacities. And these capacities have also eluded
investigators from other psychological camps. It is probably true that
some capacities, like the making of metaphors, will turn out to be part
of the basic cognitive equipment of all human beings, while others, like
the capacity to synthesize different bodies of information, require a
culture that has cultivated these encyclopedic skills over a long period.

Shifting Demands

Two 1997 events symbolize tidal shifts in world culture: The defeat of
chess champion Gary Kasparov by the IBM "Deep Blue" computer pro-

gram proved once and for all that a machine could be "smarter"than the cleverest human performer in a domain long cherished by the intelligentsia. And the cloning of the sheep Dolly by the Scottish scientist Ian Wilmut and his colleagues demonstrated the potential to engage in the most profound experiments of genetic engineering. Some people would like to turn their backs on these events, because they fear a world in which machines dominate human beings or because they don't want to see people play God by controlling the genetic options of future generations. I share these reservations, though I doubt whether it is possible to prevent human beings from exploring such possibilities. However impressive, Dolly and Deep Blue are products of technology; they are neither good nor evil in themselves. We humans, operating individually and as a corporate body, must judge how the technology that spawned these "creatures" should be used or not used.

Many of us would welcome a society in which drudgery is eliminated because robots carry out mindless work. But a society freed of much human labor can turn in two opposite directions. We might be freed to exercise higher powers of mind in the arts or in other creative spheres, or we might surrender to the pursuit of mind-numbing entertainment, either benign (like television comedies or soap operas) or malignant (the bread and circuses held in amphitheaters during the decline of Rome). As a species, we remain free to become smart or stupid, moral or immoral, in various ways.

The options offered by genetic engineering are even sharper. Even those who are repelled by the idea of cloning or more aggressive forms of eugenics understand the appeal of testing for the lethal gene of, say, Huntington's chorea and, if possible, turning it off. But the decisions first exercised in the realm of bodily disease will sooner or later reverberate in the corridors of personality and intellect. We have to ask whether we want to eliminate the genes that give rise to dyslexia, and we may have to ask whether we will tolerate genetic engineering aimed

at producing individuals who excel at mathematics, chess, music making, or the less appealing capacity to manipulate others. The identification of new intelligences and a superior understanding of how they
operate will stimulate geneticists to probe the biological underpinning
of these capacities and, by the same token, geneticists' discoveries will
alert us to the possibility of new or different configurations among
human intellectual capacities.

No single authority has the right to make decisions in crucial realms
like artificial intelligence or genetic engineering. But this does not
mean that the opposite is true: that these decisions do not belong to
anybody or that marketplace forces should be allowed to determine
what is done. We cannot have a society in which people abdicate personal responsibility, dismiss the need to debate issues, and reject out-
right approaches that might be reasonable. Human societies can and
must participate actively in decisions that affect the health and well-
being of the planet. The primary responsibility rests upon those who
actually work in fields like engineering or genetics. They know the field
best and therefore have the potential to discern misapplications before
those become clear to outsiders. But because intimacy is rarely correlated with disinterestedness, I place an equal burden of responsibility
on those who work in neighboring fields, who have enough familiarity
to make informed judgments, and also can take a neutral or broader
stance. We must not remove responsibility from those who are closest
to the action. But ordinary citizens sometimes have better instincts
than those whose lives are immersed in a discipline. The problem is
that ordinary citizens are typically poorly informed and so are easy
prey to misrepresentations and deceptions.

I place hope in four groups: better-trained journalists who can clarify options for the public, political leaders who have studied the issues
and are able to explain them, ordinary citizens who are willing to
inform themselves about the issues enough to share the decision-mak-

ing burden with experts, and leaders or "trustees" of domains who will put aside their own ambitions to promote a wider good. Unfortunately, rewards in our society today favor none of these options. Yet the stakes could not be higher: If we do not make the most informed decisions—I might even say the most *intelligent* decisions—about our genetic and cultural destinies, we may find it has become too late.

For the next millennium, I nominate a new virtue: *species humility*. In the past, we honored those (like St. Francis) who were humble, even as we scorned leaders and groups guilty of hubris. But we are now one, inextricably bound world, and the unimaginable, in many forms, has become possible. As a species, we must somehow arrive at decisions about what we will do and what we will not, about which Pandora's boxes to open and which to keep shut. We have eliminated smallpox and polio, and we stand on the verge of eliminating biological warfare and land mines. Perhaps we can also agree not to manipulate the intellectual capacities of future generations.

GREATER INDIVIDUATION:
A CHALLENGE FOR THE FUTURE

A wondrous feature of life is that we humans differ from one another, and, despite the homogenization of the world, our differences show no sign of declining. Indeed, the opposite is the case. Humans evolved to live in small groups, with similar experiences from one day to the next and from one generation to the next. In such milieus, the number of "models for living" were small. We now live in a global village, with rapid change and constant contact with thousands of others. The more experiences we have, the more media we are exposed to, the more people we interact with, the greater the differences that are likely to emerge. Diversity is the order of the millennium.

If the past millennium ushered in greater democracy, this one should usher in greater individuation—individuation, not in the sense of self-ishness or self-seeking, but in the sense of knowledge about and respect for each individual. We already can know a great deal about individuals, and we are learning even more from genetics, psychology, and other behavioral and biological sciences. Information widely available in databases will allow us to determine how we resemble and differ from one another and will empower us to make more judicious life decisions.

We cannot avoid moral issues. Individual information can be used to manipulate us; intelligent programmed agents can serve us what they *think* we want or what they *want* us to want. And there is no guarantee that we will make sensible use of information about ourselves. In certain spheres we will not want to dote on our individuality; we hope, for example, that everyone will honor the laws of driving and will show civility to each other on the road. But when it comes to learning, using our minds well, and informing others and being informed by others, there need be no limitations. Knowledge need not be competitive; we can all increase our own knowledge and the knowledge of others without end, without the peril of zero-sum situations. Indeed, information about our own minds and the minds of others can be mobilized to broaden our understandings in myriad ways and to open up new vistas.

Everyone acknowledges the importance of science and technology, but it is also important to remember the necessity for the arts and the humanities. The sciences deal with general principles, universal laws, and broad predictions; the arts and humanities deal with individuality. We learn about seminal historical figures in their individuality; we explore the psyches of diverse (and often perverse) characters in literature; we gain from artists' and musicians' reflections of their own emotional lives through their works. Every time we are exposed to a new individual—in person or in spirit—our own horizons broaden. And the possibilities of experiencing different consciousnesses never diminish. The humanist of classical times said, "Nothing human is alien to me"; and the saga of individual consciousnesses cannot be reduced to formulas or generalizations.

Here, we connect to multiple human intelligences. Granted only our species membership, we are fundamentally alike. Factoring in each person's unique genetic blueprint, we become capable of achieving different potentials, and our different family and cultural milieus ensure that we will eventually become distinct human beings. Because our genes and our experiences are unique and because our brains must figure out meanings, no two selves, no two consciousnesses, no two minds are exactly alike. Each of us is therefore situated to make a unique contribution to the world. In the recognition of our individuality, we may discover our deepest common tie—that we are all joint products of natural and cultural evolution. And we may discover why we must join forces, in a complementary but synergistic way, to make sure that Nature and Culture survive for future generations.

NOTES

CHAPTER 1. INTELLIGENCE AND INDIVIDUALITY

page

2 The role of symbol analysts is discussed in R. Herrnstein and C. Murray, *The Bell Curve* (New York: Free Press, 1994) and in R. B. Reich, *The Work of Nations: Preparing Ourselves for Twenty-first Century Capitalism* (New York: Knopf, 1991).

2 F. Galton's views on intelligence are described in his *Inquiries into Human Faculty and its Development* (New York: Dutton, 1883); and *Hereditary Genius: An Inquiry into Its Laws and Consequences*. London: Watts, 1892.

4 The Emerson comment "Character is more important" is quoted in the frontispiece for Robert Coles, *The Moral Intelligence of Children* (New York: Random House, 1997).

CHAPTER 2. BEFORE MULTIPLE INTELLIGENCES

8 See R. Herrnstein and C. Murray, *The Bell Curve* (New York: Free Press, 1994).

8 For opinions on Herrnstein and Murray's ideas, see S. Fraser (ed.), *The Bell Curve Wars; Race, Intelligence and the Future of America* (New York: Basic Books, 1995): and R. Jacoby and N. Glauberman (eds.), *The Bell Curve Debate: History, Documents, Opinions* (New York: Times Books, 1995).

8 See G. Myrdal, *An American Dilemma* (New York: Harper, 1944).

8 For my views on "rhetorical brinkmanship," see H. Gardner, "Cracking open the IQ box; Review of *The Bell Curve* by R. Herrnstein and C. Murray," in *American Prospect* 30, (Winter 1995): 71–80.

9 For critical scholarly reviews of *The Bell Curve*, see J. Cawley,

J. Heckman, and E. Vytacil, *Cognitive Ability and the Rising Return to Education* (Cambridge: National Bureau of Educational Research, 1998); B. Devlin et al., *Intelligence, Genes, and Success: Scientists Respond to the Bell Curve* (New York: Springer, 1997); C. S. Fischer, *Inequality by Design* (Princeton, N.J.: Princeton University Press, 1996); and U. Neisser (ed.), *The Rising Curve* (Washington, D.C.: The American Psychological Association, 1998).

9 See A. Jensen, "How much can we boost IQ and scholastic achievement?" *Harvard Educational Review* 39, no. 1 (1969): 1–123.

10 See D. Goleman's two books, *Emotional Intelligence* (New York: Bantam Books, 1995); and *Working with Emotional Intelligence* (New York: Bantam Books, 1998).

11 Details on the history of intelligence testing appear in H. Gardner, *Frames of Mind: The Theory of Multiple Intelligences* (New York: Basic Books, 1983); H. Gardner, M. Kornhaber, and W. Wake, *Intelligence: Multiple Perspectives* (Fort Worth, Tex.: Harcourt Brace, 1996); R. J. Sternberg, *Beyond IQ* (New York: Cambridge University Press, 1985); and A. Binet and T. Simon, *The Development of Intelligence in Children* (1916; reprint, New York: Arno Press, 1973).

12 For details on Stern's development of the intelligence quotient, see W. Stern, "The Psychological Methods for Testing Intelligence," in *A Sourcebook in the History of Psychology*, eds. R. J. Herrnstein and E. G. Boring (1912; reprint, Cambridge, Mass.: Harvard University Press, 1965).

12 For the work of Terman and Yerkes, see L. Terman, *The Measurement of Intelligence* (Boston: Houghton Mifflin, 1916); and R. M. Yerkes, *Psychological Examining in the United States Army* (Washington, D.C.: U. S. Government Printing Office, 1921).

13 A discussion of the debate between Lippmann and Terman is found in W. Lippmann, "Readings from the Lippmann-Terman Debate," in *The IQ Controversy: Critical Readings*, eds. N. Block and G. Dworkin (1922–1923; reprint, New York: Pantheon Books, 1976).

13 Boring, "Intelligence is what . . ." is in E. G. Boring, "Intelligence as the tests test it," *New Republic*, 6 June 1923, pp. 35–37.

14 For the work of Charles Spearman, see his "'General Intelligence' Objectively Determined and Measured," *American Journal of Psychology* 15(1904): 201–93.

14 For the work of L. L. Thurstone, see his "Primary Mental Abilities," *Psychological Monographs* 1(1938).

14 Guilford's "factors of the intellect" are described in J. P. Guilford, *The Structure of Intelligence* (New York: McGraw Hill, 1967).

14 A discussion of factor analysis and the intelligence debates is found in S. J. Gould, *The Mismeasure of Man* (New York: Norton, 1981; rev. ed., 1995).

14 Charles Darwin's remark to Francis Galton is quoted in P. Bowler, "Defining Darwinist," *Times Literary Supplement*, 21 November 1998, p. 30.

15 For a discussion of the heritability issue, see T. J. Bouchard and P. Propping, *Twins as a Tool of Behavioral Genetics: Report of the Dahlem Workshop on What Are the Mechanisms Mediating the Genetic and Environmental Determinants of Behavior* (Chichester, U.K.: Wiley, 1993); and R. Plomin, *Genetics and Experience: The Interplay Between Nature and Nurture* (Thousand Oaks, Calif.: Sage, 1994).

15 The arguments against heritability are presented in S. Ceci, *On Intelligence . . . More or Less: A Bio-Ecological Treatise on Intellectual Development* (Englewood Cliffs, N.J.: Prentice Hall, 1990); M. W. Feldman and S. P. Otto, "Twin Studies, Heritability, and Intelligence," *Science* (1997): 278; and R. Lewontin, S. Rose, and L. Kamin, *Not in Our Genes: Biology, Ideology, and Human Nature* (New York: Pantheon Books, 1984).

16 For a discussion of how genes and environments interact, see S. Scarr and K. McCartney "How people make their own environments: A theory of genotype-environment effects," *Child Development* 54(1983): 424–35.

16 On the issue of IQ-score differentials between black and white Americans, see U. Neisser (ed.), *The Rising Curve* (Washington D.C.: American Psychological Association, 1998); A. Jensen, *Bias in Mental Testing* (New York: Free Press, 1980); and C. Steele, "A threat in the air: How stereotypes shape intellectual identity and performance," *American Psychologist* 52 (1997) 613–29.

17 On the relationship between intelligence-test biases and social class, see N. Lemann, "The structure of success in America," *The Atlantic Monthly*, August 1993, pp. 41–60; and *The Big Test* (New York: Farrar, Straus & Giroux, 1999); D. Owen, *None of the Above: Behind the Myth of Scholastic Aptitude* (Boston: Houghton Mifflin, 1985); and P. Greenfield, "You can't take it with you" [See "The cultural evolution of IQ" in U. Neisser, *The Rising Curve* (Washington,

D.C.: American Psychological Association, 1998), pp. 81–123]. On the correlation between test scores and ZIP codes, see P. Sacks, *Standardized Minds* (New York: Basic Books, 1999).

19 For more about neuroscientists' views on intelligence, see H. Gardner, *The Mind's New Science* (New York: Basic Books, 1985); and S. Pinker, *How the Mind Works* (New York: Norton, 1997).

20 The efficiency of neural signaling is discussed in A. Jensen, "Why is reaction time correlated with psychometric *g*?" *Current Directions in Psychological Science* 2, no. 2(1993): 53–56.

20 Brain plasticity during the early years of life is discussed in M. Diamond and J. Hopson, *Magic Trees of the Mind* (New York: Dutton, 1998); and W. Greenough, J. E. Black, and C. S. Wallace, "Experience and brain development," *Child Development* 58(1987): 539–59.

20 On new trends in computer science that relate to the concept of intelligence, see D. Rumelhart and J. McClelland, *Parallel Distributed Processing* (Cambridge, Mass.: MIT Press, 1986); and J. Elman et al., *Rethinking Innateness* (Cambridge, Mass.: MI theory Press, 1996).

22 For details about the work of R. J. Sternberg, see his *Beyond IQ.*

24 The work of other psychologists who have recently examined neglected aspects of intelligence is discussed in J. Greeno, "The situationality of knowing, learning, and research," *American Psychologist* 53, no. 1 (January 1998): 5–26; J. Lave, "Situated learning in communities of practice," in *Perspectives in Socially Shared Cognition*, eds. L. B. Resnick, J. M Levine, and S. D. Teasley (Washington, D.C.: American Psychological Association, 1991), pp. 63–82; D. R. Olson, *Media and Symbols* (Chicago: University of Chicago Press, 1974); R. Pea, "Practices of Distributed Intelligence and Designs for Education," in *Distributed Cognitions,* ed. G. Salomon (New York: Cambridge University Press, 1993), pp. 47–87; D. Perkins, *Outsmarting IQ* (New York: Free Press, 1995); and G. Salomon, *Distributed Cognitions* (New York: Cambridge University Press, 1993).

24 Recent books on other kinds of intelligence include R. Coles, *The Moral Intelligence of Children* (New York: Random House, 1997); D. Goleman, *Emotional Intelligence* (New York: Bantam, 1995); R.J. Sternberg, *Successful Intelligence* (New York: Simon & Schuster, 1997); and H. Gardner et al., *Intelligence: Multiple Perspectives* (New York: Harcourt Brace, 1996).

24 For an introduction to the contemporary landscape, see H. Gardner, M. Kornhaber, and W. Wake, *Intelligence: Multiple Perspectives*

(New York: Harcourt Brace, 1996).

CHAPTER 3. THE THEORY OF MULTIPLE INTELLIGENCES: A PERSONAL PERSPECTIVE

27 For details about the author's early life, see H. Gardner, *To Open Minds: Chinese Clues to the Dilemma of Contemporary Education* (New York: Basic Books, 1989).

27 The work of these psychologists, who strongly influenced the author's early research career, is described in J. S. Bruner, *The Process of Education* (Cambridge, Mass.: Harvard University Press, 1960); H. Gruber and J. Vonèche, *The Essential Piaget* (New York: Basic Books, 1978); N. Goodman, *Languages of Art* (Indianapolis: Hackett, 1976); and N. Geschwind, *Selected Papers* (Boston: Reidel, 1974).

30 The ravages of brain injury are described in H. Gardner, *The Shattered Mind: The Person After Brain Damage* (New York: Vintage, 1976).

32 For more about the organization of brain capacities in left-handers, see M. Annett, *Left, Right, Hand, and Brain: The Right Shift Theory* (Hillsdale, N.J.: Erlbaum, 1985); and S. Coren (ed.), *Left-handedness: Behavioral Indications and Anomalies* (Amsterdam: North Holland Publishing, 1990).

32 The "modularity" view of the human brain is described in J. Barkow, L. Cosmides, and J. Tooby, *The Adapted Mind: Evolutionary Psychology and the Generation of Culture* (New York: Oxford University Press, 1992); N. Chomsky, *Rules and Representation* (New York: Columbia University Press, 1980); J. A. Fodor, *The Modularity of Mind* (Cambridge, Mass.: MIT Press, 1983); and S. Pinker, *How the Mind Works* (New York: Norton, 1997).

32 The Project on Human Potential is described in H. Gardner, introductory note, *Frames of Mind*, and Gardner, *To Open Minds*, op. cit., chapter 5.

36 The emerging field of evolutionary psychology is discussed in J. Barkow et al., *The Adapted Mind*; S. Mithen, *The Prehistory of the Mind* (London: Thames & Hudson, 1996); S. Pinker, *How the Mind Works* (New York: Norton, 1997); and E. O. Wilson, *Sociobiology* (Cambridge, Mass.: Harvard University Press, 1975).

37 The notion of symbol systems is discussed in H. Gardner, "Extraor-

dinary cognitive achievements: a symbol systems approach," in *Theoretical Models of Human Development*, volume 1 of *The Handbook of Child Psychology*, 5*th* ed., ed. R. M. Lerner (New York: Wiley, 1997).

38 The relation between symbols systems and the human brain is discussed in T. Deacon, *The Symbolic Species* (New York: Norton, 1997).

39 For the abilities of autistic people, see F. Happé, *Autism: An Introduction to Psychological Theory* (Cambridge, Mass.: Harvard University Press, 1995).

39 The characteristics of prodigies are discussed in D. Feldman, *Nature's Gambit* (New York: Basic Books, 1986); and E. Winner, *Gifted Children* (New York: Basic Books, 1996).

40 For a discussion of how activities can draw on discrete brain and mental capacities, see M. Kinsbourne, "The control of attention by interaction between the cerebral hemispheres," in *Attention and Performance* (New York: Academic Press, 1983), pp. 239–56.

41 Social intelligence and emotional intelligence are considered in R. Rosnow et al., "Intelligence and the epistemics of interpersonal assessment: Testing some implications of Gardner's theories," *Intelligence* 19(1994): 93–116; and P. Salovey and J. Mayer, "Emotional intelligence," *Imagination, Cognition, and Personality* 9(1990): 185–211.

CHAPTER 4. ARE THERE ADDITIONAL INTELLIGENCES?

48 "Folk taxonomies" are discussed in B. Berlin, *Ethnobiological Classification: Principles of Categorization of Plants and Animals in Traditional Societies* (Princeton, N.J.: Princeton University Press, 1992).

48 Darwin "born a naturalist" is quoted in J. Browne, *Voyaging,* volume 1 of *Charles Darwin: A Biography* (New York: Knopf, 1995).

48 Wilson describes his background in his book *Naturalist* (Washington D.C.: Island Press/Shearwater Books, 1994).

49 For details about Geermat Vermig, see C. K. Yoon, "Getting the Feel of a Long-Ago Arms Race," *New York Times*, 7 February 1995, Science section, p. 8.

49 On "biophilia," see E. O. Wilson, *Biophilia* (Cambridge, Mass.: Harvard University Press, 1984).

49 On birds' ability to indicate which forms in photographs are

humans, see G. M. Edelman, *The Wordless Metaphor: Visual Art and the Brain* (New York: Whitney Museum, in press); R. Herrnstein and D. Loveland, "Natural concepts in pigeons," *Journal of Experimental Psychology: Animal Behavior Processes*: 2(1976): 285–302; and R. Wasserman, "The conceptual abilities of pigeons," *American Scientist* 83(1994): 246–55.

50 The scale from novice to expert for a budding naturalist is discussed in S. Carey, *Conceptual Change in Childhood* (Cambridge, Mass.: MIT Press, 1985); and F. Keil, "The birth and nurturance of concepts by domains: The origins of concepts of living things," in *Mapping the Mind*, ed. L. Hirschfield and S. A. Gelman (New York: Cambridge University Press, 1994), pp. 234–54.

50 For more on the work of biologically oriented scientists, see M. Csikszentmihalyi, *Creativity* (New York: HarperCollins, 1996); A. Roe, *The Making of a Scientist* (New York: Dodd, Mead, 1953); C. Taylor and F. Barron, *Scientific Creativity, Its Recognition and Development* (New York: Wiley, 1964); and H. Zuckerman, *Scientific Elites* (New York: Free Press, 1977).

51 For more on the clinical brain-damage literature, see J. Konorski, *Integrative Activity of the Brain: An Interdisciplinary Approach* (Chicago: University of Chicago Press, 1967); and J. Nielsen, *Agnosia, Apraxia, and Aphasia: Their Value in Cerebral Localization* (New York: Hoeber, 1946).

51 Experimental findings are discussed in A. Caramazza et al., "The organization of lexical knowledge in the brain: Evidence from category- and modality-specific deficits," in *Mapping the Mind*, eds. L. Hirschfield and S. Gelman (New York: Cambridge University Press, 1994), pp. 68–84; A. Damasio and H. Damasio, "Recent trends in cognitive neuroscience," lecture presented at the Center for Advanced Study in the Behavioral Sciences, Stanford, Calif., June 1995; A. Martin, C. L. Wiggs, L. Ungerleider, and J. W. Haxby, "Neural correlates of category-specific knowledge," *Nature* 379 (1996): 649–52; and E. Warrington and R. Shallice, "Category-specific semantic impairments," *Brain* 107(1984): 829–54.

51 For details on the neural networks involved in face recognition, see C. B. Gross, "Visual functions of infero-temporal cortex," in *Handbook of Sensory Physiology, VII/3*, ed. R. Jung (New York: Springer Verlag, 1973), pp. 451–82; and E. Rosch, C. Mervis, W. Gray, D. Johnson, and P. Bayes-Braem, "Basic objects in natural cate-

gories," *Cognitive Psychology* 8(1976): 382–439.

55   For more on ways of achieving spiritual states, see D. Goleman, *The Meditative Mind* (New York: Putnam, 1988); and K. Wilber, *The Eye of Spirit* (Boston: Shambhala, 1997).

57   Phenomenology of the spiritual is discussed in J. Mishlove, *Roots of Consciousness* (Tulsa, Okla.: Council Oaks Books, 1993), p. 66.

57   The significance of one's spiritual effects on others is discussed in A. Storr, *Feet of Clay* (New York: Free Press, 1996).

57   The role of charisma in religious and spiritual processes is discussed in H. H. Gerth and C. W. Mills, *From Max Weber: Essays in Sociology* (New York: Oxford University Press, 1958).

61   Pope John XXIII's painstaking training is discussed in H. Gardner, *Leading Minds* (New York: Basic Books, 1995).

61   How a lama proves his mettle is described in "Tibetans Call Boy Reincarnation of No. 2 Monk," *New York Times*, 14 May 1995, p. A4.

62   For a discussion of early humans' grappling with existential issues, see Csikszentmihalyi, *Creativity*; and Storr, *Feet of Clay*.

62   Early humans' artwork and dance are discussed in W. Burkert, *Creation of the Sacred: Tracks of Biology in Early Religions* (Cambridge, Mass.: Harvard University Press, 1995).

63   Consciousness in its fullest senses is discussed in E. Havelock, *Preface to Plato* (Cambridge, Mass.: Harvard University Press, 1963); and J. Jaynes, *The Origins of Consciousness in the Breakdown of the Bicameral Mind* (Boston: Houghton Mifflin, 1974).

63   Temporal-lobe epilepsy is discussed in D. Bear, R. Freeman, D. Schiff, and M. Greenberg, "Interictal behavioral changes in patients with temporal lobe epilepsy," in *American Psychiatric Association Annual Review*, no. 4(1985), ed. R. E. Hales and A. J. Frances; N. Geschwind, "Behavioral change in temporal lobe epilepsy," *Archives of Neurology*: 34(1977), 453; and E. La Plante, *Seized* (New York: HarperCollins, 1993).

63   For more about the possible adaptive significance of ultimate concerns, see S. Pinker, *How the Mind Works* (New York: Norton, 1997).

63   Heightened attention in "flow states" is discussed in M. Csikszentmihalyi, *Flow* (New York: HarperCollins, 1990).

63   The brain centers mobilized in flow states are described in R. Orn-

stein, *The Nature of Human Consciousness* (San Francisco: Freeman, 1973).

64 Studies of identical twins' religiosity are discussed in T. Bouchard, "Sources of human psychological differences: The Minnesota study of twins reared apart," *Science* 250(1990): 223–28.

64 For another view of the plausibility of spiritual intelligence, based on the several criteria, see R. Emmons, "Is spirituality an intelligence?" *International Journal for Psychology of Religion* (1999), in press, and my response "A Case against Spiritual Intelligence," *Ibid.*

66 Proust, "It is inconceivable. . . " is from M. Proust, *Remembrance of Things Past,* vol. 3, trans. C. K. Scott Moncrieff, T. Kilmartin, and A. Mayor (New York: Random House), pp. 380–81.

CHAPTER 5. IS THERE A MORAL INTELLIGENCE?

67 For another perspective on the disjunction between description and prescription, see L. Kohlberg "From Is to Ought: How to commit the naturalistic fallacy and get away with it in the study of mental development," in *Cognitive Development and Epistemology,* ed. T. Mischel (New York: Academic Press, 1971), pp. 151–235.

69 On emotional intelligence and a set of recommended behaviors, see D. Goleman, *Emotional Intelligence* (New York: Bantam Books, 1985).

69 Scholars' attempts to delineate a moral domain are discussed in W. Damon, *The Moral Child* (New York: The Free Press, 1988); M. Hoffman, "Affective and cognitive processes in moral internalization," in *Social Cognition and Social Behavior,* ed. E. T. Higgins et al. (New York: Cambridge University Press, 1981); L. Kohlberg, *The Psychology of Moral Development* (New York: Harper & Row, 1984); A. MacIntyre, *After Virtue* (Notre Dame, Ind.: Notre Dame University Press, 1981); J. Rawls, *A Theory of Justice* (Cambridge, Mass.: Harvard University Press, 1971); E. Turiel, "The development of morality," in *Handbook of Child Psychology,* vol. 3, ed. N. Eisenberg (New York: Wiley, 1998), pp. 863–932; and B. Williams, *Ethics and the Limits of Philosophy* (Cambridge, Mass.: Harvard University Press, 1985).

70 Differing views in the way society defines what is moral are discussed in R. Shweder, M. Mahaputra, and J. Miller, "Culture and moral

development," in J. Kagan and S. Lamb (eds.), *Emergence of Morality in Young Children* (Chicago: University of Chicago Press, 1987), pp. 1–83; and E. Turiel, *The Development of Social Knowledge: Morality and Convention* (New York: Cambridge University Press, 1983).

71 For more on children's sense of right and wrong, see J. Kagan, *The Nature of the Child* (New York: Basic Books, 1984).

71 The characteristic development trajectory for a moral sense is discussed in Damon, *The Moral Child*; and Kohlberg, *The Psychology of Moral Development*.

71 For information about the sense of right and wrong in primates, see F. B. M. de Waal, *Good Natured: The Origins of Right and Wrong in Humans and Other Animals* (Cambridge, Mass.: Harvard University Press, 1996).

71 Evolutionary psychologists' views are discussed in J. Tooby and L. Cosmides, "Psychological Foundations of Culture," in *The Adapted Mind: Evolutionary Psychology and the Generation of Culture*, eds. J. Barkow, L. Cosmides, and J. Tooby (New York: Cambridge University Press, 1992); and R. Wright, *The Moral Animal* (New York: Vintage, 1995).

71 The association between pathology and a sense of right and wrong is discussed in A. Damasio, *Descartes' Error* (New York: Putnam, 1994).

72 For studies of the mental makeup of creators and leaders, see H. Gardner, *Creating Minds* (New York: Basic Books, 1993); *Leading Minds* (New York: Basic Books, 1995); and *Extraordinary Minds* (New York: Basic Books, 1997).

72 On the moral sense of creative people, see M. Csikszentmihalyi, *Creativity* (New York: HarperCollins, 1996).

73 For the moral concerns of gifted children, see E. Winner, *Gifted Children* (New York: Basic Books, 1996).

73 More information about Pope John XXIII can be found in Gardner, *Leading Minds*.

74 Self-understanding as related to moral concerns is discussed in Damasio, *Descartes' Error*; P. Salovey and J. Mayer, "Emotional intelligence," *Imagination, Cognition, and Personality* 9(1990): 185–211.

75 The rights and obligations of robots were considered by K. Warwick in a presentation at the World Economic Forum in Davos, Switzerland, 30 January 1998.

76 For research on the issue of moral judgments, see L. Kohlberg; and C. Gilligan, *In a Different Voice* (Cambridge, Mass.: Harvard University Press, 1982).

76 For a discussion of moral behaviors, see S. Milgram, "Group pressure and action against a person," *Journal of Abnormal and Social Psychology* 69(1964): 137–43; K. Keniston, *Young Radicals* (New York: Harcourt Brace & World, 1968); and S. P. Oliner and P. M. Oliner, *The Altruistic Personality: Rescuers of Jews in Nazi Europe* (New York: Free Press, 1988).

CHAPTER 6. MYTHS AND REALITIES ABOUT MULTIPLE INTELLIGENCES

79 For more about memes, see R. Dawkins, *The Selfish Gene* (Oxford: Oxford University Press, 1976).

81 On the need for assessment to occur in a comfortable setting with familiar materials, see H. Gardner, *Multiple Intelligences: The Theory in Practice* (New York: Basic Books, 1991).

81 For details of Project Spectrum, see Gardner, *Multiple Intelligences*; and also H. Gardner, D. H. Feldman, and M. Krechevsky (eds.), *Project Zero Frameworks for Early Childhood Education* (New York: Teachers College Press, 1998).

82 For more on the collaborations with Csikszentmihalyi and Feldman, see D. Feldman, M. Csikszentmihalyi, and H. Gardner, *Changing the World: A Framework for the Study of Creativity* (Westport, Conn.: Greenwood Publishing Co., 1994).

83 On the topic of style, see J. Kagan and N. Kogan, "Individual variation in cognitive processes," in *Carmichael's Manual of Child Psychology*, vol. 1, ed. P. H. Mussen (New York: Wiley, 1970).

84 Silver's intriguing proposal appears in H. Silver, R. Strong, and M. Perini, "Integrating learning styles and multiple intelligences," *Educational Leadership* 55, no. 1 (September 1997): 22–29.

85 For a discussion of social intelligence, see R. Rosnow et al., "Intelligence and the epistemics of interpersonal assessment: Testing some implications of Gardner's theories," *Intelligence* 19(1994): 93–116.

85 A "theory of mind" is discussed in J. Astington, *The Child's Discovery of the Mind* (Cambridge, Mass.: Harvard University Press, 1993).

86 For more on the minds of autistic children, see F. Happé, *Autism: An Introduction to Psychological Theory* (Cambridge, Mass.: Harvard University Press, 1995).

86 On the link between musical and spatial capacities, see F. H. Rauscher, G. L. Shaw, and K. N. Ky, "Musical and spatial task performance," *Nature* 365(1993): 611; and F. H. Rauscher, G. L. Shaw, and K. N. Ky, "Listening to Mozart enhances spatial-temporal reasoning: Towards a neurophysiological basis," *Neuroscience Letters* 185(1995): 44–47.

87 For research on general intelligence (*g*), see the notes for chapter 2.

87 For research on heritability and genetics, see the notes for chapter 2, and M. J. Chorney et al., "A quantitative trait locus associated with cognitive ability in children," *Psychological Science* 9, no. 3 (May 1998): 159–66.

87 For a discussion of the dynamic interaction between genetic and environmental factors, see H. Gardner. T. Hatch, and B. Torff, "A Third Perspective: The Symbol Systems Approach," in *Intelligence, Heredity, and Environment*, eds. R. J. Sternberg and E. Grigorenko (New York: Cambridge University Press, 1997), pp. 243–68.

88 For more about the Suzuki Music Talent Education Program, see H. Gardner, *Frames of Mind*.

CHAPTER 7. ISSUES AND ANSWERS REGARDING
MULTIPLE INTELLIGENCES

94 On linguistic information being mobilized by visual information, see P. Rozin, "The evolution of intelligence and access to the cognitive unconscious," *Progress in Psychobiology and Physiological Psychology* 6(1976): 245–80.

95 On bodily performances that involve computation, see J. A. S. Kelso, *Dynamic Patterns: The Self-Organization of Brain and Behavior* (Cambridge, Mass.: MIT Press, 1996); E. Thelen and L. B. Smith, "Dynamic Systems Theories," in *Handbook of Child Psychology*, vol. 1, ed. R. Lerner (New York: Wiley, 1998), pp. 563–634.

101 For a discussion of horizontal faculties versus a vertical view of mind, see J. A. Fodor, *The Modularity of Mind* (Cambridge, Mass.: MIT Press, 1983).

104 Different kinds of memory are discussed in D. Schacter, *Searching for Memory* (New York: Basic Books, 1997).

106 For a critique of critical thinking, see M. Kornhaber and H. Gardner, "Critical Thinking Across Multiple Intelligences," in *Learning to Think: Thinking to Learn: The Proceedings of the 1989 OECD Conference,* eds. S. Maclure and P. Davies (Oxford: Pergamon Press, 1991), pp. 147–68.

109 For information about MI theory in schools that highlight the arts, see the preliminary results of the SUMIT Project (Schools Using Multiple Intelligences Theory) directed by Mindy Kornhaber at Harvard Project Zero, at http://pzweb.harvard.edu/SUMIT

109 On group differences in intelligences and their possible meanings, see H. Gardner, *Frames of Mind*; and E. Winner, *Gifted Children*.

110 Details about Carol Gilligan's work are found in C. Gilligan, *In a Different Voice* (Cambridge, Mass.: Harvard University Press, 1982).

111 The spatial intelligence of rodents is discussed in K. Cheng, "A purely geometric module in the rat's spatial representation," *Cognition* 23(1986): 149–78.

CHAPTER 8. THE INTELLIGENCES OF CREATORS AND LEADERS

115 On the distinctions among different intellectual virtues, see Gardner, *Multiple Intelligences*; and Gardner, *Extraordinary Minds*.

116 On creativity, see Gardner, *Creating Minds* (New York: Basic Books, 1993); and M. Csikszentmihalyi, *Creativity* (New York: HarperCollins, 1996).

118 The question "Where is creativity?" is discussed in M. Csikszentmihalyi, "Society, culture, and person: A systems view of creativity," in *The Nature of Creativity*, ed. R. Sternberg (New York: Cambridge University Press, 1998), pp. 325–38.

119 For a discussion of long-time immersion in a domain, see J. R. Hayes, *The Complete Problem Solver,* 2nd ed. (Hillsdale, N.J.: Erlbaum, 1989).

120 Personalities of creators are explored in F. Barron, *Creative Person and Creative Process* (New York: Holt, Rinehart & Winston, 1969).

123 On the intelligences of some famous creators, see Gardner, *Creating Minds*, chap. 10.

125 For an elaborated view of leadership, see Gardner, *Leading Minds* (New York: Basic Books, 1995).
126 More about Thatcher is found in H. Gardner, *Leading Minds*, chap. 12; and H. Young, *The Iron Lady: A Biography of Margaret Thatcher* (New York: Farrar, Straus & Giroux, 1989).
129 Louis Gerstner at IBM is discussed in Gardner, *Leading Minds*, p. 144.

CHAPTER 9. MULTIPLE INTELLIGENCES IN THE SCHOOLS
135 For general discussions of the assessment of multiple intelligences, see H. Gardner, *Multiple Intelligences* (New York: Basic Books, 1993), chaps. 10–11.
136 The Spectrum classroom is discussed in *Multiple Intelligences*, chap. 6; and H. Gardner, M. Krechevsky, and D. Feldman (eds.), *Project Zero Frameworks for Early Childhood Education* (New York: Teachers College Press, 1998).
140 The staff of the New City School has written about this approach in two books: *Celebrating Multiple Intelligences* (1994) and *Succeeding with Multiple Intelligences* (1996). These may be obtained from the school in St. Louis, or from various distributors, such as National Professional Resources or Zephyr Press.
148 On the work of Ernesto Cortes and the Alliance Schools Network, see D. Shirley, *Community Organizing for Urban School Reform* (Austin, Tex.: University of Texas Press, 1997).
154 East Asian educational approaches are described in H. Stevenson and J. Stigler, *The Learning Gap: Why Our Schools are Failing and What We Can Learn from Japanese and Chinese Education* (New York: Simon & Schuster, 1992).

CHAPTER 10. MULTIPLE APPROACHES TO UNDERSTANDING
160 For a discussion of education as a basis for enhanced understanding, see M. S. Wiske (ed.), *Teaching for Understanding* (San Francisco: Jossey-Bass, 1998); and also D. Cohen et al., *Teaching for Understanding* (San Francisco: Jossey-Bass, 1993).
162 For more about students' difficulties in understanding important ideas, see G. Wiggins and J. McTighe, *Understanding by Design* (Alexandria, Va.: ASCD, 1998); H. Gardner, *The Unschooled Mind:*

How Children Think, and How Schools Should Teach (New York: Basic Books, 1991); and H. Gardner, *The Disciplined Mind: What All Students Should Understand* (New York: Simon & Schuster, 1999).

165 For more about the "Teaching for Understanding" approach, see Wiske, *Teaching for Understanding*; and T. Blythe, *The Teaching for Understanding Guide* (San Francisco: Jossey-Bass, 1998).

167 Examples of the true, the beautiful, and the good are discussed further in H. Gardner, *The Disciplined Mind* (New York: Simon & Schuster, 1999).

171 See S. Milgram, *Obedience to Authority* (New York: Harper & Row, 1974).

177 For new scholarship about the Holocaust that clarifies the involvement of ordinary citizens in Hitler's plans, see D. Goldhagen, *Hitler's Willing Executioners* (New York: Knopf, 1996).
Mihaly Csikszentmihalyi, William Damon, and I are exploring these issues of responsibility in a large-scale research project. We expect to publish our initial findings shortly.

177 Punctuated equilibrium is discussed in Stephen Jay Gould, *Wonderful Life* (New York: Norton, 1993).

178 The views of conservative educational critics are described in E. D. Hirsch, *The Schools We Need and Why We Don't Have Them* (New York: Doubleday, 1996).

CHAPTER 11. MULTIPLE INTELLIGENCES IN THE WIDER WORLD

184 Children's museums are discussed in H. Gardner, *The Unschooled Mind: How Children Think and How Schools Should Teach* (New York: Basic Books, 1991), chap. 11; and Please Touch Museum and Harvard Project Zero, *Project Explore: A two-year study on how and what young children learn in children's museums* (Cambridge, Mass.: Please Touch Museum and Harvard Project Zero, October 1998).

188 For information on MUSE, see J. Davis et al., *The Muse Guide: A Training Manual for Using Muse Tools* (Cambridge, Mass.: Harvard Graduate School of Education, 1997). Available from Harvard Project Zero, Longfellow Hall, Cambridge, MA 02138.

189 The visual thinking curriculum is based on the research of Abigail

Housen and was developed by Housen in conjunction with Philip Yenawine at the Museum of Modern Art. See A. Housen, "Three methods for understanding museum audiences," *Museum Studies Journal* 2, no. 4(1987): 41–49. For information on the Visual Thinking Curriculum, contact the Dept. of Education, Museum of Modern Art, 11 W. 53rd Street, New York, NY 10022.

189 For a general discussion of developmental stages in viewing works of art, see M. Parsons, *How We Understand Art* (New York: Cambridge University Press, 1987).

192 On shareholders in Britain, see G. Mulgan, *Connexity* (London: Chatto and Windus, 1997).

192 On the civic function of schools, the best source is still the writings of John Dewey. See R. Archambault (ed.), *John Dewey on Education: Selected Writings* (Chicago: University of Chicago Press, 1964). See also C. Glickman, *Democracy as Education* (San Francisco: Jossey-Bass, 1998); and D. Meier, *The Power of Their Ideas* (Boston: Beacon Press, 1995).

193 For more on "hot-button" topics, see P. Graham, *Sustain Our Schools* (New York: Hill & Wang, 1992).

193 The new business environment is discussed in P. Senge, *The Fifth Discipline: The Art and Practice of the Learning Organization* (New York: Doubleday, 1990).

194 Not much has yet been written about the use of MI ideas in business and the workplace. One scholar who has worked on this issue is Joyce Martin at Australian Catholic University (see appendix D). Karen Pennar has written about it in "How Many Smarts Do You Have?" *Business Week*, 16 September 1996, pp. 104–8.

199 For further discussion of businesses and personal intelligences, see D. Goleman, *Working with Emotional Intelligence* (New York: Bantam Books, 1998); and P. Drucker, "Managing oneself," *Harvard Business Review* (April–May 1999): 65–74.

CHAPTER 12. WHO OWNS INTELLIGENCE?

205 The Golden Rule is discussed in A. Etzioni, *The New Golden Rule* (New York: Basic Books, 1996).

205 Moral reasoning tests are compared with moral behaviors in A. Colby and W. Damon, *Some Do Care* (New York: Free Press, 1992).

205 On the men who laid the plans to implement the Final Solution, see D. Patterson, *When Learned Men Murder* (Bloomington, Ind.: Phi Delta Kappan Educational Foundation,1996).

206 See D. Goleman, *Emotional Intelligence* (New York: Bantam, 1995).

210 Identifying the genes for general intelligence: M.J. Chorney, K. Chorney et al., "A quantitative trait locus associated with cognitive ability in children," *Psychological Science,* 9, no. 3 (May 1998): 159–66.

211 Intelligences used in concert: E. Hutchins, "The Social Organization of Distributed Intelligence," in *Perspectives in Socially Shaped Cognition,* ed. L. B. Resnick, J. M. Levine, and D. Teasley (Washington, D.C.: American Psychological Association, 1995), pp. 283–307; T. Kidder, *The Soul of a New Machine* (Boston: Little, Brown, 1981).

213 The forerunners of *Homo sapiens* are discussed in S. Mithen, *The Prehistory of the Mind* (London: Thames & Hudson, 1996).

215 On the cloning of the sheep Dolly, see G. Kolata, *Clone: The Road to Dolly and the Path Ahead* (New York: Morrow, 1998.)

APPENDIX A

BOOKS AND ARTICLES BY HOWARD GARDNER

I. Authored by Howard Gardner

Gardner, H. (1983). *Frames of mind: The theory of multiple intelligences.* New York: Basic Books. Selected by five book clubs. British Edition, W. Heinemann. Translated into Spanish, Japanese, Italian, Hebrew, Chinese, French, and German. Basic Books Paperback, 1985.

Gardner, H. (1984, June). Assessing intelligences: A comment on "Testing intelligence without IQ tests" by Robert Sternberg. *Phi Delta Kappan,* 699–700.

Gardner, H. (1984). The development of competence in culturally-defined domains. In R. Shweder & R. Levine (Eds.), *Culture Theory: Essays on Mind, Self, and Emotion.* New York: Cambridge University Press.

Gardner, H. (1985). On discerning new ideas in psychology. *New Ideas in Psychology, 3,* 101–104.

Gardner, H. (1985). Towards a theory of dramatic intelligence. In J. Kase-Polisini (Ed.), *Creative Drama in a Developmental Context.* University Press of America.

Gardner, H. (1987). The assessment of intelligences: A neuropsychological perspective. In M. Meier, A. Benton & L. Diller (Eds.), *Neuropsychological Rehabilitation.* London: Churchill Publishers.

Gardner, H. (1987). An individual-centered curriculum. In *The schools we've got, the schools we need.* Washington, DC: Council of Chief State School Officers and the American Association of Colleges of Teacher Education.

Gardner, H. (1987). The theory of multiple intelligences. *Annals of Dyslexia, 37,* 19–35.

Gardner, H. (1988). Beyond a modular view of mind. In W. Damon (Ed.), Child Development Today and Tomorrow (222-239). San Francisco: Jossey-Bass Also in W. Damon (Ed.) (1987), New Directions for Child Development, Tenth Anniversary Edition.

Gardner, H. (1993). *Frames of Mind, Tenth Anniversary Edition* (with new introduction). New York: Basic Books. Translated into Swedish, German, Portuguese, Spanish, Italian, Chinese (Taiwan), French, Norwegian, Hebrew and Slovenian. Selected by three book clubs. Tenth Anniversary British Edition, London: HarperCollins (Fontana Press), 1993.

Gardner, H. (1988). The theory of multiple intelligences: Educational implications. In *Language and the World of Work in the 21st Century*. Published by Massachusetts Bureau of Transitional Bilingual Education.

Gardner, H. (1988). Mobilizing resources for individual centered education. In R. Nickerson and P. Zodhiates (Eds.), *Technology in education: Looking toward 2020*. Hillsdale, NJ: Lawrence Erlbaum.

Gardner, H. (1988, Summer). Multiple intelligence in today's schools. *Human Intelligence Newsletter, 9*, (2), 1–2.

Gardner, H. (1988, Fall). Challenges for museums: Howard Gardner's theory of multiple intelligences. *Hand to Hand, 2* (4), 1–7. Salt Lake City, UT: Children's Museum Network.

Gardner, H. (1989). Intelligences. In K. Jervis and A. Tobler (Eds.), *Education for democracy: Proceedings from the Cambridge School Conference on progressive education*. Weston, MA: The Cambridge School. Reprinted in *Putney Post*, Winter 1992, 16–20 & 30.

Gardner, H. (1990). Building on the range of human strengths. *The Churchill Forum, 12* (1), 1,2,7.

Gardner, H. (1990). The difficulties of school: Probable causes, possible cures. *Daedalus, 119* (2), 85–113. Reprinted in S. Graubard (Ed.) (1991), *Literacy* (85–113). New York: Hill and Wang.

Gardner, H. (1990). Intelligence in seven steps. In D. Dickinson (Ed.), *Creating the future*. Aston Clinic, England: Accelerated Learning Systems, Inc., pp. 68–75. Also published in *Intelligent connections, 1*, (1), Fall 1991, pp. 1, 3, 7, 8; in *Harvard Graduate School of Education Alumni Bulletin, 36*, (1), Fall 1991, pp. 17–19. Reprinted in *Provoking Thoughts, 4*(2), 1992.

Gardner, H. (1991). Cognition: A Western Perspective. In D. Goleman and R. A. F. Thurman (Eds.), *MindScience: An East-West dialogue* (75–87). Boston: Wisdom Publications. Based on a paper delivered at *Symposium on Mind Science: The Dialogue Between East and West*. Symposium conducted at the Massachusetts Institute of Technology, Cambridge, MA, March 1991.

Gardner, H. (1991). The nature of intelligence. In A. Lewin (Ed.) *How we think and learn*. Washington: National Learning Center, pp. 41–46.

Gardner, H. (1992, Autumn). From intelligence to intelligences and beyond. *Synapsia: The International Brain Club Journal, 3* (3), 5–8. Paper presented at the Young Presidents' Organization, Boston, 1991.

Gardner, H. (1992, Fall). A new edition of *Frames of mind. Developing Human Intelligence. New Horizons for Learning, 13,* 1, pp. 10–11.

Gardner, H. (1993). *Multiple Intelligences: The theory in practice.* New York: Basic Books. Translated into Spanish, Portuguese, Italian, French, Chinese (Taiwan), Hebrew, and Korean. Selected by three book clubs. Excerpted in the magazine *Behinderte in Familie, Schule und Gesellschaft, vol.* 2, 1997. Abridged, Danish translation, 1997, Copenhagen: Glydendal Undervisning

Gardner, H. (1993). The "intelligence-giftedness" complex. In H. Rosselli and G. MacLauchlan (Eds.), *Blueprinting for the future.* Proceedings from the *Edyth Bush Symposium on Intelligence,* The University of Southern Florida, Tampa, FL.

Gardner, H. (1993). Intelligence and intelligences: Universal principles and individual differences. [An essay on "Diagnosis of Mental Operations and Theory of the Intelligence."] Prepared for Festschrift in honor of the 80th birthday of Professor Barbel Inhelder. Archives de psychologie, 61 (238), 169-172.

Gardner, H. (1993). Les dimensions de l'intelligence spatiale. *MScope Revue,* 6, 45-53.

Gardner, H. (1993, Fall). Music as Intelligence. *Kodaly Envoy,* 20 (1), 14-21.

Gardner, H. (1993). Opening minds. *Demos,* Issue no. 1, pp. 1–5. Reprinted: G. Mulgan (Ed.), *Life after politics: New thinking for the twenty-first century* (101–110). London: Fontana Press, 1997.

Gardner, H. (1993). The relationship between early giftedness and later achievement. *Ciba Conference, No. 178* (175–186). Chichester: John Wiley and Sons. Paper presented at *The Origins and Development of High Ability,* CIBA, London, England.

Gardner, H. (1993, Fall). "Choice Points" as multiple intelligences enter the school. *Intelligence Connections, 3,* (1).

Gardner, H. (1993, Autumn). The unschooled mind: Why even the best students in the best schools do not understand. *International Schools Journal,* 26, 29–33. Originally presented as the *Alec Peterson Lecture to the International Baccalaureate Conference,* Geneva, Switzerland, December, 1992. See also *IB World Magazine* (1993).

Gardner, H. (1993, Winter). The school and the work place of the future. *Synapsia: The International Brain Club Journal,* 22–26.

Gardner, H. (1994). Are Intelligence Tests Intelligent? In R. H. Ettinger, R. L. Crooks, and J. Stein (Eds.), *Psychology: Science, behavior, and life*, 3d edition. Fort Worth: Harcourt Brace College Publishers, pp. 214-221.

Gardner, H. (1994). Entry on Multiple Intelligences theory. In R. Sternberg (Ed-in-Chief), *Encyclopedia of Human Intelligence*, vol. 2 (740-742). New York: Macmillan.

Gardner, H. (1994). Multiple intelligences: A view from the arts. Issues 1994, 5–22. Based on a talk delivered to a conference of the Art Educators of New Jersey, October 1993.

Gardner, H. (1994). On intelligence. In R. H. Ettinger, R. L. Crooks, and J. Stein, *Psychology: Science, behavior, and life* (515–521). Fort Worth, TX: Harcourt Brace.

Gardner, H. (1994, Jan). Multiple intelligences. *Quest*, published by Kumon Institute of Education, Korea.

Gardner, H. (1995). Perennial antinomies and perpetual redrawings: Is there progress in the study of mind? In R. Solso and D. Massaro (Eds.), *Science of the mind: 200l and beyond* (65–78). New York: Oxford University Press.

Gardner, H. (1995, Fall). Limited visions, limited means: Two obstacles to meaningful educational reform. *Daedalus, 124*, (4), 101–105.

Gardner, H. (1995, Aug/Sept). ECT Interview of the Month. *Early Childhood Today, 10*, (1), 30–32.

Gardner, H. (1995, Sept). Why would anyone become an expert? [Critique of A. Ericsson and N. Charness, Expert performance: Its structure and acquisition]. *American Psychologist, 50*, (9), 802–804.

Gardner, H. (1995, Nov). Reflections on multiple intelligences: Myths and messages. *Phi Delta Kappan, 77*, (3), 200–209. Reprinted: *International Schools Journal, 15*, (2), 8–22, European Council of International Schools. Reprinted: K.G. Duffy (Ed.), Annual Editions: Psychology 97/98 (101-105), Guilford, CT: Dushkin, 1997. Reprinted: K. M. Cauley, F. Linder, and J.H. McMillan (Eds.), *Annual Editions: Educational Psychology 97/98* (108–112), Guildford, CT: Dushkin, 1997. Reprinted, translated: E. Beck et al. (Eds.), *Lernkultur im Wandel* (45–60), St. Gallen: UVK, Fachverl. für Wiss. und Studium, 1997.

Gardner, H. (1995, Dec). 'Multiple Intelligences' as a catalyst. *English Journal, 84*, (8), 16-18.

Gardner, H. (1995, Dec 26). The meaning of multiple intelligence [sic]. *Post-Dispatch* (St. Louis, MO), 15B.

Gardner, H. "Is Musical Intelligence Special?" In Ithaca Conference '96: Music as Intelligence, A Sourcebook, ed. V. Brummett, Ithac, N.Y.: Ithaca College, 1997. (Based on a conference keynote, September 1996.)

Gardner, H. (1996). Zur Entwicklung des Spektrums der menschlichen

Intelligenzen. *Beitrage zur Lehrerbildung, 14*, (2), 198-209.

Gardner, H. (1996, Nov). Probing more deeply into the theory of multiple intelligences. *NASSP Bulletin*, pp. 1–7.

Gardner, H. (1997). Developmental Views of Multiple Intelligence [*sic*]. In G. O. Mazur (Ed.), *Twenty-year commemoration to the life of A.R. Luria (1902–1977)* (61–79). New York: Semenenko Foundation.

Gardner, H. (1997, March 1). Our many intelligences: Kinds of minds. *The Mini Page*. A children's supplement to local newspapers, edited by Betty Debnam, © Universal Press Syndicate.

Gardner, H. (1997, Sept). Multiple Intelligences as a partner in school improvement. *Educational Leadership, 55*, (1), 20–21.

Gardner, H. (1997, Sept). Fostering diversity through personalized education: implications of a new understanding of human intelligence. [*Journal of UNESCO's International Bureau of Education*], *Prospects, 27*, (3), 347–363. Translated and Reprinted: French, *Perspectives, 27*, (3), 369–387; Spanish, *Perspectivas, 27*, (3), 371–389; Russian; Chinese; Arabic.

Gardner, H. (1997, Sept). Truth, Beauty, and Goodness: Education for All Human Beings. Interview with John Brockman, [www.edge.org]. Reprinted, B. Presseisen (Ed.), *Teaching for intelligence I: A collection of articles*, Arlington Heights, IL: SkyLight Publishing, 1999.

Gardner, H. (1998). Extraordinary cognitive achievements: A symbols systems approach. In W. Damon (Ed.-in-Chief), *Handbook of child psychology, 5th ed., vol. 1: Theoretical models of human development* (415–466). New York: Wiley.

Gardner, H. (1998). A multiplicity of intelligences. *Scientific American Presents: Exploring Intelligence* (A special issue of *Scientific American*), pp. 19–23.

Gardner, H. (1998, March 19). An intelligent way. (London) *Independent*, Education Supplement, pp. 4, 5 [A response to John White, *Do Howard Gardner's Multiple Intelligences Add Up?* London: Inst. of Education University of London, 1998].

Gardner, H. (1998, November 9). Letter to the Editor in Reply to Collins "Seven Kinds of Smart" (Oct 19, 1998). *Time*.

Gardner, H. (1999). Are there additional intelligences? The case for naturalist, spiritual, and existential intelligences. In J. Kane (Ed.), *Education, Information and Transformation* (111–131). Upper Saddle River, NJ: Prentice-Hall. Reprinted: *Gifted Education Press Quarterly, 11*, (2), Spring 1997, pp. 2–5.

Gardner, H. (1999). Multiple approaches to understanding. In C. M. Reigeluth (Ed.), *Instructional-design theories and models: A new-*

paradigm of instructional theory. Mahwah, NJ: Erlbaum Associates.

Gardner, H. (1999, Feb). Who owns intelligence? *Atlantic Monthly,* pp. 67–76.

Gardner, H. (1999, Sept). Howard Gardner debates James Traub on multiple intelligences. *Cerebrum: The Dana Forum on Brain Science, 1,* (2).

Gardner, H. (in press). "Intelligence." Entry in the *Fontana/Norton Dictionary of Modern Thought.*

Gardner, H. (in press). Is there a moral intelligence? To appear in M. Runco (Ed.), *Perspectives on Creativity Series.* Cresskill, NJ: Hampton Press.

Gardner, H. (in press). A case against spiritual intelligence. Submitted to *International Journal for the Psychology of Religion.* R. Paloutzian, Ed.

II.   *Coauthored by Howard Gardner*

Baker, L., Gardner, H. et al. (1993). Intelligence and its inheritance: A diversity of views. In T. Bouchard and P. Propping (Eds.), *Twins as a tool of behavioral genetics* (85–108). Chichester, England: Wiley.

Baum, S., Viens, J., and Slatin, B., in consultation with H. Gardner (in preparation). *Pathways to multiple intelligences: A guide to implementation.* Submitted to American Psychological Association.

Blythe, T., White, N., and Gardner, H. (1995). Teaching practical intelligence. *What research tells us* [series of booklets]. West Lafayette, IN: Kappa Delta Pi.

Boix-Mansilla, V. & Gardner, H. (1997, Jan.). Of Kinds of Disciplines and Kinds of Understanding. *Phi Delta Kappan, 78,* (5), 381–386.

Chen, J-Q. & Gardner, H. (1997). Alternative assessment from a multiple intelligences theoretical perspective. In D. Flanagan, J. Genshaft, and P. Harrison (Eds.), *Contemporary intellectual assessment: Theories, tests, and issues* (105–121). New York: Guilford Press. Reprinted: B. Torff (Ed.), *Multiple Intelligences and Assessment,* Arlington Heights, IL: IRI Skylight, 1997.

Gardner, H. & Checkley, K. (1997, Sept). [Interview] The first seven. . . and the eighth: A conversation with Howard Gardner. *Educational Leadership, 55,* (1), 8–13.

Gardner, H., Feldman, D. H., and Krechevsky, M. (Gen eds.) (1988). *Project zero frameworks for early childhood education: volume: volume 1. Building on children's strengths: The experience of project spectrum.* Volume authors Chen, J-Q., Krechevsky, M., and Viens, J. with E. Isberg. New York: Teachers College Press.

Gardner, H., Feldman, D. H., and Krechevsky, M. (Gen eds.) (1998). *Project zero frameworks for early childhood education: volume 2, Project spectrum early learning activities.* Volume author Chen, J-Q., with E. Isberg and M. Krechevsky. New York: Teachers College Press.

Gardner, H., Feldman, D. H., and Krechevsky, M. (Gen eds.) (1998). *Project frameworks for early childhood education: volume 3, Project sprectrum preschool assessment handbook.* Volume author Krechevsky, M. New York: Teachers College Press.

Gardner, H. & Hatch, T. (1989). Multiple intelligences go to school. *Educational Researcher, 18,* 4–10.

Gardner H., Hatch, T., and Torff, B. (1997). A third perspective: The symbol systems approach. In R. Sternberg and E. Grigorenko (Eds.), *Intelligence, heredity, and environment* (243–268). New York: Cambridge University Press.

Gardner, H., Kornhaber, M., and Wake, W. (1996). *Intelligence: Multiple perspectives.* Fort Worth, TX: Harcourt Brace. Translated into Portuguese and Croatian.

Gardner, H. & Schmidt, R. (1992, Fall). [Interview with Howard Gardner]. *Learning 2001, 3,* (3), 4–6.

Gardner, H. & Shores, E. F. (1995, Summer). [Interview] Howard Gardner on the eighth intelligence: Seeing the natural world. *Dimensions of Early Childhood,* 5–7.

Gardner, H. & Viens, J. (1990). Multiple intelligences and styles: Partners in effective education. *The Clearinghouse Bulletin: Learning/Teaching Styles and Brain Behavior, 4,* 2, pp. 4–5. Seattle, Washington: Association for Supervision and Curriculum Development.

Gardner, H. & Walters, J. (1988). *Managing intelligences* (Tech. Rep. #33). Cambridge, MA: Harvard University Graduate School of Education, Harvard Project Zero.

Gardner, H., Walters, J., and Hatch, T. (1992). If teaching had looked beyond the classroom: The development and education of intelligences. *Innotech Journal, 16* (1), 18–36.

Goldman, J. & Gardner, H. (1988). Multiple paths to educational effectiveness. In D.K. Lipsky and A. Gartner (Eds.), *Beyond separate education: Quality education for all students* (121–140). Baltimore: Brookes.

Granott, N. & Gardner, H. (1994). When minds meet: Interactions, coincidence, and development in domains of ability. In R. J. Sternberg and R. K. Wagner (Eds.), *Mind in context: Interactionist perspectives on human intelligence* (171–201). New York: Cambridge University Press.

Hatch, T. & Gardner, H. (1986). From testing intelligence to assessing competences: A pluralistic view of intellect. *The Roeper Review, 8,*

147–150.

Hatch, T. & Gardner, H. (1988, Nov/Dec). How Kids Learn: What Scientists Say. *Learning88*, pp. 36–39.

Hatch, T. & Gardner, H. (1990). If Binet had looked beyond the classroom: The assessment of multiple intelligences. *International Journal of Educational Research*, 415–429. Reprinted (abridged): *Innotech Journal, 16* (1), 1992, 18–36. Reprinted: *NAMTA Journal, 21*, (2), 1996, 5–28. Reprinted: B. Torff (Ed.), *Multiple Intelligences and Assessment*, Arlington Heights, IL: IRI Skylight, 1997.

Hatch, T. & Gardner, H. (1993). Finding cognition in the classroom: An expanded view of human intelligence. In G. Salomon (Ed.), *Distributed cognitions* (164–187). New York: Cambridge University Press.

Kornhaber, M. & Gardner, H. (1993, March). Varieties of excellence and conditions for their achievement. Paper prepared for Commission on Varieties of Excellence in the Schools, New York State. New York: The National Center for Restructuring Education, Schools and Teaching.

Kornhaber, M. L. & Gardner, H. (1995). Solving for *g* and beyond. *Triumph of discovery: A chronicle of great adventures in science* (121–123). New York: Henry Holt and Co., Inc. and Scientific American, Inc. Selected by Quality Paperback Club and Book of the Month Club.

Krechevsky, M. & Gardner, H. (1990). Multiple intelligences, multiple chances. In D. Inbar (Ed.), *Second chance in education: An interdisciplinary and international perspective* (69–88). London: The Falmer Press.

Krechevsky, M. & Gardner, H. (1994). Multiple intelligences in multiple contexts. In D. K. Detterman (Ed.), *Current topics in human intelligence: volume 4, Theories of intelligence* (285–305). Norwood, NJ: Ablex Publishing Corp.

Krechevsky, M., Hoerr, T., and Gardner, H. (1995). Complementary energies: Implementing MI theory from the laboratory and from the field. In J. Oakes and K. H. Quartz (Eds.), *Creating new educational communities* (166–186). 94th Yearbook of the National Society for the Study of Education (Part I). Chicago, IL: Univ. of Chicago Press.

Malkus, U., Feldman, D. H., and Gardner, H. (1988). Dimensions of mind in early childhood. In A.D. Pelligrini (Ed.), *The psychological bases of early education* (25–38). Chichester, U.K.: Wiley.

Ramos-Ford, V., Feldman, D. H., and Gardner, H. (1988, Spring). A new look at intelligence through Project Spectrum. *New Horizons in Learning*, 6, 7, 15.

Ramos-Ford, V. & Gardner, H. (1991). Giftedness from a multiple intelligences perspective. In N. Colangelo and G. Davis (Eds). *The handbook of gifted education* (55–64). Boston: Allyn and Bacon.

Solomon, B., Powell, K., and Gardner, H. (1999). Multiple intelligences and creativity. In M. Runco and S. Pritzker (Eds.-in-Chief), *Encyclopedia of Creativity*. San Diego, CA: Academic Press.

Torff, B. & Gardner, H. (1999). The vertical mind: The case for multiple intelligences. In M. Anderson (Ed.), *The Development of Intelligence*. London: University College London Press, pp. 139-159.

Veenema, S. & Gardner, H. (1996, Nov/Dec). Multimedia and Multiple Intelligences. *The American Prospect*, pp. 69–75. Based on a presentation at M.I.T. at Cambridge, Mass. on June 4, 1996.

Viens, J., Chen, J-Q., and Gardner, H. (1997). Theories of Intelligence and Critiques. In J. L. Paul, et al. (Eds.), *Foundations of Special Education* (122–141). Pacific Grove, CA: Brooks-Cole.

Walters, J., Krechevsky, M. and Gardner, H. (1985). *Development of musical, mathematical, and scientific talents in normal and gifted children* (Tech. Rep. #31). Cambridge, MA: Harvard University Graduate School of Education, Harvard Project Zero.

Wexler-Sherman, C., Gardner, H., and Feldman, D. (1988). A pluralistic view of early assessment: The Project Spectrum approach. *Theory into Practice*, 27, 77–83.

White, N., Blythe, T., and Gardner, H. (1992). Multiple intelligence theory: Creating the thoughtful classroom. In A. Costa, J. Bellanca, and R. Fogarty (Eds.), *If mind matters: A foreword to the future*, 2 (127–134). Palatine, IL: Skylight Publishers.

Wolf, D., Bixby, J., Glenn, J., and Gardner, H. (1991). To use their minds well: Investigating new forms of student assessment. In Gerald Grant (Ed.), *Review of Research in Education* (31–74). Washington: AERA.

Zessoules, R. & Gardner, H. (1991). Authentic assessment: Beyond the buzzword and into the classroom. In V. Perrone (Ed.), *Expanding student assessment* (47–71). Arlington, VA: Association for Supervision and Curriculum Development.

APPENDIX B

OTHER WORKS ABOUT THE THEORY OF MULTIPLE INTELLIGENCES

Dates and/or addresses provided when available.
Works available only in languages other than English appear with asterisks (**).

I. Selected Books and Monographs

Adams, C. M. and Callahan, C. M. (in press). Psychometric properties of a checklist to assess multiple intelligences.

Alejandre, S., Braatz-Brown, L., and Haskell, A. *Mathematical moments in music, magic, and mime.* Riverside, CA: University of California.

Armstrong, T. (1987). *In their own way: discovering and encouraging your child's personal learning style.* Los Angeles: J.P. Tarcher (distributed by St. Martin's Press, New York).

Armstrong, T. (1991). *Awakening your child's natural genius: Enhancing curiosity, creativity, and learning ability.* New York: Putnam Publishing Group.

Armstrong, T. (1993). *Seven kinds of smart: discovering and using your natural intelligences.* New York: Plume/Penguin.

Armstrong, T. (1994). *Multiple intelligences in the classroom.* Alexandria, VA: Association for Supervision and Curriculum Development. Also available in Spanish.

Arnold, E. Brilliant brain becomes brainy. MI application for K-3 classroom. Tucson, AZ: Zephyr Press.

Arnold, E. The MI Strategy Bank. Available through Zephyr Press.

Arulmani, G. and Nag-Arulmani, S., Eds. (1992). Multiple Intelligneces for Simulation. Bangalore, India.

Barkman, R. Science Through Multiple Intelligences. Available through Zephyr Press.

Bellança, J. *Active learning handbook for the multiple intelligences classroom.* Palatine, IL: IRI/Skylight.

Bellanca, J., Chapman, C., and Swartz, E. (1995). *Multiple assessments for multiple intelligences*. Palatine, IL: IRI/Skylight.

Berman, S. *A multiple intelligences road to a quality classroom*. Palatine, IL: IRI/Skylight.

Benzwie, T. *A moving experience: Dance for lovers of children and the child within*. Zephyr Press catalog.

Benzwie, T. *Moving experiences: Connecting arts, feelings, and imagination*. Zephyr Press Catalog.

Berman, S. *Project learning for the multiple intelligences classroom*. Palatine, IL: IRI/Skylight.

Boggeman, S., Hoerr, T., and Wallach, C. (Eds.). *Succeeding with multiple intelligences: Teaching through the personal intelligences*. Palatine, IL: IRI/Skylight.

Bowen, J., King, C., and Hawkins, M. *Square pegs: Building success in school and life through MI*. Tucson, AZ: Zephyr Press.

Bower, B., Lobdell, J., and Swenson, L. (1993). *History alive: Engaging all learners in diverse classrooms*. Menlo Park, CA: Addison Wesley.

Brewer, C. and Campbell, D. (1991). *Rhythms of learning: Creative tools for developing lifelong skills*. Tucson, AZ: Zephyr Press.

Bruetsch, A. (1994). *Multiple intelligences: Lesson plan book*. Tucson, AZ: Zephyr Press.

Callahan, C. M. et al. (1995, Sept). *Project SMART: Using a Multiple Intelligences Model in Identifying and Promoting Talent in High Risk Students*. Research Monograph 95136. Charlottesville, VA: National Center on the Gifted and Talented.

Campbell, B. (1994). *The Multiple intelligences handbook: Lesson plans and more*. Stanwood, WA: Campbell and Associates.

Campbell, B., Campbell, L., and Dickinson D. (1993). *Teaching and learning through multiple intelligences*. Tucson, AZ: Zephyr Press.

Carreiro, P. *Tales of Thinking: Multiple intelligences in th in the classroom*. Available through Zephyr Press.

Chapman, C. *If the shoe fits: How to develop multiple intelligences in the classroom*. Palatine, IL: IRI/Skylight.

Chapman, C. and Freeman, L. *Multiple intelligences centers and projects*. Palatine, IL: IRI/Skylight.

Chapman, C. et al. *Multiple assessments for multiple intelligences, 3rd ed.*. Palatine, IL: IRI/Skylight.

Charbonneay, M. and Reider, B. (1995). *The integrated elementary classsroom*. Boston: Allyn and Bacon.

Center for Arts in the Basic Curriculum, Inc. (1994). *The balanced mind: An educational and societal imperative*. Available from CABC, 58 Fearing

Rd., Hingham, MA 02043.

Costa, A., Bellanca, J., and Fogarty, R. (1993). *If minds matter: A foreword to the future.* Palatine, IL: IRI/Skylight Publishing.

Cullen, L. (1995). *Solid gold for kids: Musical energizers.* Scarb of the semester. *San Francisco: Jossey Bass. [Includes discussion of MI at the college level.]*

De Amicis, B. *A daily dose: Integrating MI into your curriculum.* Tucson, AZ: Zephyr Press.

Diaz-Lefebvre, R. (1999). *Coloring outside the lines: Applying multiple intelligences and creativity in teaming.* New York: John Wiley & Sons, Inc.

Duffy, D. and Jones, J. W. (1995). *Teaching with the rythms of the semester.* San Francisco: Jossey-Bass. [Includes discussion of MI at the college level.]

Dryden, G. and Vos Groenendal, J. (1993). *The learning revolution.* Rolling Hills Estate, CA: Jalmar Press.

Eisner, E. (in press). *Creating strength-based programs for adults with dementia: A practical resource for assessing and prescribing strength-based activities.* Austin, TX: Pro-ed, Inc. (to appear in 2000).

Ellison, L. (1993). *Seeing with magic glasses: A teacher's view from the front line of the learning revolution.* Arlington, VA: Great Ocean Publishers [1823 North Lincoln St., Arlington, VA 22207].

**Filograsso, N. (1995). *Howard Gardner: Un Modello di Pedagogica Modulare.* Rome: Anicia Publishers.

Fischer, L. and Jansen, J. *Brain works: A multiple intelligences teaching model for primary grades.* Available from Brainworks, P.O. Box 6082, Edmonds, WA 98026–6082.

Fogarty, R. *Problem-based learning and other models for the multiple intelligences classroom.* Palatine, IL: IRI/Skylight.

Fogarty, R. and Bellanca, J. (Eds.). (1995). *Multiple intelligences: A collection.* Palatine, IL: IRI/Skylight.

Fogarty, R. and Stoehr, J. (1995). *Integrating curricula with multiple intelligences: Teams, themes, and threads.* Palatine, IL: IRI/Skylight.

Glock, J. et al. (1999). *Discovering the Naturalist Intelligence.* Tucson, AZ: Zephyr Press, P. O. Box 66006, Tucson, AZ 85728. Telephone: 800–232–2187.

Granter, B. and Murray, A. (1997). *Bethany's Children.* Cambridge, MA: Learning Society, Inc.

Green, J. *The Green Book.* Nashville, TN: Professional Desk References, Inc.

Haggerty, B. *In the year of the boar.* Available from Instructional Materials Development, San Diego Public Schools, 4100 Normal Street, San Diego, CA 92103–2682.

Haggerty, B. *Introduction to the theory of multiple intelligences*. Available from Instructional Materials Development, San Diego Public Schools, 4100 Normal Street, San Diego, CA 92103–2682.

Haggerty, B. *Multiple intelligence theory and instructional design: Creating literature units for teaching across the curriculum*. Available from Instructional Materials Development, San Diego Public Schools, 4100 Normal Street, San Diego, CA 92103–2682.

Haggerty, B. (1994). *Teaching guide for Paul Fleischman's Joyful noise: poetry for two voices*. Menlo Park, CA: Addison Wesley.

Haggerty, B. (1995). *Nurturing intelligences: a guide to multiple intelligences theory and teaching*. Menlo Park, CA: Addison Wesley.

Haggerty, B. (1996). *Teaching guide for Mildred Taylor's Roll of thunder, hear my cry*. Menlo Park, CA: Addison Wesley.

Haggerty, B. (1996). *Teaching guide for Russell Freedman's Lincoln: A photobiography*. Menlo Park, CA: Addison Wesley.

Hague, Douglas. (1993). *Transforming the dinosaurs*. London: Demos.

Hannaford, C., Sharer, C., and Zachery S. *Education in motion: A practical guide to whole brain-body integration for everyone*. Zephyr Press catalog.

Healy, J. (1987). *Your child's growing mind: A parents guide to learning from birth*. Garden City, NY: Doubleday.

Healy, J. (1990). *Endangered minds: Why our children don't think*. New York: Simon & Schuster.

Hench, M. and Li, J. (1994). *Diverse Universe: Uses of Howard Gardner's theories of multiple intelligence in the television program "Lift Off."* Melbourne: Australian Children's Television Foundation.

Hoerr, T. R. (1996). *Implementing Multiple Intelligences: The New City School Experience*. Bloomington, IN: Phi Delta Kapa Educational Foundation.

Hoerr, T. (1999). *Becoming a multiple intelligences school*. Arlington, VA: Association and curriculum development.

Hopper, B., Chamberlain, V. and Jack, B. *An introduction to the theory of multiple intelligences*. Lancashire, England: Centre for the Promotion of Holistic Education, Edge Hill College of Higher Education.

Hopper, B., Chamberlain, V. and Jack, B. *Multiple intelligence theory in the primary school*. Lancashire, England: Centre for the Promotion of Holistic Education, Edge Hill College of Higher Education.

Hopper, B, Chamberlain, V. and Jack, B. *Multiple intelligence theory in the secondary school*. Lancashire, England: Centre for the Promotion of Holistic Education, Edge Hill College of Higher Education.

Jasmine, J. (1995). *Addressing diversity in the classroom*. Westminster, CA: Teacher Created Materials, Inc.

Kagan, S. and Kagan, L. (1998). *Cooperative learning and multiple intelligences*. San Clemente, CA: Kagan Cooperative Learning.

Kagan, S. and Kagan, M. *Multiple Intelligences: The Complete MI Book*. San Clemente, CA: Kagan Cooperative Learning.

Kelly, L. *Challenging Minds: Thinking skills and enrichment activities*. Tucson, AZ: Zephyr Press.

Kline, P. (1988). *The everyday genius*. Arlington, VA: Great Ocean Publishers [1823 North Lincoln St., Arlington, VA 22207].

Kovacs, E. (1999) *Writing with multiple intelligences*. Portland, OR: Blue Heron Publishing Co.

Kovalik, S. (1993). ITI: *The model—integrated thematic instruction*. Vilage of Oak Creek, AZ: Books for Educators [P.O. Box 20525, Oak Creek, AZ 86341].

Lazear, D. *Seven ways of teaching*. Palantine, IL: IRI/Skylight.

Lazear, D. *Eight ways of teaching*. Palatine, IL:IRI/ Skylight.

Lazear, D. *Intelligence builders for every student: Forty-four exercises to expand MI in your classroom*. Tucson, AZ: Zephyr Press.

Lazear, D. (1991). *Seven ways of knowing: Teaching for multiple intelligence: A handbook of techniques for expanding intelligence* [foreword by Howard Gardner]. Palantine, IL: IRI/Skylight Publishers.

Lazear, D. (1992). *Teaching for the multiple intelligences*. Bloomington, IN: Phi Delta Kappa.

Lazear, D. (1993). *Seven pathways of learning: Teaching students and parents about multiple intelligences*. Tucson, AZ: Zephyr Press.

Lazear, D. (1994). *Seven multiple intelligence approaches to assessment*. Tucson, Arizona: Zephyr Press.

Lazear, D. (1995). *Multiple intelligence approaches to assessment: Solving the assessment conundrum*. Tucson, AZ: Zephyr Press.

Lazear, D. (1996). *Step beyond your limits*. Tucson, AZ: Zephyr Press.

Lazear, D. (1998). *The Rubrics Way: Using MI to Assess Understanding*. Tucson, AZ: Zephyr Press.

Li, R. (1996). *A Theory of conceptual intelligence: Thinking, learning, creativity, and giftedness*. Westport, CT: Praeger.

Majoy, P. (1993). *Doorways to learning: A model for developing the brain's full potential*. Tucson, AZ: Zephyr Press.

Margulies, N. *Yes, You Can Draw* [book and videotape]. Available from the author, 709 Wenneker, St. Louis, MO 63124.

Marks–Tarlow, T. (1996). *Creativity inside out: Learning through multi-

ple intelligences [with a foreword by Howard Gardner]. Menlo Park, CA: Addison–Wesley.

Martin, H. *Multiple intelligences in the mathematics classroom.* Palatine, IL: IRI/Skylight.

McGrath, H. and Noble, T. (1995). *Seven ways at once: Classroom strategies based on the seven intelligences.* Melbourne, Australia: Longman Publishers.

Miller, L. *The Smart profile: A qualitative approach for describing learners and designing instruction.* Austin, TX: Smart Alternatives, Inc. (P.O. Box 5849, Austin, TX 78763).

Miller, L. *Your personal smart profile.* Austin, TX: Smart Alternatives, 1991 (P.O. Box 5849, Auxtin, TX 78763).

Miller, L. *What we call smart.* San Diego, CA: Singular Publishing Group (4284 – 41st St., San Diego, CA 92105).

Mollan–Masters, R. *You are smarter than you think.* Ashland, OR: Reality Productions, 1992 (6245 Old Highway 99 South, P.O. Box 943, Ashland, OR 97520).

National Curriculum and Text Book Board. (1998). *Multiple ways of teaching and learning: A guidebook for primary school teachers.* Dhaka, Bangladesh: N.C.T.B.B.

New City School. (1994). *Celebrating multiple intelligences: Teaching for success.* St. Louis, MO: New City School.

New City School (1995). *Succeeding with multiple intelligences: teaching through the personal intelligences,* Boggeman, S., Hoerr, T., and Wallach, C. (Eds.). St. Louis, MO: New City School. Available from Zephyr Press, P. O. Box 66006, Tucson, AZ 85728.

New City School. (1996). *Succeeding with multiple intelligences: Teaching through the personal intelligences.* St. Louis, MO: New City School.

Nicholson-Nelson, K. (1998). *Developing students' multiple intelligences.* New York: Scholastic Professional Books.

O'Connor, A. and Callahan–Young, S. (1994). *Seven windows to a child's world: One hundred ideas for the multiple intelligences classroom.* Palatine, IL: IRI/Skylight Publishing.

O'Neill, L. *Matching multiple intelligences to careers: A teacher's manual for discovering and developing your natural talents.* Tucson, AZ: Zephyr Press.

O'Neill, L. *Matching multiple intelligences to careers: A guidebook for discovering and developing your natural talents and designing career paths.*

Patterson, M. K. (1997). *Everybody can learn: Engaging the bodily-kinesthetic intelligence in the everyday classroom.* Tucson, AZ: Zephyr Press.

**Perticari, P. (1996). *Attesi imprevisti: uno squardo ritrovato su difficolta di Insegnamento/Apprendimento e diversita delle intelligenze a scuola.* Turin, Italy: Bollati Boringhieri.

Peterson, D. *Seven ways to success—Aptitude and interest measure for high school students.* Available from the author, Watchung Hills Regional High School, 108 Stirling Rd., Warren, NJ 07060.

Piirto, Jane. (1992). *Understanding those who create.* Dayton, OH: Psychology Press.

Rainey, F. (1991). *Multiple intelligences: Seven ways of knowing.* Denver: Colorado Dept. of Education, Gifted and Talented Education.

Robinson, E. (1991). *Care givers' annual 1991: A guide to multiple intelligences for the elderly.* Available from the author, Life Enhancement Research, P.O. Box 3756, Salem, OR 97302.

Robinson, J. *A Literature teaching guide.* San Diego, CA: San Diego City Schools.

Rogers, M. (1995). *Working styles of high and low achieving children in the seven intelligence domains of Howard Gardner's theory of multiple intelligences.* Available from the author, University of South Florida, Tampa, Florida.

Rose C. and Goll, L. (1992). *Accelerating your learning.* Buckinghamshire: Accelerated Learning Systems.

Rose, L. *Developing intelligences through literature: ten theme-based units for growing minds.* Tucson, AZ: Zephyr Press.

Roth, K. (1998). *The naturalist intelligence.* Palatine, IL: IRI/Skylight

**Santoianni, Flavia. (1996). *Didattica Configuarzionale: Modelli Multipli A Coordinate Modulari.* Naples, Italy: Edizioni Scientifiche Italiane.

Shearer, B. (1996). *The MIDAS: multiple intelligences developments assessment scales. A guide to assessment and education for the multiple intelligences.* Columbus, OH: Original Works. Available from the author, 519 S. DePeyster St., Kent, OH 44240.

Shelton, L. (1991).*Honoring Diversity: A multidimensional learning model for adults.* Available from California State Library Foundation, South San Francisco Public Library, 840 W. Orange Ave. So., San Francisco, CA 94080.

Smagorinsky, P. (1991). *Expressions: Multiple intelligences in the English class. Theory and research in practice.* National Council of Teachers of English.

Sollman, C. (1994). *Through the cracks.* Worcester, MA: Davis Publications, Inc

**Starlight Elementary School. *How I am Smart/Como Soy Inteligente* (written by 22 elementary school children). Available from Starlight Elementary School Learning Academy, 313 W. Winton Ave., Suite 373, Hayward, CA 94544.

Teele, S. (1992). *The Teele inventory of multiple intelligences.* Available from the author, P.O. Box 7302, Redlands, CA 92374.

Teele, S. (1992). *The role of multiple intelligences in the instructional process.* Riverside, CA: University of California.

Teele, S. (1992). *Teaching and assessment strategies appropriate for the multiple intelligences.* Riverside, CA: University of California.

Teele, S. (1995). *The multiple intelligences school: A place for all students to excel.* Redlands, CA: Citrograph Printings. Available from the author, P.O. Box 7302, Redlands, CA 92374.

Thornburg, D. (1989). *The role of technology in teaching to the whole child: Multiple intelligences in the classroom.* Los Altos, CA: Starsong Publications.

Tobias, C. (1995). *The way they learn: How to discover and teach to your children's strengths.* Colorado Springs, CO.

Tolson, S. *Multiple intelligences: General research capsule.* Brevard County, Florida: Florida Diagnostic and Learning Resource System.

Torff, B. (Ed.). *Multiple intelligences and assessment: a collection of articles.* Palatine, IL: IRI/Skylight.

Ulrey, J. and Ulrey, D. *Learning through the seven intelligences: Thematic units for the primary, multiage classroom.* Available from the authors, 377 13th St., Del Mar, CA.

Vail, P. (1987). *Smart kids with school problems: Things to know and ways to help.* New York: Dutton.

Vialle, W. and Perry, J. (1995). *Nurturing multiple intelligences in the Australian classroom.* Melbourne, Australia: Hawker Brownlow Education.

Wahl, M. *Math for humans: Teaching math through seven intelligences.* Palatine, IL: IRI/Skylight.

Ward-Prewitt, B. *Learning styles and performance assessment: A model teaching guide.* Columbia, CT: The Learner's Dimension (P.O. Box 6, Columbia, CT 06237).

Wass, L. (1991). *Imagine that: Getting smarter through imagery practice.* Rolling Hills Estates, CA: Jalmar Press. Also available from the author, P.O. Box 443, Glenville, NC 28736.

Wayne, S. (1997). *Practical Themes for Busy Teachers.* Melbourne, Australia: Hawker Brownlow Education.

Weber, E. (1995). *Creative learning from inside out: A collaborative learning and teaching approach for high school.* Vancouver, BC: Edusserv.

Weber, E. (1999). *Roundtable learning: building understanding through enhanced MI strategies.* Tucson, AZ: Zephyr Press.

Weber, E. (1999). *Student Assessment That Works: A Practical Approach.* Boston: Allyn and Bacon.

Wilkens, D. *Multiple intelligences activities.* Tucson, AZ: Zephyr Press.

Willard-Holt, C., and Holt, D. (1998). *Applying multiple intelligences to gifted education: I'm not just an I.Q. score!* Manassas, VA: Gifted Education Press.

Williams, W., Blythe, T., White, N., Li, J., Sternberg, R., and Gardner, H. (1996). *Practical Intelligence for School.* New York: HarperCollins.

Young, K. A. *Constructing Buildings, Bridges, and Minds.* Portsmouth, NH: Heinemann.

II. Selected Articles and Reviews

Allis, S. (1999, July 11) The master of *un*artificial intelligence. *Boston Globe,* pp. D1, 5.

Altman, L. (1991, Sept 24). Can the brain provide clues to intelligence? *New York Times.*

Andrews, G. Howard Gardner's multiple intelligences theory as a framework for the teaching of mathematics. Available from the author, RD #2 Ballard Rd., Rm. 250, St. Albans, VT 05478.

Armstrong, T. (1993, Sept). Home is where the learning is: 25 ways to help your child. *Family Circle.*

Armstrong, T. (1994, Sept 5). Smart Kids. *Family Circle,* p. E1.

Aschettino, E. (1986, March). Children aren't always traditionally smart. *Massachusetts Elementary Educator.*

Association of Youth Museums. (1993, July/Aug). Opening Minds with Howard Gardner. *Association of Youth Museum News, 1,* (4).

Atchity, K. (1984, Feb 26). Profound thoughts on the thinking process. *Los Angeles Times.*

Bailey, J. (1995, Sept). Seven kinds of smart. *Working Mother.*

Baldwin, A. (1994). The seven-plus story: Developing hidden talent among students in socioeconomically disadvantaged environments. *Gifted Child Quarterly, 38,* (2).

**Barth, B. M. (1999, March). Mettre en valeur les différences individuelles. *Journal des instituteurs et des institutrices* (7), 73–74.

Beem, E. (1993, Dec 10). What did you do in school today? I participated in collaborative problem solving and sold coat hangers. *Maine Times, 26,* (11).

Black, S. (1994, Jan). Different kinds of smart. *The Executive Educator*, pp. 24–27.

Black, S. (1997, Aug). Branches of Knowledge. *American School Board Journal*, pp. 35–37.

Black, S. (1998, Oct). How are you smart? *American School Board Journal*, pp. 26–29.

Blumenthal, R. (1996, Sept 1). Tap your child's special strengths. *Family Circle*.

Bolanos, P. (1994). From theory to practice: Indianapolis's Key School applies Howard Gardner's MI theory to the classroom. *The School Administrator, 51*, (1).

Bornstein, M. (1986). Review of *Frames of Mind*. *Journal of Aesthetic Education, 20*, (1).

Bottom Line/Personal (1992, June 30). What parents can do to help their kids learn better: An interview with Dr. Howard Gardner, pp. 9–10.

Bouchard, T. (1984, July 20). Review of *Frames of Mind*. *American Journal of Orthopsychiatry*.

Bruce, S. (1995). Using multiple intelligences in art connections at the Cummer Museum of Art. Unpublished paper available from the author, 2294 East Park Ave., Tallahassee, FL 32301.

Bruner, J. (1983, Oct 27). State of the Child. Review of *Frames of Mind*. *New York Review of Books*.

Bryant, P.(1984, June 8). A Battery of Tests. Review of *Frames of Mind*. *Times Higher Education Supplement*.

Buescher, T. (1985). Seeking the roots of talent: An interview with Howard Gardner. *Journal for the Education of the Gifted, 8*, (3), pp. 179–187.

Business Wire. (1994, Oct 19). The Harold McGraw, Jr. Prize in Education.

Campbell, B. Multiple intelligences in the classroom. *Cooperative Learning, 12*, (1), pp. 24–25. Reprinted from *In Context*, Number 27, Winter 1991.

Campbell, L. (1997). Variations on a theme: How teachers interpret MI theory. *Educational Leadership, 55*, (1).

Carroll, J. (1984). An artful perspective on talents. Review of *Frames of Mind*. *Contemporary Psychology, 29*, (11).

Carroll, J. (1985). Like minds, like sympathies: Comments on the interview with Howard Gardner. *New Ideas in Psychology, 3*, (1).

Chapman, C. and Schrenko, L. (1993, Winter). Multiple intelligences: If the shoe fits. *High Expectations*, Network newsletter of IRI/Skylight Publisher, Palatine, IL.

Chideya, F. (1991, Dec 2). Surely for the spirit but also for the mind: Arts

PROPEL as one of the outstanding educational programs in the world. *Newsweek*.

Clinchy, B. (1984). Review of *Frames of Mind*. *Boston University Journal of Education, 166*, (2).

Cohen, L. (1995, Aug/Sept). A classroom for every child. *Early Childhood Today, 10*, (1), pp. 35–40.

Cohen, M. (1990, Dec 12). Test questions: A subject for the '90s. *Boston Sunday Globe*, Learning Section.

Collins, J. (1998, Oct 19). Seven kinds of smart. *Time*, pp. 94–96.

Cromwell, R and Croskery, B. (1995, Fall). Will a tiny ripple become a tidal wave: Building a new paradigm through multiple intelligences. *Florida ASCD Journal*.

Deitel, B. (1990, May 20). The key to education. (Louisville, KY) *Courier Journal*.

Dezell, M. (1995, Aug 20). Studying with a 'student of genius.' *Boston Globe*, pp. B21, 24.

Diaz-Lefebvre, R. et al. (1998, Jan). What if they learn differently: Applying multiple intelligences theory in the community college. *Leadership Abstracts, 11*, (1). Available from the League for Innovation in the Community College, 26522 La Alameida, Ste. 370, Mission Viejo, CA 92691.

Diaz-Lefebvre, R. and Finnegan, P. (1997, Oct/Nov). Coloring outside the lines: Applying the theory of multiple intelligences to the community college setting. *Community College Journal*.

Education USA. (1985, Dec 16). Voices against the testing "explosion".

Eisenmann, L. (1984, July). Neuropsychology sheds new light on intelligence. Review of *Frames of Mind*. *American School Board Journal*.

Eisner, E. (1998). Creating strength-based intervention for geriatric persons with neurological progressive dementias. Hand-out from presentation to the American Speech-Language and Hearing Assn. annual convention in San Antonio, TX, November 21, 1998.

Eisner, E. (1994). Putting multiple intelligences in context: Some questions and observations. *Teachers College Record, 95*, (4).

Eisner, E. (1998, Oct.) Target activities that focus on strengths. *Case Management Advisor*, pp. 166–167.

Ellison, L. (1992). Using multiple intelligences to set goals. *Educational Leadership, 50*, (2), pp. 69–72.

English Journal, 84, (8), December 1995. Special issue devoted to articles on MI, with a particular emphasis on using MI in high school classrooms.

Fagella, K. and Horowitz, J. (1990, Sept). Different child, different style.

Instructor, pp. 49–54.

Feierabend, J. (1995, Summer). Music and intelligence in the early years. *Early Childhood Connections: Journal of Music- and Movement-Based Learning, 1*, (3).

**Folgarait, A. (1996, June 29). ¿Somos más intelligentes? *Noticieas* [Argentina].

Glacken, B. (1994, Sept 19). And how is your bodily kinesthetic IQ? *The Irish Times*, City Edition, p.14.

Glazer, S. (1993, July 30). Intelligence testing. *The CQ Researcher, 3*, (28), pp. 649–672.

Gold, De. (1988, March 30). Early testing said to have "long–term negative effects." *Education Week*.

Goleman, D. (1986, Feb 18). Influencing others: Skills are identified. *New York Times*.

Goleman, D. (1986, March 11). Psychologists study sources of influence and power. *New York Times*.

Goleman, D. (1986, Nov 9). Rethinking the value of intelligence tests. *New York Times*.

Goleman, D. (1988, April 5). New scales of intelligence rank talent for living. *New York Times*, Science Times.

Goleman, D. (1990, Oct 2). The study of play yields clues to success. *New York Times*, Science Times.

Gonzales, J. The dramatic intelligence and Gardner's theory of multiple intelligences: connecting drama to science pedagogy. Available from Dept. of Theatre, Bowling Green State University, Bowling Green, OH 43403–4236.

Gray, J. and Viens, J. (1994, Winter). The theory of multiple intelligences: Understanding cognitive diversity in school. *Phi Kappa Phi National Forum*.

Greenhawk, J. (1997). Multiple intelligences meet standards. *Educational Leadership, 55*, (1).

Grimes, S. (1998, Spring/Summer). How are your students smart? The theory of multiple intelligences. *Exchange, 16*, (1) (newsletter of the Learning Disabilities Network).

Grimm, M. (1986, Oct). Mind benders. *Creativity*.

Guskin, S. et al. (1992). Do teachers react to 'multiple intelligences'? Effects of teachers' stereotypes on judgments and expectancies for students with diverse patterns of giftedness/talent. *Gifted Child Quarterly, 36*, (1).

Hack, M. (1993, Oct 12). Your Child's Learning Style. *Staten Island Advance*.

Hall, B. (1986, Aug). "Portfolio" proposed as adjunct to SAT score.

Christian Science Monitor.

Hammer, S. Stalking intelligence: I.Q. isn't the end of the line: You can be smarter. *Science Digest.*

Hatch, T. (1993). From research to reform: Finding better ways to put theory into practice. *Educational Horizons, 71,* (4), pp. 197–202.

Hatch, T. (1997, March). Getting specific about multiple intelligences. *Educational Leadership, 54,* (6).

Hatch, T. (1998, March). How comprehensive can comprehensive reform be? *Phi Delta Kappan, 79,* (7), p. 518.

Hatch, T. and Seidel, S. (1997, Winter). Putting student work on the table. *National Forum, 77,* (1), p. 18. [The Honor Society of Phi Kappa Phi: Celebration of Excellence.]

Healy, Y. (1994, Sept 13). There's more than one kind of intelligence: Interview with Howard Gardner. *The Irish Times,* City Edition, p.8.

Healy, Y. (1995, Jan 24). Understanding intelligence: Education pioneer Howard Gardner on the human mind. *The Irish Times,* pp.8–9.

Hennepin County (MN). (1993, Sept). Seven ways we learn. *Essentials, 18,* (5), pp. 6–7. Newsletter for Hennepin County Foster Parents.

Hoerr, T. (1992, Oct). How our school applied multiple intelligences theory. *Educational Leadership, 50,* (2), pp. 67–68.

Hoerr, T. (1993, Aug/Sept). New dimensions of intelligence. *Education St. Louis.*

Hoerr, T. (1994, Fall). The multiple intelligence approach to giftedness. *Contemporary Education, 66,*(1).

Hoerr, T. (1994). How the New City School approaches the multiple intelligences. *Educational Leadership, 52,* (3).

Hoerr, T. (1996, Aug). Multiple Intelligences. *Learning,* Publication of The Education Center, Inc.

Hoerr, T. (1996, Winter). Education: One size does not fit all. *Private School Administrator.*

Hoerr, T. (1997, Sept/Oct). Call of the wildlife: The naturalist intelligence offers more than one way to help students understand and learn. *Learning.*

Hoerr, T. (1997). Frog ballets and musical fractions. *Educational Leadership, 55,* (1).

Hoerr, T. R. (1998, Fall). Letter to Network Members. *Intelligence Connections, 8,* (3). See also: Faculty Collegiality through Implementing Multiple Intelligences, *Intelligence Connections 5,* (2); and Using MI: A Work in Progress, *Intelligence Connections 7,* (2).

Horn, M. and Steder, J. (1992, March 30). Looking for a renaissance: The campaign to revive education in the arts. *U.S. News and World*

Report.

Jacobson, R. (1986, July). As SAT endures, new testing methods are sought. *The Chronicle of Higher Education.*

Jean, M. (1999, March). MI, the GED and Me. *Focus on basics*, 3, (A), pp. 3–5.

Johnson, C. (1990). Howard Gardner: Redefining intelligence. *Cardinal Principles*, p. 23. Publication of the University of Louisville College of Education.

Johnson–Laird, P. (1984, May 11). More faculties than one. Review of *Frames of Mind.* (London) *Times Literary Supplement.*

Kallenbach, S. & Viens, J. (Eds). (1999). MI Grows up: Multiple Intelligences Theory in the Adult Education Classroom. Unpublished paper of the Adult Multiple Intelligences Study, National Ctr. for the Study of Adult Learning and Literacey (NCSALL) and Harvard Projects Zera. Cambridge, MA: Harvard Graduate School of Education.

Kendel, R. Intelligence: Dr. Howard Gardner's multiple intelligences. *Effective Classrooms: The In–Service Newsletter.* Available from the author, 1810 Park Ave., Richmond, VA 23220.

Klein, P. (1997). Multiplying the problems of intelligence by eight. *Canadian Journal of Education,* 22, pp. 377–394. See also: H. Gardner, A Reply to Perry Klein, *CJE, 21,* (2), 1998, pp. 96–102. See also: P. Klein, A Response to Howard Gardner, *CJE, 23,* (1), 1998, pp. 103–112.

Knox, R. (1995, Nov 5). Brainchild. *Boston Globe Magazine.*

Kolata, G.(1989, April 9). Project SPECTRUM explores many-sided minds. *New York Times.*

Kornhaber, M. (1998, Fall). Schools Using Multiple Intelligence [sic] Theory. *LD Matters*, pp. 1–2, 11. Publication of the Parents & Educators Resource Center, San Mateo, CA.

Kornhaber, M. and Krechevsky, M. (1995). Expanding definitions of learning and teaching: Notes from the MI underground. In P. Cookson and Schneider, B. (Eds.), *Transforming schools.* New York: Garland Press.

Kornhaber, M., Krechevsky, M., and Gardner, H. (1990). Engaging intelligence. *Educational Psychologist,* 25, 177–199.

Krechevsky, M. (1991). Project SPECTRUM: An innovative assessment alternative. *Educational Leadership,* 48, pp. 43–48.

Krechevsky, M. and Seidel, S. (1998). Minds at Work: Applying Multiple Intelligences in the Classroom. In R. J. Sternberg and W. M. Williams (Eds.), *Intelligence, Instruction, and Assessment* (pp. 17–42). Mahwah, NJ: Lawrence Erlbaum Assoc.

Latham, A. (1997). Quantifying MI's gains. *Educational Leadership, 55,* (1).

Lehigh Valley Arts-in-Education Coalition. (1996, June). Dr. Howard

Gardner's Multiple Intelligences. *artLINKS*, pp. 1–2.

Leonard, L. (1990, Aug). Storytelling as experiential education. *Journal of Experiential Education, 13*, (2), pp. 12–17.

Levenson, T. (1984, Jan). Review of *Frames of Mind*. *Discover Magazine*, p. 79.

Levin, H. (1994). Multiple intelligence theory and everyday practices. *Teachers College Record, 95*, (4).

**Liebendorfer, W. (1995, Nov). Wieviele Arten von Intelligenz gibt es? *Erziehungskunst: Monatsschrift zur Padagogik Rudolf Steiners. 59.* Jg., Heft 11.

Maker, C., Nielson, A., and Rogers, J. (1994, Fall). Multiple intelligences: Giftedness, diversity, and problem-solving. *Teaching Exceptional Children, 27*, pp. 1–19.

Marshall, M. (1981, July 26). Musical Wunderkinds. *Boston Globe Magazine*.

Martin, A. and Weingartner, H. (1994). Modules, domains, and frames: Toward a neuropsychology of intelligence. In D. Detterman (Ed.), *Current topics in human intelligence, volume 2: Is mind modular or unitary?* (pp. 117–139). Norwood, NJ: Ablex.

McFarland, V. (1998). An investigation of the problem of identification in the under-representation of culturally diverse students in gifted and talented programs in Utah schools. Unpublished paper. Ogden, UT: Weber State University.

McKean, K. (1985, Oct). Intelligence: New ways to measure the wisdom of man. *Discover*.

McLellan, H. (1994). Virtual reality and multiple intelligences: Potentials for higher education. *Journal of Computing in Higher Education, 5*, (2), pp. 33–66.

Miller, L. (1988, Summer/Fall). Multiple intelligences offer multiple ways to become literate. *Update*.

Miller, G. (1983, Dec 25). Varieties of intelligence. Review of *Frames of Mind*. *New York Times Book Review*.

Miller, N. (1986, March 18). Changing your mind. (Boston) *Phoenix*.

Moorman, M. (1989, Summer). The great art education debate. *ARTnews*.

Morgan, H. (1996). An analysis of Gardner's theory of multiple intelligences. *Roeper Review, 18*, (4).

Morris, C. (1992, Sept/Oct). Gardner's multiple intelligences in our classrooms. *Teaching Today, 11*, (1).

Nelson, K (1995, July/Aug). Nurturing kids' seven ways of being smart. *Instructor*, pp. 26–34.

O'Connell, S. (1994, Oct 6). Off line: Creative tensions. *The Guardian Online*, p. T–11.

Obler, L. (1984, May). Plus ça change. Review of *Frames of Mind*. *The Women's Review of Books, 1*, (8).

Ohler, J. (1998, March). The Promise of MIDI technology: a reflection of musical intelligence. *Learning and Leading with technology* (pp. 6–10). Publication of the International Society for Technology in Education, Eugene, OR.

Ohler, J. (1998, March). Getting in touch with the musician within: Conducting a MIDI workshop for all ages. *Learning and Leading with technology* (pp. 11–12). Publication of the International Society for Technology in Education, Eugene, OR.

Ohler, J. (1998, March). Creating a MIDI [Musical Instrument Digital Interface] workstation for your classroom. *Learning and Leading with Technology* (pp. 13–15). Publication of the International Society for Technology in Education, Eugene, OR.

Olson, L. (1988, Jan 27). Children flourish here: Eight teachers and a theory changed a school world. *Education Week*.

Olson, L. (1988, Nov 16). In Pittsburgh: New approaches to testing track arts "footprints." *Education Week, 8*, (11).

Olson, L. (1989, Sept/Oct). A Revolution of Rising Expectations. *Teacher Magazine*.

Page, J. (1986, Dec). From bright to dull: The different kinds of intelligence. *Minneapolis Star and Tribune*.

Page, J. (1987, Jan 22). Your brain is not a computer. *San Francisco Chronicle*.

Park, L. et al. (1992). Giftedness and psychological abuse in borderline personality disorder: Their relevance to genesis and treatment. *Journal of Personality Disorders, 6*, (3), pp. 226–240.

Pennar, K. (1999, Sept. 16). How many smarts do you have? *Business Week*, pp. 104–108.

Plucker, J., Callahan, C., and Tomchin, E. (196, Sept.). Wherefore art thou, multiple intelligences? Alternative assessments for identifying talent in ethinically diverse and low income students. *Gifted Child Quarterly*, 40, (2), pp. 81–92.

Price, S. (1985, Oct). An I.Q. to live by: Developing personal intelligence. *Human Potential*.

Rafe, K. Benjamin Franklin—The Character Within the "Autobiography". Benjamin Franklin Institute of Global Education. Web: <branklin.edu//hubs/global/rafe02.html>.

Rafe, K. with L. Hotaling. Is the Passport to Success in Multicultural Education Through the Theory of Multiple Intelligences? Benjamin FranklinInstitute of Global Education. Web: <bfranklin.edu//hubs/global/rafe01.html>.

Reid, C., and Romanoff, B. (1997). Using multiple intelligence theory to identify gifted children. *Educational Leadership, 55*, (1).

Reidy, J. (1994, Oct 18). Educating for happiness. *The Irish Times*, City Edition, p.14.

Roberts, F. (1985, March). The trouble with back to basics. *Parents*.

Rochester, M. (1995, Nov 27). The Three Stooges as Geniuses. *St. Louis Post*.

Rosnow, R. (1991, May). Inside rumor: A personal journey. *American Psychologist*, pp. 484–496.

Rosnow, R., Skedler, A., Jacger, M. and Rind, B. (1994). Intelligence and the epistemics of interpersonal acumen: Testing some implications of Gardner's theory. *Intelligence, 19*, pp. 93–116.

Rosselli, H. and MacLauchan, G. (1992). Blue printing fromn the future: Proceedings from the Edith Bush symposium on intelligence, Univ. of South Florida, Tampa, FL.

Rothman, S. and Snyderman, M. (1987, Feb). Survey of expert opinion on intelligence and aptitude testing. *American Psychologist*.

Rusch, Liz (1999, Sept). Differend kinds of smart. *Child*, pp. 78–80

Salsberry, T. and Miller, S. (199, April 22) Female superintendents: Perceptions of their use of multiple intelligences. Presented at the American Education Research Assn. Annual Meeting, Montréal, Quebec.

Scarr, S. (1985). An author's frame of mind. Review of *Frames of Mind*. *New Ideas in Psychology, 3*, (1).

Scialabba, G. (1984, March/April). Mindplay. Review of *Frames of Mind*. *Harvard Magazine*.

Scherer, M. (1985, Jan). How many ways is a child intelligent? *Instructor and Teacher*.

Scherer, M. (1997). Teaching for multiple intelligences. *Educational Leadership, 55*, (1).

Schmidt, R. (1992, Fall). Interview with Howard Gardner. *Learning 2001*.

Schwager, I. (1986, Summer). Different children, different gifts. *Sesame Street Parent's Guide*.

Shaughnessy, M. (1985). What's new in I.Q.: Contemporary analysis with implications for gifter/talented/creative. *Creative Child and Adult Quarterly, 10*, (2).

Silver, H., Strong, R. and Perini, M. (1997). Integrating learning styles and multiple intelligences. *Educational Leadership, 55*, (1).

Simon, N. (1985, Aug). Your child's imagination. *Parents*.

Sloane, B. (1990, Jan 7). Flouting tradition, some educators begin to change A–to–F grading system. *Chicago Tribune School Guide.*

Smagorinsky, P. (1995, Feb). Constructing meaning in the disciplines: reconceptualizing writing across the curriculum as composing across the curriculum. *American Journal of Education.*

Smerechansky-Metzger, J. (1995). The quest for multiple intelligences. *Gifted Child Today, 18,* (3).

Snow, R. (1985, Nov). Review of *Frames of Mind. American Journal of Psychiatry.*

Stein, R. Multiple intelligences: A community learning campaign. *Teachers Reflections on Schooling in Rural Alaska,* pp.17–21.

Sternberg, R. (1983, Winter). How much gall is too much gall? A Review of *Frames of Mind. Contemporary Education Review, 2,* (3), pp.215–224.

Sternberg, R. (1994). Reforming school reform: Comments on *Multiple Intelligences: The theory in Practice. Teachers College Record, 95,* (4).

Stovsky, R. (1995, Jan 10). Disabled or different? *St. Louis Post Dispatch.*

Strahan, D. et al. (1996). Teaching diversity through multiple intelligences: Student and teacher responses to instructional improvement. *Research in Middle Level Education Quarterly, 19,* (2).

Strong, M. (1985, Jan). The seven kinds of smart: How does your child score? *Redbook.*

Sutherland, S. (1984, April 26). Grand organization in mind. Review of *Frames of Mind. Nature, 308.*

Think Magazine. Creating the climate for thinking with multiple intelligences.

Thompson, K. Cognitive and analytical psychology. Review of *Frames of Mind. San Francisco Jung Institute Library Journal, 5,* (4).

Traub, J. (1998, Oct 26). Multiple Intelligences Disorder. *The New Republic,* pp. 20–23.

Trumbull, M. (1994, Sept 20). Design invigorates schools–and students. *Christian Science Monitor,* p.12.

Turnbull, C. (1984, Jan 1). The seven 'intelligences'. *The Philadelphia Inquirer.*

Ullmann, H. (1998, April 23). Dreaming the best at IPS [about the Key Renaissance School]. (Indianapolis) *Nuvo Newsweekly,* pp. 18–21.

Viadero, D. (1994, Feb 2). The world of difference. *Education Week.*

Viadero, D. (1995, Nov 8). Expert testimony. *Education Week.*

Vialle, W. (1997). In Australia: Multiple intelligences in multiple settings. *Educational Leadership, 55,* (1).

Vialle, W. (1991). Tuesday's children: A study of five children using multiple intelligences theory as a framework. *Dissertation Abstracts*

International.

Voices against the testing "explosion." *Education USA*, December 16, 1985.

Weinreich–Haste, H. (1985). The varieties of intelligence: An interview with Howard Gardner. *New Ideas in Psychology, 3*, (1).

Weiss, S. (1999, March). Interview with Howard Gardner. NEA Today. [Full I-view available online at <www.nea.org/neatoday/9903/gardner.html>]

White, J. (1998). *Do Howard Gardner's Multiple Intelligences Add Up?* London: Inst. of Education University of London. See also: H. Gardner, An Intelligent Way to Progress: A Reply to John White, *The (London) Independent*, Education section, March 19, 1998, pp. 4,5.

Williams, G. (1990, April). Radical class acts. *Omni, 12*, (7).

Willard-Holt, C. and Holt, D. (1997, Spring). Multiple intelligences and gifted education. *Gifted Education Press Quarterly*. Available from Gifted Education Press, 102 Yuma Court, P.O. Box 1586, Manassas, VA 20108.

Willis, S. (1994, Oct). The well–rounded classroom: Applying the theory of multiple intelligences. *ASCD Update, 36*, (8).

Winn, M. (1990, April 29). New views of human intelligence. *New York Times*, Good Health Magazine.

Wohlwill, J. (1985). The Gardner–Winner view of children's visual–artistic development: Overview, assessment, and critique. *Visual Arts Research, 11*.

Woo, E. (1995, Jan 20). Teaching that goes beyond IQ. *Los Angeles Times*.

World Education-National Ctr. For the Study of Learning and Literacy. (1999, March). Adult multiple intelligences. *Focus on Basics, 3*, (A), special issue. Available through World Education/NCSALL, 44 Farnsworth St., Boston, MA 02210-1211.

III. Theses/Dissertations/Papers

Alexander, L. (1964). The writings of Howard Gardner and their implications for music education (Dept. of Music, Michigan State University).

**Antonietti, Alessandro. La Teoria delle intelligenze multiple anche una teoria implicita dell 'intelligenza? Available from author: Dipartmento di Psicologia, Centro Ricerca Technologie dell'Istruzione, Universita Cattolica del Sacro Cuore, Milan, Italy.

**Araya, Roberto, ed. (1997). Conferencia de Howard Gardner en Chile: Intelligencias multiples en educacion. AutoMind Education.

Armstrong, T. Describing strengths in children identified as "learning disabled" using Howard Gardner's theory of multiple intelligences as an organizing framework. *Dissertation Abstracts International.*

Chen, J. (1993). Building on children's strengths: Examination of a project SPECTRUM intervention program for students at risk for school failure. *Dissertation Abstracts International.*

Davis, R. Learning how to learn: Technology, the seven intelligences and learning. Paper presented at the Spring CUE Conference, Palm Springs, CA, May, 1991.

**Donolo, Danilo. Manifestaciones de la inteligencia y actividades escolares. Presented to Viii Encuentro de Investigacion Educativa: formacion y practica. Available from author: Santa Fe 649, 5800 Rio Cuartoi, Cordobe, ARGENTINA

Grow, G. Writing and the seven intelligences. Available from the author: Division of Journalism, Florida A&M University, Tallahassee, FL 32307

Hanafin, J. Assessment and the theory of multiple intelligences: An overview. In *Towards new understandings: Assessment and the theory of multiple intelligences.*

Lohman, D. Intelligence: A question of values. Paper delivered at Annual Meeting of the National Council on Measurement in Education, New Orleans, April 1994.

Lucks, N. A study of the proposed benefits of combining the theories of learning styles and multiple intelligences for use in the classrooms. Available from the author: P.O. Box 1324, Warren, PA 16365

Maio, J. Fostering the multiple intelligences in your child. Presentation to Pennsylvania Association for Gifted Education Affiliate Weekend, Carlisle, PA, 1997.

Martin, J. (1999, Jan) Assessment in Multiple Intelligences. Doctoral Dissertation for Loyola University, Chicago.

Mitchell, J. The Theory of Multiple Intelligences as a Theoretical Foundation for Art Appreciation. Available from the author: Art Department, Anderson College, Anderson, SC 29621.

Mumme, R. Figurative frames and tacit tropes, from Giambattista Vico to Howard Gardner: Toward the possibility of a tropological–logical intelligence. Available from the author: University of Southern Florida at Fort Myers, 8111 College Parkway SW, Fort Myers, FL 33919

Roselli, H. and Taylor, E. (1998, April 16).Operationalizing Gardner's entry points. Paper presented to American Educational Research Association, San Diego, CA.

Rubin, J. Multiple intelligence: From theory to practice: the Javits seven-plus gifted and talented program. Paper delivered at the Esther Katz Rosen Symposium on the Psychological Development of Gifted Children, Lawrence, Kansas, February 1992. Also available from the author: Javits 7+ Gifted and Talented Program, Community School District 18, 755 E. 10th Street, Brooklyn, NY 11236

**Santoianni, Flavia. Configurational didactics: Teaching in multiple models. Unpublished doctoral dissertation: Università degli Studi di Napoli Federico II, Via Petrarca 203/A, 80122 Napoli, Italy.

Slatin, B. The emerging role of the principal in restructuring for enrichment education. Unpublished doctoral dissertation, Fordham University, 1994.

Starnes, W., Barton, J., and Leibowitz, D. Using multiple intelligences to identify and nurture young potentially gifted children. Paper delivered at the Esther Katz Rosen Symposium on the Psychological Development of Gifted Children, February 1992. Also available from the author: Early Childhood Gifted Model Program, 850 Hungerford Drive, Rockville, MD 20850.

Tubb, L. Gifted deaf students: Case studies describing profiles of domains of intelligence. Available via the author: Teacher Education, Louisiana Tech University, P.O. Box 3161, Ruston, LA 71272–0001.

Vialle, W. (1991). Tuesday's children: A study of five children using multiple intelligences theory as a framework. *Dissertation Abstracts International.*

APPENDIX C

VIDEOS, NEWSLETTERS, AND MISCELLANY

Works in languages other than English appear with asterisks(**).

Video

MI: Intelligence, Understanding, and the Mind. (1996) R. DiNozzi, Producer. Los Angeles, CA: Into the Classroom Media. One hour presentation with Question & Answer.

Creativity and Leadership: Making the Mind Extraordinary. (1998) R. DiNozzi, Producer. Los Angeles, CA: Into the Classroom Media. One hour presentation with Question & Answer.

How are kids smart? Multiple Intelligences in the Classroom. (1995) Port Chester, NY: National Professional Resources.

Optimizing Intelligences: Thinking, Emotion & Creativity. (1998) Port Chester, NY: National Professional Resources. Featuring Howard Gardner, Mihaly Csikszentmihalyi, and Daniel Goleman.

Multiple Intelligences and the Second Language Learner. (1998) Port Chester, NY: National Professional Resources.

The Multiple Intelligences Series. (1994) Alexandria, VA: Association for Supervision and Curriculum Development.

Multiple Intelligences: Developing Intelligences for Greater Achievement. (1995) Salt Lake City, UT: Video Journal of Education.

**Howard Gardner y Thomas Hoerr Sobre Intelligencias Múltiples.* (1997) Santiago, Chile: AutoMind Educación. Videographed live in Santiago, Chile, July 14, 1997. Spanish-language.

Changes Unfold: A Documentary on Multiple Ways of Teaching and Learning. (1998) Bangladesh: UNICEF.

Newsletters

MI Bulletin. Newsletter of the Multiple Intelligences, Curriculum and Assessment Project, Aine Hyland (Ed.). Dublin, Ireland: University College Cork.

Intelligence Connections: Newletter of the ASCD Network Teaching for Multiple Intelligences. T. Hoerr (Ed.). Available from the New City School, 5209 Waterman Ave., St. Louis, MO 63108

MI-News. E-mail newsletter. C. Morris (Ed.). Available from Multiple Intelligences Research and Consulting [subscribe-mi-news@xc.org].

Instructional and miscellaneous materials

Active Minds. MI-based teaching materials catalog. Atlanta, GA: Sportime International.

Adventures of the MI way gang. A series of small books for children which introduce and explain each of the intelligences. Loretta Saff, 11738 Lipsey Rd., Tampa, FL 33618

The balancing act: A multiple intelligences approach to curriculum, instruction, and assessment (videotapes and guides). Palatine, IL: IRI/Skylight.

Bright ideas. Educational computer software programs and in-home software seminars. Addie Swartz, President, What a Bright Idea, Inc., P.O. Box 1034, Concord, MA 01742.

Common miracles: The new revolution in learning. ABC News Special with Peter Jennings. MPI Home Video, 16101 So. 108 Ave., Orland Park, IL 60462.

Consortium for Whole Brain Learning. L. Ellison, ed. 1078 Cedar View Dr., Minneapolis, MN 55405.

Cooperative learning and multiple intelligences. Audio and videotapes presented by Spencer and Laurie Kagan. Available through The LPD Video Journal, 1–800–572–1153.

Deike, R. *Stone Wall Secrets* and *Stone Wall Secrets Teacher's Guide: Exploring Geology in the Classroom*. Zephyr Press, Tucson, AZ.

Exploring Our Multiple Intelligences. Marcia D'Arcangelo and Kathy Checkley (Producers). CD-ROM available from the Association for Supervision and Curriculum Development, 1703 N. Beauregard St., Alexandria, VA 22311–1714. Web: [http://www.ascd.org]

Harvard Project Zero. Web site with background, projects listing, and product information [http://pzweb.harvard.edu].

Have you used your eight intelligences today? Activity pad. Palatine, IL: IRI/Skylight.

How are kids smart? Video featuring Dr. Howard Gardner and the Fuller Elementary School in Gloucester, MA. (Teachers and Administrator's Versions available.) Zephyr Press.

Identifying talents among multicultural children. Booklet partially focused on MI theory, by Bella Kranz. Phi Delta Kappa Educational Foundation.

Intelligence Connections. Newsletter of the ASCD network on the teaching for multiple intelligences. Edited by Tom Hoerr, New City School, St. Louis, MO and available through ASCD, Alexandria, VA.

The joy of thinking: A multimedia celebration. A multimedia curriculum tool program for grades K–8. Zephyr Press.

Kid smart posters. Donna Kunzler. Zephyr Press.

Lift off. Multiple intelligences video program for 3–8 year olds produced by the Australian Children's Television Foundation..

The Magic Seven: Tools for building your multiple intelligences. Interactive Comics, vol.2 by Nancy Marguilies. Comic book appropriate for all ages. Zephyr Press, 1995.

Managing the disruptive classroom: Strategies for educators. Videocassette program and facilitator's guide to applying reality therapy in the classroom. Agency for Instructional Technology, Box A, Bloomington, IN, 47402–0120.

Maps, mindscapes, and more . . . Nancy Margulies. Zephyr Press, Tucson, Arizona, 1993.

MI daily activity calendar. Available from Loretta Saff, 11738 Lipsey Road, Tampa, FL 33618.

MI in action: Your school and the multiple intelligences. Videotape with David Lazear. Zephyr Press.

The MIDAS challenge: A guide to career success. MI-oriented career guidance workbook for students by C. Branton Shearer, Multiple Intelligence Research and Consulting, 519 S. DePeyster Street, Kent, OH 44240

Multiple intelligences and the second-language learner. Videotape presented by J Gusman. Available through National Professional Resources.

Multiple intelligences family home learning kit Video tapes. Citizens Education Center, 310 First Avenue South #330, Seattle, WA 98104.

Multiple intelligences from theory to practice. Two audio tapes; on tape 1, "Intelligence in Seven Phases," Howard Gardner explains MI; tape 2, "Applying Multiple Intelligences in the Classroom," Linda Campbell discusses practical applications. IRI/Skylight.

Multiple intelligences in action MI curriculum tools from training videos to practical classroom materials, in collaboration with David Lazear. Zephyr Press, Tucson, Arizona, 1995.

Multiple intelligences lesson plan book. Anne Bruetsch. Zephyr Press, 1–800–232–2187.

Multiple intelligences school network. Consortium of schools committed to systemic reform, utilizing MI. 200 E. Wood Street, Suite 274, Palatine, IL60067.

Multiple intelligences starter package With David Lazear, published by Zephyr Press, Tucson, Arizona, 1995.

Multiple intelligences. Kit with audio and video tapes as well as several handbooks and the book Multiple intelligences in the classroom by Thomas Armstrong. Alexandria, VA: Association for Supervision and Curriculum Development, 1995.

Multiple intelligences. Audio and videotapes presented by Howard Gardner and David Lazear. Available through The LPD Video Journal, 1–800–572–1153.

Multiple intelligences: Discovering the giftedness in all. Videotape by Thomas Armstrong. Zephyr Press, 1–800–232–2187.

Pad o' posters: Have you used your seven intelligences today? Pad of paper intended to increase students' awareness of seven intelligences. IRI/Skylight Publishers, 1994

Playmaking: The latest in the integration of the arts in educaton. (1998). East Brunswick, NJ: Creative Educational Systems.

Provoking thoughts game. Card game of critical thinking exercises in each of the seven intelligences. Institute for the Development of Educational Alternatives (IDEA. Inc.), 404 NW 1st Street, P.O. Box 1004, Austin, MN 55912.

The Quick smart profile. Personal analyses and intelligences profiles provided for everyday life, by Lynda Miller, Ph.D. and Lynn C. Miller, Ph.D. Smart Alternatives, Inc., P.O. Box 5849, Austin, TX 78763.

**Quinto Año de Educación Básica. (1998). Series of teachers guides [*Matemáticas, Lenguaje, Estudios Sociales, Ciencias Naturales*] produced for the Santillana Foundation, Madrid, Spain.

Reinventing our schools. A video interview with Howard Gardner. AIT Customer Service, Box A, Bloomington, IN 47402–0120

Rogers multiple intelligences indicator. Available from J. Keith Rogers, 149C MCKB, Brigham Young University, Provo, UT 84602.

Schools Using M. I. Theory (SUMIT) Project, Harvard Project Zero. See descriptive Web site http://pzweb.harvard.edu/Research/SUMIT.htm

Summer Stars. A summer camp based on MI. Contact Marylou Cantrell, South School, Gower Rd., New Canaan, CT 06840.

Tap your 7 intelligences: Multiple intelligence posters for the classroom By David Lazear and Nancy Margulies. Zephyr Press, 1995.

Theater in motion: Educational theater, participatory educational theater (creative drama) and the seven intelligences. A set of exercises for teachers and artists. Fanelli, Leslie. Available from Theater in Motion, 121–25 6th Avenue, Queens, NY 11356

Who's smart, what's smart: The MI brain game. Game show format. Zephyr Press, 1996.

Who's smart, what's smart: An introduction to MI for kids. Videotape. Zephyr Press.

APPENDIX D

CONTACTS ON MULTIPLE INTELLIGENCES THEORY
AND ITS APPLICATIONS

United States

James Allen
Univ. of Rio Grande &
Rio Grande Community College
Rio Grande, OH 45674

Tom Armstrong
P.O. Box 548
Cloverdale, CA 95425

Jim Bellenca
IRI SkyLight
2626 S. Clearbrook Dr.
Arlington Heights, IL 60005–4626

Patricia Bolanos
Key Learning Community
725 N. New Jersey St.
Indianapolis, IN 46202

Sheila Callahan-Young
Milton Fuller School
4 Schoolhouse Rd.
Gloucester, MA 01930

Bruce and Linda Campbell
17410 Marine Dr.
Stanwood, WA 98292–6740

Jackie Chen
The Erikson Institute
420 North Wabash Ave.
Chicago, IL 60611

Rene Diaz-Lefebvre
Glendale Community College
6000 W. Olive Ave.
Glendale, AZ 85302

Dee Dickinson
New Horizons for Learning
P.O. Box 15329
Seattle, WA 98115–0329

Launa Ellison
Consortium for Whole Brain
    Learning
1078 Cedar View dr.
Minneapolis, MN 55405-2129

Peter Everson
Everson Leadership Coaches
5 Strathmore Lane, Suite 3
Madison, CT 06443

Ellen Fabrikant
1816 Sonett Street
El Cajon, CA 92109

Robin Fogarty
SkyLight Training and Publishing
2626 S. Clearbrook Dr.
Arlington Heights, IL 60005–4626

Jo Gusman
Educational Consultant
New Horizons in Education
Sacramento, CA

Brian Haggerty
San Diego City Schools
Dana Administration Center,
    Room 189
1775 Chatsworth Blvd.
San Diego, CA 92107–3709

Terry Hanson
Pinecrest Elementary School
Hastings, MN

Tom Hatch
Carnegie Foundation for the
    Advancement of Teaching
555 Middlefield Rd.
Menlo Park, CA 94025

Lois Hetland
Project Zero
Longfellow Hall, 3rd Fl.
Harvard Graduate School of
    Education
Cambridge, MA 02138

Tom Hoerr
New City School
5209 Waterman Ave.
St. Louis, MO 63108

Robert W. Johnston
OmniMind Center, Educational
    Gerontology
P.O. Box 195
Sunderland, MA 01375–0195

Mindy Kornhaber
Project Zero
Longfellow Hall, 3rd floor
Harvard Graduate School of
    Education
Cambridge, MA 02138

Mara Krechevsky
Project Zero
Longfellow Hall, 3rd floor
Harvard Graduate School of Edu-
    cation
Cambridge, MA 02138

David Lazear
New Dimensions of Learning
729 W. Waveland, Suite G
Chicago, IL 60613

Ann Lewin
1577 Cherry Park Dr.
Memphis, TN 38120

Stephanie Pace Marshall
Illinois Math and Science Academy
1500 W. Sullivan Rd.
Aurora, IL 60506–1039

Gregory Miller
Dept. of Fine and Performing Arts
Univ. of Rio Grande &
Rio Grande Community College
Rio Grande, OH 45674

Anna O'Connor
Milton Fuller School
4 Schoolhouse Road
Gloucester, MA 01930

Sally Osberg, Director
Children's Discovery Museum
180 Woz Way
San Jose, CA 95110

Jane Piirto
Talent Development Education
Ashland University
Ashland, OH 44805

Hilda Rosselli
Univ. of Southern Florida
College of Education
Tampa, FL 33620–8350

Branton Shearer
1316 S. Lincoln St.
Kent, OH 44240

Ronald Strumbeck
Potential Unlimited
4500 Great Lakes Dr. South
Clearwater, FL 33762

Bruce Torff
Hofstra University
School of Education
Dept. of Curric. & Teaching
Hempstead, NY 11549

John Turnbull
P.O. Box 620
Southampton, NY 11969

Julie Viens
Project Zero
Longfellow Hall, 3rd floor
Harvard Graduate School of
   Education
Cambridge, MA 02138

Roger Wagner
Wagner Publishing, Inc.
El Cajon, CA

Ellen Weber
Secondary Education
Houghton College
Houghton, NY 14744

Argentina

Antonio Battro
Battro y Denham
Billinghurst 2574, Piso 1
1425 Buenos Aires
Argentina

Marita Cabarrou Gottheil,
   Directora
Paidós
Defensa 599 – 1st Piso
1065 Buenos Aires
Argentina

Paula Pogre
Colegio Aula XXI
11 de Septiembre 3168
Buenos Aires
Argentina

Australia

David and Elaine Brownlow
Hawker Brownlow Education
1123A Nepean Highway
Highett, Melbourne, VIC 3190
Australia

Dr. Patricia Edgar
Australian Children's Television
   Foundation
Level 3, 145 Smith St.
Fitzroy, VIC 3065
Australia

Wilma Vialle
Faculty of Education
Univ. of Wollongong
Wollongong NSW 2522
Australia

Anne Feehan, Deputy Principal
Strathcona Baptist Girls' Grammar
   School
34 Scott Street
Canterubry, VIC 3126
Australia

Dr. Helen McGrath
Deakin University
221 Burwood Highway
Burwood, VIC 3125
Australia

Toni Noble
Australian Catholic University
179 Albert Rd.
Strathfield, NSW 2135
Australia

Joyce Martin
Australian Catholic University
179 Albert Rd.
Strathfield, NSW 2135
Australia

Bangladesh

Mira Mitra
UNICEF -BSL Complex
1 Minto Road
Dhaka, 1000
Bangladesh

Brazil

Amélia de Borja
Rua Dr. Franco de Rocha,
   339–33A
Sao Paulo, SP CEP 05015–040
Brazil

Chile

Roberto Araya
AutoMind
Providencia 591, Piso 5
Santiago
Chile

China

Dr. Jin Li
Brown University
School of Education
Providence, RI 02912

Meiru Tu
Nanjing Normal University
122 Ninghai Rd.
Nanjing 210009
China

Zhilong Shen
Beijing Institute of Light Industry
11 Fucheng Road
Beijing 100037
China

Denmark

Hans Hendrik Knoop
Royal Danish School of
    Educational Studies
Lucernemarken 1
5260 Odense S
Denmark

Kirsten Gibson
Waves Education ApS
Kildevej 1 B
DK–2960 Rungsted Kyst
Denmark

Mogens Hansen
Royal Danish School of
    Educational Studies
Emdrupborg, Emdrupvej 101
2400 Copenhagen, NV
Denmark

Ms. Eva Jagd Mauritzen
Gyldendal Undervisning
Klareboderne 3
1001 Copenhagen K
Denmark

England

Tom Bentley
Demos
9 Bridewell Place
London EC4V 6AP
England

Dr. Anna Craft
School of Education
The Open University
Milton Keynes MK7 6AA
England

Helen Haste
Dept. of Psychology
Univ. of Bath
Bath BA2 7AY
England

John Greenacre
Teaching & Learning Systems
11 Fairoak Dr.
Eltham Heights, London SE9 2QG
England

Tim Brighouse
Birmingham City Council
Education Dept.
Margaret Street
Birmingham B3 3BU

Geoff Mulgan
Policy Unit
10 Downing Street
London, England

Finland

Marjut Haussila
Laajalahdentie 4
00330 Helsinki
Finland

France

Britt Mari Barth
Institut Supériur de Pédagogie
3, rue de l'Abbaye
75006 Paris
France

Philip Champy
Editions Retz
1, rue du Depart
75014, Paris
France

Odile Jacob
Editions Odile Jacob
15 Rue Soufflot
75005 Paris
France

Ireland

Yvonne Healy
Irish Times
P.O. Box 74
10–16 D'Olier St.
Dublin 2
Ireland

Kathleen Lynch
University College Dublin
Equality Studies Center
Library Building
Belfield, Dublin, 4
Ireland

Aine Hyland
University College, Cork
Education Dept.
M.I., Curric. and Assess't Proj.
Cork
Ireland

Israel

Nancy Ras
The Betz Foundation
P.O. Box 9456
61093 Tel Aviv
Israel

Dan Sharon
Branco Weiss Institute
P.O. Box 648 – 40 Hantke St.
96782 Jerusalem
Israel

Italy

Carlina Rinaldi
Reggio Children
Piazza Della Vittoria, 6
42100 Reggio Emilia
Italy

Prof. Nando Filograsso
Via Gaspari, 21
S. Silvestro
65132 Pescara
Italy

(Inge and Carlo Feltrinelli,
    Publishers)
Giangiacomo Feltrinelli Editore
Società per Anzioni
Via Andegari 6
20121 Milan
Italy

Korea

Woo Youp SHIM
Chuncheon National Univ. of Edu-
    cation
Sucksa-dong 339
Chuncheon-si
Korea 200–703

Myung-Hee Kim
Inst. for Educational Research
College of Education
Hanyang Univ.
17 Haengdang-dong, Soungdong-ku
Seoul
Korea

Sweden

Lars Lindstrom
Stockholm Institute of Education
P.O. Box 34103
S–100 26 Stockholm
Sweden

Helena Wallenberg
Carpe Vitam Foundation
Lemshaga Sateri
130 35 Ingaro
Sweden

Ingemar Svantesson
Brain Books
P.O. Box 344
55115 Jöngköping
Sweden

Taiwan

Mr. & Mrs. Show-Chung Ho or
Sing-Jung Chang
Hsin-Yi Foundation
75 Sec 2 Chung Chung S Road
Taipei
Taiwan

Mei-Hung Chiu
National Taiwan Normal
    University
Graduate Inst. of Science
    Education
88, Ting-chou Rd.
Taipei 11718
Taiwan

INDEX